KU-284-957

# Housing Design Quality

## Through policy, guidance and review

Matthew Carmona

London and New York

First published 2001
by Spon Press
11 New Fetter Lane, London EC4P 4EE

Simultaneously published in the USA and Canada
by Spon Press
29 West 35th Street, New York, NY 10001

*Spon Press is an imprint of the Taylor & Francis Group*

© 2001 Matthew Carmona

The right of Matthew Carmona to be identified as the Author of this Work has been asserted by him in accordance with the Copyright, Designs and Patents Act 1988

Typeset in Arial by MHL Typesetting Limited, Coventry
Printed and bound in Great Britain by Bell & Bain Ltd, Glasgow

All rights reserved. No part of this book may be reprinted or reproduced or utilised in any form or by any electronic, mechanical, or other means, now known or hereafter invented, including photocopying and recording, or in any information storage or retrieval system, without permission in writing from the publishers.

The publisher makes no representation, express or implied, with regard to the accuracy of the information contained in this book and cannot accept any legal responsibility or liability for any errors or omissions that may be made.

*British Library Cataloguing in Publication Data*
A catalogue record for this book is available from the British Library

*Library of Congress Cataloging in Publication Data*
Carmona, Matthew.
     Housing design quality: through policy, guidance, and review / Matthew Carmona.
          p. cm.
     Includes bibliographical references and index.
     1. Housing policy – England. 2. Housing – England. I. Title.

     HD7333.A3 C384 2001
     363.5′8′0941 – dc21                                                    00-046315

     ISBN 0-419-25650-4 pbk ·

# Housing Design Quality

This book directly addresses the major planning debate of our time – the delivery and quality of new housing development. As pressure for new housing development in England increases, a widespread desire to improve the design of the resulting residential environments becomes ever more apparent.

In recent years central government has come to accept the need to deliver higher quality living environments, and the important role of the planning system in helping to raise design standards. *Housing Design Quality: Through policy, guidance and review* focuses on this role and in particular on how the various policy instruments available to planning authorities can be used in a positive manner to deliver higher quality residential developments.

Part One of the book provides the theoretical and policy context for the in-depth research to follow. Debates on housing design and planning control are explored, alongside an in-depth review of government guidance and an exploration of the key theoretical constructs prescribed for effective design control process. The role of urban design and the nature of the residential development process are also discussed.

Part Two constitutes the empirical heart of the work and examines current practice and innovation in the control of residential design. The results of a country-wide survey and content analysis of residential design policy and guidance is discussed as a means to review mainstream practice and the priorities of planning authorities in attempting to influence residential design quality. A range of innovative experiences in delivering housing design quality through planning action is also examined. These are supplemented throughout the book by case studies on which the analysis is based.

Finally, Part Three of the book offers a detailed agenda for delivering housing design quality; it assesses the latest and complementary policy initiatives from central government on residential design and concludes with a look to the future.

**Matthew Carmona** is an architect and a planner whose research interests lie in the interstices between those two established professions – the areas of urban design, design policy and control, and latterly urban renaissance. He is Senior Lecturer at the Bartlett School of Planning, University College London.

LIVERPOOL JMU LIBRARY

3 - 1111  00908  9242

To Sarah

# Contents

# Preface

This book evaluates current practice and innovation in the local authority control of private sector residential design through the English planning process. It is written in the light of increasing pressure for new residential development, alongside increasing condemnation of the standard products of the volume housebuilders, and the frequently unimaginative attempts of the public sector to influence the design of such development.

The research has been undertaken as a means to make recommendations on improving the practice and effectiveness of the planning process in influencing housing design quality through means of planning policy, design guidance and design review. Although based on an in-depth examination of English practice, many of the problems and possible solutions as well as the theoretical discussions are universal. The findings will therefore be of interest around the UK and overseas.

Part 1 of the book provides the theoretical and policy context for the empirical research. In this, the debates on housing design and planning control are explored – both in a contemporary and historical context – alongside an in-depth review of government guidance and an exploration of the key theoretical constructs prescribed in the literature for effective design control process. The role of urban design and the nature of the residential development process in influencing the final outcomes are also explored in some depth.

Part 2 constitutes the empirical heart of the work and examines current practice and innovation in the control of residential design. Part 2 begins by taking a snap shot of opinion from across the full range of stakeholders in the design/development process. The results of a country-wide survey and content analysis of residential design policy and guidance is next discussed as a means to review mainstream practice and the priorities (national and local) of planning authorities in attempting to influence residential design quality. Finally, a range of innovative experiences in delivering housing design quality through planning action are examined. These are supplemented by insets placed throughout the book briefly illustrating the case studies on which the analysis is based.

Part 3 contains the recommendations for improving effectiveness that flow from the analysis in Parts 1 and 2. A detailed agenda for delivering housing design quality is offered, before attention turns to the latest and complementary policy initiatives from Central Government on residential design. Part 3 concludes with a look to the future, and argues that as the fundamental drivers underpinning established approaches to delivering residential environments change, the requirement for a robust, informed and fair planning process becomes ever more vital.

# Acknowledgements

The writing of this book has involved the contributions, both wittingly and unwittingly, of more people than I can ever hope to recall, from formal interviews to casual conversations, from practitioners, professionals and colleagues to friends and relations. The book is immeasurably richer as a result. In particular, the work would have been impossible without the direct contributions of the 376 local authorities that sent me information on their design policies and guidance. This represents a considerable investment in time and money for which I am extremely grateful.

Of the practitioners that have given up time to contribute directly I reserve special thanks to: Mark Alcock, Michael Brackenbury, David Bradley, Kim Cooper, Nigel Davies, James Doe, Lisa Jackson, Barbara McLoughlin, David Oliver, Patrick Ross, Alan Stones, Jerry Unsworth and Denis Varcoe. I would also like to thank Professor Brian Goodey and Professor John Taylor for encouraging me to write the book in the first place and to Caroline Mallinder for her support in bringing it to press.

My greatest thanks however go to three people, who in different ways have been decisive in shaping my work so far; to Professor John Punter, to Dr. Taner Oc, and last but not least to my wife Sarah for putting up with me.

Thank you.

# Part One:
# The context for delivering quality

# Chapter 1

# Housing design quality and control: the need for research

**Across the world**

Over the course of the twentieth century, much of the English-speaking world has been characterised – amongst other traits – by inhabitants that demonstrate:

- a strong preference for home ownership;
- a strong preference for more rural (less urban) lifestyles;
- a consequential acceptance of suburbia – for gardens, greenery, privacy and low density living; and
- therefore by a gradual embrace of a car culture.

By the end of the twentieth century, where we choose to live, our patterns of living and the intrinsic nature of the homes and home environments that such trends have given rise to, are being questioned and often profoundly criticised. In America, the edge city phenomenon continues to sweep all before it. Characterised as America's sprawling 'new frontier' (Garreau, 1991), much of it disconnected, introspective, sometimes gated, always car dominated and often lacking in social focus (Southworth and Parthasarathy, 1996). In Australia, the need to address the new sustainable agenda has led to a questioning of car dominated extensive patterns of growth, and, as in America (Katz, 1994), to attempts to define a new set of design principles to inform rapid suburban growth (Western Australian Planning Commission, 1997).

In the UK, where pressures on land resources are far greater and where debates about the nature and quality of the residential environment have a particularly long and turbulent history (Ravetz, 1995), contemporary debates about the nature and quality of new housing development have been particularly intense. This book examines just one aspect of this debate – the potential of the planning process to positively intervene in the delivery of better quality residential design – in just one part of the UK – England.[1] Nevertheless, although different in detail (administrative, contextual and development process), it is hoped that the

[1] The research focuses on English practice in residential design control. Scotland, Wales and Northern Ireland are subject to different legislative regimes and systems of planning guidance, and therefore are not covered directly by the study. Nevertheless, the close relation of the systems in Scotland, Northern Ireland and Wales to the one pertaining in England means that the key research findings will be of direct relevance to those systems also.

practices discussed and lessons learnt through this analysis will have much wider application to debates on residential design and the public sector role in influencing its quality across the world.

### The housing numbers game

In England, the Department of the Environment's (DoE[2]) 1992b household forecast (published in 1995) raised the projected numbers of new households to 4.4 million over the 25-year period beginning 1991. It in turn raised questions about the need for new houses versus the desire to protect the environment and contain urban sprawl. The figure represented a 70 per cent increase on the previous 25-year forecast and began a heated debate, the focus of which was well summed up in the title of the Town and Country Planning Association (TCPA) publication 'The People – Where Will They Go?' (Breheny and Hall, 1996), itself echoing the question posed by Ebenezer Howard in his famous 'Three Magnets' diagram of 1898 (see Fig. 1.1).

That famous and enduring diagram reflected Howard's powerful vision, to capture in one place the best of town and country – in the Garden City. Although beautifully interpreted in places like Welwyn Garden City or Hampstead Garden Suburb, the reality was soon diluted

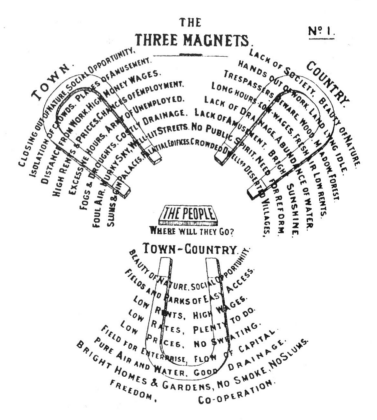

Fig. 1.1  *The Three Magnets (Howard, 1898).*

---

[2]  In 1997, during the period of the research, the DoE was amalgamated with the Department of Transport to form the new Department of the Environment, Transport and the Regions (DETR). Each acronym is used in the book in its appropriate historical context.

to an evolving but formula-based suburban solution. With such solutions, many of the advantages of town and country envisaged by Howard were lost in a market, rather than social or environmental driven interpretation of the living environment (see Figs 1.2 and 1.3).

The result has been an increasing perception that new housing development is bad, and that such development, particularly on greenfield land, far from enhancing the environment, increasingly destroys the distinctive qualities of place. Although often tied up in romantic and perhaps unduly rosy notions of the past, the perception that new-build housing is bland, ubiquitous and unresponsive to local character is widely held (Popular Housing Forum, 1998, pp. 15–17). Such perceptions go a long way to explaining the controversial nature, both locally and nationally, of any proposals to increase housing provision, particularly when planned on virgin ('greenfield') land.

These attitudes mark something of a paradox, in that research has consistently shown that anti-urban sentiments remain strong in the UK and aspirations for a rural (or at least suburban) lifestyle remain keen (URBED *et al.*, 1999, pp. 4–6); yet equally, that greenfield land and particularly rural land should be protected, if necessary by building at higher densities where development does occur (Popular Housing Forum, 1998, p. 58). In England, this latter and strongly-held 'national view' drove much of the subsequent debate following publication of the projected 4.4 million household requirement (a figure subsequently reduced to 3.8 million over the period 1996 to 2021).

The household forecast was accompanied about the same time by the setting of a new government target for 50 per cent of all new housing development to be built on re-used ('brownfield') urban land (HM government, 1995a). The pronouncement encouraged some environmentalists to argue for a more hard-line approach to residential development, rejecting such massive projections as unfounded and potentially disastrous, and supporting a much higher percentage of urban compaction and brownfield land re-use; this at a time when building of housing was already achieving the desired 50 per cent re-use of urban land (DETR, 1997). Such arguments and the unprecedented public and press interest in the issue swayed the DoE which, in the 1996 Green Paper 'Household Growth: Where Shall We Live?', increased its aim by 10 per cent to advocate 60 per cent construction of new houses on brownfield sites (DoE, 1996c, para. 7.9).

*Fig. 1.2 The suburban dream: Hampstead Garden Suburb, 1906.*

The context

The approach

The layout

The homes

*Fig. 1.3  The suburban reality: 'Anywhere', 1999.*

Together the evidence was clear. First, a household requirement in excess of the total numbers of houses built in the inter-war period was needed in England (Oliver *et al.*, 1981, p. 13) – a requirement with the potential to have at least as great an impact on British towns and cities and their surrounding countryside as suburban expansion did back then. Second, that whatever the division between brown and greenfield sites, based on the evidence of private sector development in England in the twentieth century, much of the new housing is likely to be 'suburban' in nature – the corollary of which will be a massive expansion of, and demand for, the products of the volume housebuilders (see Chapter 4). Finally, that one of the major planning and urban design challenges of the subsequent twenty years, will be observed in the potential of the public sector to ameliorate this impact and contribute to making the new housing allocations more acceptable to local populations through improved design – one of the claims made of better design in government guidance (DoE, 1997b, para. 15; DoE, 1992b, para. 4). A series of initiatives (discussed in Chapter 10) has been started to meet this challenge.

Simply put, to avoid building more than 40 per cent of the projected homes on greenfield land, where their impact would be both environmentally and socially unsustainable, ways need to be found to increase and sustain housing construction on brownfield land whilst maintaining design quality, existing residential area amenity and the support of established communities. Hand in hand with such efforts, the design quality of any necessary development on greenfield sites will need to be improved in urban design and landscape terms in order to ameliorate environmentally the impact of new housing on the edges of settlements and into the countryside. In this context, the potential of planning authorities to encourage and require better residential design through statutory control and positive guidance would seem of paramount importance.

### An investment reaps dividends

It is hoped that developments in central government policy on design and planning in the late 1990s (see Chapters 3 and 10) herald a more broadly based and widely accepted framework for controlling the design of residential development than that which currently exists in England. A broadly based acceptance of design control is necessary because in the final analysis the power to develop – or to invest elsewhere – lies in the hands of developers guided by their professional advisors and only rarely in the hands of politicians and their planners. Nevertheless, within this context some writers have observed that the value of design is gaining a wider acceptance and is now in demand across a series of levels – because people want better places to live, because developers are pursuing a better product, and because politicians want to be associated with better decisions (Gleave, 1990, p. 63).

Unfortunately, the effectiveness of any system of reviewing design is particularly difficult to measure as decisions made on design are constrained by a wide range of often conflicting factors, particular to the circumstances of the locality (DoE, 1995a, p. 3). In the case of residential design these are summed up in Fig. 1.4. Nevertheless, those authorities who have begun to make appropriate investments in the necessary tools with which to establish a

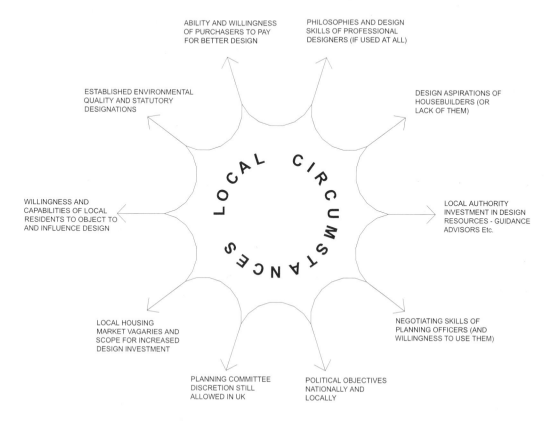

*Fig. 1.4  Local circumstances and their influence on residential design control.*

robust, contextually relevant framework for residential design control, are beginning, in turn, to report dividends in a local acceptance that quality design increasingly represents a prerequisite for development (Brackenbury, 1994, p. 73). In such places, design tends to be seen less as an afterthought or as a subject for protracted haggling after the important decision on whether to develop or not has already been made. Instead, design is seen as an important part of the development process, in which early investment by developers is both necessary and appropriate (Carmona, 1996b, p. 180). Such practice is evident in an increasing number of authorities, but is still rare enough that its impact on a national scale has been limited (see Chapters 7 and 8).

Characteristic of many such places is a full hierarchy of design guidance, established to ensure full coverage and dissemination of a planning authority's design objectives – design policy in local plans, local and/or county design guides, flexible design standards (i.e. for residential roads), site-specific design briefs and area appraisal – in which each level of the hierarchy acts to further develop and elucidate the one above (see Chapter 5). Support for such hierarchical approaches has been implicitly given in new government guidance on design, because of the 'greater certainty to all those involved' that clear guidance gives (DoE, 1997b, para. A2).

Nevertheless, evidence for increased effectiveness remains largely anecdotal as little empirical research has yet been done which attempts to measure – across one land use type – how effective such an integrated hierarchy can be. The intention has been to start to fill this research gap by focusing on the design of private sector residential development. The work relates to, and in part develops, research which focused in depth on one level in the hierarchy – design policies in local plans – although across the full range of land use types (Punter and Carmona, 1997a).

**Residential design control – a research gap**

'There can be no doubt about the major planning issue in the UK . . . It is how much housing we are going to need over the next 20 years, and where we are going to put it' (Breheny and Hall, 1996, p. 39). There can be equally little doubt about what, above anything else, will occupy the thoughts and activities of all those upon whom such decisions impact (the planning officers, local councillors, housebuilders, designers and the many affected local populations) over the next twenty years following acceptance of the housing projections; namely, how to implement the resulting allocations on the ground in environmentally and socially sustainable, locally acceptable and contextually compatible ways.

In the light of such pressures, and the fact that across the western world most people live in what can be characterised as suburban locations, it is surprising that only a minority of design and design policy research has ever addressed a concern for residential areas. Furthermore, that in the UK, the vast majority of planning policy has been concerned with either urban or rural issues, with residential areas often receiving hardly a mention (Hooper, 1994). Residential design-based research has been noticeable by its absence in recent years for a number of reasons:

- because the public sector involvement in housing provision has declined (a rich source of research in the past);
- because the perceived free hand given to the housebuilding industry in the 1980s rendered such research ineffective (see Chapter 2); and
- because the focus of much academic endeavour in recent years has switched to the problems and opportunities offered by design in town and city centres.

This reflects the findings of the Design Policies in Local Plans research, which revealed the general failure of planning authorities to relate design policies to different contexts – in particular to suburban contexts (Punter and Carmona, 1997a). The lack of research, and the need to examine the impact of residential design guides in particular, was also confirmed in government consultation on means to enhance 'Quality in Town and Country' (DoE, 1996b, paras. 4.5.3 and 4.5.7). Such work, the analysis suggests, 'is overdue if past experience is to inform future guidance'.

### Research aim and objectives

The particular aim of the research has been:

To evaluate current practice and innovation in local authority control of private sector residential design through the planning system, as a means to make recommendations on improving the effectiveness of residential design control.

The research aim was subdivided into seven detailed objectives:

**Objective 1.** To explore the evolving framework for design control in England and the attitudes of the key stakeholders in the planning and development process to that new framework.

**Objective 2.** To review critically the prevalence and hierarchical structure of residential design policy and guidance – county and district/unitary – and how up-to-date the different forms of guidance are in practice.

**Objective 3.** To evaluate the content, prescription and analytical basis of residential design policy and guidance and the regional emphasis of authorities – county and district/unitary.

**Objective 4.** To analyse the preparation and use of residential design policy and guidance in practice.

**Objective 5.** To assess any innovative practice in, and possible future directions of, residential design control.

**Objective 6.** To evaluate the roles of different forms of local design guidance – county design guides, district design guides, design codes, design frameworks and briefs – used in controlling residential development.

**Objective 7.** To propose a new government framework for controlling the design of residential development.

### Limitations to the research scope

Although the perspectives of the full range of stakeholders involved in the process of controlling residential design are reviewed in detail in Part 1 of the book (utilising primary and secondary sources), the key empirical elements of the research – in Part 2 – largely focus on residential design control from the perspective of the authorities delivering the service. In this respect, the research is not intended to be a definitive study of residential design control effectiveness. Such a study would require, in addition, a more focused project by project study of the results of local authority intervention in residential design outcomes on the ground, and of the impact of such controls on the operations of the other key stakeholders in the process. Nevertheless, the current research does offer the first stage of such a wider study of residential design control effectiveness, while an agenda for the next stage is briefly discussed in Chapter 9.

### The book structure

Part 1 of the book deals with the context for the research and effectively constitutes a wide-ranging literature review. By its nature, this part of the book departs from the strict remit of residential design to encompass the control of design more widely, although with an emphasis on residential design. This was inevitable because the process of controlling residential design sits within a broader framework for controlling design *per se*. The literature is used in Part 1 of the book as a means to explore, and underpin, an analysis framework for the empirical research in Part 2.

In dealing with the broad context for the work, Part 1 has begun in this chapter with an introductory justification for the research and with a brief review of the work. In Chapter 2 the contemporary debates on residential design control are placed in an historical context. The chapter culminates in a review of the government planning guidance on design and residential design in place throughout the period of the content analysis discussed in Chapter 7 – up to (but not including) the mould-breaking guidance contained in (revised) PPG1 (DoE, 1997b). In Chapter 3, this new design guidance is examined in depth alongside a review of the wider design debate and of roles of the different stakeholders in the process. Ten themes of design control are identified and the impact of the new framework for control on these themes is examined. Chapter 4 goes on to examine the speculative residential house – both as a product, and as regards the processes inherent in its delivery. The roles and motivations of the housebuilder and house buyer form the major focus of the chapter. Part 1 concludes with Chapter 5 in which some of the key theoretical requirements prescribed in the literature for effective design control systems are discussed.

Part 2 of the book contains the empirical heart of the research. Part 2 begins in Chapter 6 by making use of the rare opportunity provided by new government guidance on design to review the responses of twenty key respondents to the consultation exercise held on PPG1. By this means, a snap shot of opinion is taken across the full range of stakeholders in the design/development process, as an attempt to look to the future and identify any potential for consensus suggested across the responses examined. In the remainder of Part 2 the work focuses more specifically on residential design control as the means to address directly the key research aim. Thus, in Chapter 7 the results of a country-wide survey and content analysis of residential design guidance is discussed, reviewing mainstream practice and priorities in controlling residential design quality. The chapter concludes with an examination of the regional variations in priority afforded to residential design control. In Chapter 8 the work examines a range of innovative residential design control practice drawing on ten case studies. The case studies, which are distributed throughout the book as a series of insets (following each chapter), offer a means to explore the preparation, use and roles of the different forms of residential design guidance in controlling the design of new-build residential development.

Part 3 focuses on the future challenge faced by those involved in the process of designing and controlling new residential development. Chapter 9 draws from the research to present recommendations in the form of an agenda for improving the effectiveness of residential design control. Finally, in Chapter 10, a series of recent government initiatives in the area are examined, and the extent to which these relate to the recommendations and may, therefore, lead to a general improvement in residential quality is considered.

The book is structured so that the key empirical chapters (6, 7 and 8) address directly six of the seven key research objectives (see Fig. 1.5). The objectives are used in turn as a focus to structure the conclusions of these chapters. Chapter 9 brings these conclusions together, alongside the key findings of each section of the preceding chapters (given as bullet point

| | Research Objectives | Book Chapters | Methodological Stages | |
|---|---|---|---|---|
| Book Part 1 | 1–7 | 1 2 3 4 5 | 1 | The Context |
| Book Part 2 | 1 2 3 4 5 6 | 6 7 8 | 2 3 4 5 6 7 | Practice & Innovation |
| Book Part 3 | 7 1 5 | 9 10 | 8 1 8 | The Challenge |

*Fig. 1.5  Book structure.*

'evaluations' at the end of each section) as a method to address directly the overall research aim and the seventh research objective.

### The eight research stages

To ensure systematic analysis of the research aim and seven detailed objectives, an eight-stage methodology was adopted:

1. **Literature review** – a wide ranging residential design/design control literature review and review of existing and emerging government guidance.
2. **Key stakeholder responses** – a detailed comparative review of the responses of twenty key respondents to the consultation exercise held on the revised government guidance on design in the form of (revised) PPG1.
3. **Country-wide survey of residential design guidance** – a 100 per cent country-wide postal survey of all local authorities in England and request for examples of the full hierarchy of design guidance still in active use for controlling residential design.
4. **Content analysis** – the detailed content analysis of residential design guidance collected from all of the responding authorities utilising a detailed pro-forma to extract and analyse data.
5. **Analysis of innovative practice** – the identification of innovative practice in residential design control and its further investigation by means of two special conferences.
6. **Direct practitioner input** – the commissioning of structured practitioner papers from a number of the innovative authorities, as a further feed into the innovative case study work.
7. **Wider practitioner discussion** – discussion of the innovative practice at the two special conferences and six further academic/CPD conferences at which variously one or a number of the innovative practice case studies were presented.
8. **Research analysis and synthesis** – the detailed analysis and synthesis of outputs from stages 1 to 7 and the drawing out of recommendations and proposals for future research.

The main research instruments combined policy analysis in the form of a country-wide survey and content analysis of residential design policy and guidance, with case study analysis through a series of 'innovative practice case studies'. These instruments were supplemented by a review of wider practitioner experience of local authority practice and by a review of key stakeholder responses to revised government guidance on design.

A detailed discussion of the methodology for the key empirical chapters (6, 7 and 8) is included at the start of these chapters. Broadly, Stage 1 corresponds to Chapters 1 to 5 and to Chapter 10, Stage 2 to Chapter 6, Stages 3 and 4 to Chapter 7, Stages 5 to 7 to Chapter 8 and Stage 8 to Chapter 9 (see Fig. 1.5).

## Conclusions

The research has proved increasingly topical as the work commenced, and if the 'Analysis of Responses to the Discussion Document Quality in Town and Country' (DoE, 1996b) is to be believed then it is environmentally necessary as well. Through its focus on examining the potential local authorities possess by way of their planning powers to control the design of private sector residential development, it directly addresses a key opportunity to ameliorate environmentally the impact of the recent housing projections. The research is all the more important because the design of residential environments has suffered consistently from a lack of serious academic investigation – notwithstanding the majority of UK citizens living in 'suburban' locations – and because design control remains one of the least researched areas of planning practice – despite being the area with which planning is most readily associated by the public.

The 1996 government discussion paper – 'Household Growth – Where Shall We Live?' – suggested that 'There is growing resistance to new development which is regarded as ugly or makes places seem "just like everywhere else"'. It asked: 'What more can be done to raise the quality of design of new residential development?' (DoE, 1996c). Based on the systematic empirical research, an agenda is outlined in this book that begins to address this question. It reflects a period that since 1996 has seen increasingly rapid change in policy approaches to the question.

**INSET A: ESSEX COUNTY COUNCIL – THE 'NEW' ESSEX GUIDE**

With its dramatic move away from standards-based approaches and towards townscape and local vernacular as the basis of residential design control, the original 'Essex Design Guide' (Essex County Council, 1973) broke the mould of residential design guidance. The new guide (Essex Planning Officers Association, 1997) maintains the 'spectrum of development' at its core (see Fig. 2.3), but attempts to refine the criteria by drawing from the now considerable experience of what has worked and what has not. The aim is to prevent developers – and planners – from slipping back into unsatisfactory suburban compromises.

The strengthened core principles are boosted by a comprehensive examination and adoption of the urban design theory that filled the intervening years. Thus, issues of sustainability, mixed use, crime prevention and connectivity are taken on board, at least in part, to move practice on the ground away from the branch-and-twig, single use, introspective cul-de-sac layouts that had become dominant. Most obviously, the new emphasis is reflected in the revised title for the guide – the 'Essex Design Guide for Residential and Mixed Use Areas'. Thus, in schemes larger than 500 dwellings, the incorporation of non residential uses – facilities for residents and employment uses – and the provision of a mix of tenures and dwelling sizes becomes a requirement.

The intention of the new guide is to establish a set of principles and a process of implementation that will ensure a contextually appropriate layout structure for each site. Thus, the form, topography, natural desire lines and accesses to the site may suggest layout; while spaces should be designed against criteria established in the guide and before the resulting legible layout is (only then) 'plumbed' for traffic circulation. The changed approach has been made possible through the introduction of the 20 mph concept for residential roads in the Second Edition of Design Bulletin 32 (see Chapter 2), a move which enabled new road standards to be introduced (Billingham, 1996, p. 22).

As part of a continued emphasis on local vernacular, the implications of arranging buildings to enclose space are made more explicit, addressing a clear omission of the earlier guidance. Thus, dwellings will need to be joined together and placed forward on the street, while wide-fronted, shallow-plan house types are promoted as offering the most advantageous house type for enclosing space, producing practical garden shapes, admitting daylight and producing building forms compatible with the Essex vernacular. An appendix is included in the guide illustrating these alternative house types, in an attempt to encourage developers to move away from their 'standard', detached, square (in plan) and regimented housing solutions.

The original design guide promised much, but, despite a small number of very good schemes, often failed to deliver the high quality environments envisaged. Nevertheless, there has been a widespread perception that the majority of output – since 1973 (post guide) – has shown considerable improvement on that before (Stones, 1992, p. 17). The guide also showed that the development control system could be creative, offered townscape-derived urban design principles to a new audience, encouraged highways engineers to re-assess their hallowed rules of thumb, and reintroduced the concept that contemporary development has much to learn from the past (Smales, 1991, Sec. 9.3). Planning officers in Essex have argued that the failure of the guide to live up to its original expectations can be put down to number of factors:

- the negative approach adopted to design control by the government throughout the 1980s;

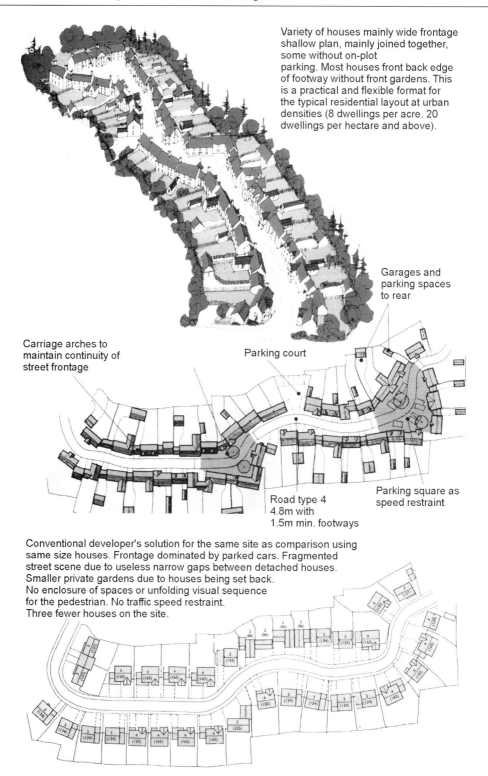

Variety of houses mainly wide frontage shallow plan, mainly joined together, some without on-plot parking. Most houses front back edge of footway without front gardens. This is a practical and flexible format for the typical residential layout at urban densities (8 dwellings per acre. 20 dwellings per hectare and above).

Garages and parking spaces to rear

Carriage arches to maintain continuity of street frontage

Parking court

Parking square as speed restraint

Road type 4
4.8m with
1.5m min. footways

Conventional developer's solution for the same site as comparison using same size houses. Frontage dominated by parked cars. Fragmented street scene due to useless narrow gaps between detached houses. Smaller private gardens due to houses being set back. No enclosure of spaces or unfolding visual sequence for the pedestrian. No traffic speed restraint. Three fewer houses on the site.

*Fig. A.1 Case study 1, informal urban street compared with typical unsatisfactory layout using standard detached house types (EPOA, 1997).*

- the lack of commitment to the guide shown by some of the district authorities, who took over responsibility for its implementation from the county almost immediately; and
- the intransigence of most developers and the compromises of planning officers.

To the list, one of the only detailed post-design guide effectiveness studies to have been undertaken of any guide (Smales, 1991, Secs. 9.2–9.3) revealed that:

- the theories and principles of the 1973 guide were based on the subjective judgements of its authors and owe little to systematic research;
- the use of jargon prevented the guide's message from reaching its wider intended audience – local populations and developers; and
- the views of residents and housebuilders were largely ignored in the guide's preparation, with the resulting guidance over-emphasising the significance of visual quality and failing to recognise the redeeming features of the housing it aimed to replace – the high levels of privacy enjoyed by residents, their possession of front gardens and play space and their legibility.

Although it is too early to examine the effectiveness of the new guide, the document begins with two distinct advantages. First, it is published at a time when design control is in a period of positive re-evaluation by government, and second, the fourteen district councils have been working hand-in-hand with the county on the production of the new guide (although the latest round of local government reorganisation may again muddy the waters).[1]

If anything, the core principles of the original guide receive a vote of confidence and a further boost in the new version. Nevertheless, in an attempt to undermine long-standing criticisms that the guide is too restrictive, the new guide contains fourteen case studies illustrating the range of spatial treatments possible when following the design principles. The most basic is the informal urban street (see Fig. A.1), which illustrates an attractive street

*Fig. A.2  'New' Essex Design Guide housing at Noak Bridge.*

[1] Local government reorganisation has reduced the number of districts under Essex County Council from fourteen to twelve, with two of the former districts receiving unitary status. It is intended that these new authorities will also adopt the guide, and will use the design service of the county council on an agency basis.

scene in which a variety of house sizes are linked and set forward onto the street to provide on-plot parking through carriage arches and generous garden sizes. The approach is contrasted with a standard developer's scheme of detached house types resulting in 'unsatisfactory suburbia' that offers fewer houses, a lower return on investment and a fragmented street scene.

The split responsibility for design between the county and districts has consistently caused problems in making necessary revisions to the Essex Design Guide. Thus, although the County has responsibility for highways design and maintains a specialist design advisory service – from which the districts may seek advice – day-to-day responsibility for design rests with the districts. Over the years the most intractable problems faced by the writers of the guide have been finding agreement over the variety of design standards used by the individual districts. The solution has been to agree to disagree on the grounds that although design concept and physical standards are inextricably interlinked, as long as individual authorities aspire to the overall design principles laid out in the document, districts should be able to impose their varying physical standards as an insert to the main guide.

Reflecting the now dominant position of the development plan, particular efforts have, however, been made to bring the new guide into line with existing local plans – a difficult task across fourteen districts. If past practice is repeated, then once adopted, it is likely that local plans will also begin to draw from the guide in the formulation of plan policy, as and when they are rolled forward. Currently, the Epping Forest plan illustrates the most comprehensive example of an Essex district explicitly complementing the design guide through its own local plan policy (Epping Forest District Council, 1994).

The disagreements over design standards nevertheless emphasise a continuing tension between the county and district authorities in an area where some degree of overlapping responsibility still applies. The original and the new guides, nevertheless, represent substantial achievements against such a background and against the continued lack of resources given to design – some districts still have no design skills specifically available to the planning department. The fact that the guide took seven years to revise clearly indicates the need for greater resources if effective implementation is to be achieved.

*Fig. A.3 'Original' Essex Design Guide housing at Woodham Ferrers.*

During the technical consultation on the new guide, the reactions from local chapters of the Royal Institute of British Architects (RIBA) and the Housebuilders Federation (HBF) were somewhat negative. Individual local developers were more positive, however, on the grounds that the guide could make their more tailored products more competitive against those of the volume housebuilders. Subsequently, the guide underwent a period of wider public consultation in order to give it the status of supplementary design guidance when finally adopted by the individual districts. To date, however, direct user research – the lack of which contributed to the perceived failings of the 1973 guide – has still not been undertaken for the new guidance. Nevertheless, since publication, a new commitment to the guide from districts and housebuilders has become apparent (although some early applications from housebuilders water down many of the principles). Nevertheless, some successful inter-pretations are already realised (see Fig. A.2), to add to the now plentiful Design Guide housing scattered throughout Essex (see Fig. A.3).

Rather than a twenty-five-year-old guide running to catch a policy train that has left it far behind, government guidance – and broader planning practice – is only just now beginning to catch the original guide with its dual emphasis on urban design and local distinctiveness. Reflecting this more positive approach to design, the Essex Guide is again rolling forward to incorporate many of the theoretical advances of the intervening years and to offer a more robust policy tool to practitioners.

# Chapter 2

# Residential design control: history and government guidance up to 1997

> Who shall decide on the nature of good design in the built environment? 'Me!' 'Me!'
> 'Me!', come the cries of response from Prince and planner, councillor and consultant,
> architect and accountant. It seems that each must believe in the virtue of their own
> opinion at the expense of others, must believe that there can be only one right
> answer. . . . This intolerance does not apply in other arts (HBF and RIBA, 1990, p. 6).

The extent to which design is recognised as a legitimate interest of the planning system
has been a matter of great controversy dating back to the evolution of planning in Britain
and its emergence out of the architectural profession. In reality the majority of decisions
planning authorities make will be design-related in one form or other, from those dealing
with settlement form and transportation, to those concerning land use mix, and from
those aimed at defining an appropriate public realm, to those concerned with individual
site layout and detailed design. To that extent planning undoubtedly remains a design
discipline, but a discipline that has rarely been fully able (or comfortable) to embrace its
design roots.

The research represents a study of contemporary residential design control practice and
is not intended, therefore, to be an historical evaluation of design control, or residential
design, both of which are well covered elsewhere (Punter, 1986; 1987; Punter and
Carmona, 1997a; Sim, 1993; Edwards, 1981; Ravetz, 1995); nor is it an evaluation of housing
policy beyond that directly concerned with design. Nevertheless, the first half of Chapter 2
constitutes a short examination of the development of residential design control (within the
wider context of general design control) as a means to understand more clearly the
evolving critiques of such control and the government framework established to guide the
process. The second half of the chapter explores the guidance regime in place during the
collection and analysis of local authority guidance examined in Chapter 7 – namely, the
period up to, but not including, the dramatic changes in policy contained in (revised)
PPG1 (1997). Again, although the framework for design established by government
guidance during this period is discussed elsewhere in greater depth (Punter and Carmona,
1997a, Ch. 3), this more focused overview allows the substantive research in Chapters 7
and 8 to be contextualised. Subsequent changes to government guidance are discussed
in Chapters 3 and 10.

## The historical context for controlling residential design

### *Public health and amenity*

The first tangible attempts to control the design of housing were the public health acts of 1874 and 1875, which were also among the earliest attempts to control the design of development *per se*, providing early testimony to the important place residential design has always had in shaping design control more generally. The so-called 'bye-law housing' that resulted from the acts provided the first important lesson for design control, namely that the minimum standards given in legislation (or guidance) very often become the maximum standards that developers will provide, thus leading to standardised uniform townscapes.

In part as a reaction to the legacy of bye-law housing and certainly as a reaction to the slum conditions in England in the nineteenth and early twentieth centuries, the Garden Cities movement inspired and led by Ebenezer Howard, first suggested an alternative vision of the English home. The components of this vision included:

- the ownership of land by the municipality with leasing to private concerns;
- a diversity of activities, including social institutions and industry;
- agriculture surrounding the garden cities to largely support it;
- a limit on population size and physical restriction by greenbelts;
- the linking together of these new communities to form larger polycentric social cities (Mumford in Howard, 1976).

In Letchworth, Welwyn Garden City and Hampstead Garden Suburb (see Fig. 1.2), Howard's ideas were interpreted by talented designers including Louis de Soissons, Barry Parker, Raymond Unwin and Sir Edwin Lutyens. Unfortunately, 'as with many visionaries, the concepts have not faired so well on the drawing boards of less talented designers' (Rudlin and Falk, 1999, p. 32). Nevertheless, the housing forms these early suburban developments inspired, produced an enduring vision of the English home that has persisted ever since.

The 1906 Hampstead Garden Suburb Act which relaxed the bye-law standards to allow the building of picturesque suburbs provided the precedent for those who drafted the first Housing and Town Planning Act in 1909. This provided for the suspension of bye-laws where such was shown to be in the interests of good planning. It intended to 'secure the home healthy, the house beautiful, the town pleasant, the city dignified and the suburb salubrious' (John Burns, ex-president of the local government board). The legislation clearly hoped that the use of statutes designed originally to facilitate a development which had (in very exceptional circumstances) achieved a very high standard of amenity, would in turn promote equally good practice elsewhere (Smith, 1974, p. 25).

In reality, because only new suburban development could be adequately controlled to secure 'proper sanitary conditions, amenity and convenience' (Section 54 [i]) few schemes were ever approved. Nevertheless, the second of these schemes in Ruislip-Northwood attempted to extend the provisions of the Act to allow the council to control the character or design of buildings by requiring the submission of full plans and particulars, and empowering them to make 'reasonable alterations' if the quality of design or repetitious use of designs and materials were 'injurious to amenity' (Punter, 1986, p. 352). With this, 'amenity' was introduced as a key test of environmental quality, a test that survives through to today and still constitutes a frequent, if ill-defined, criterion for refusing planning permission to poor quality residential development.

The 1918 Tudor Walters report – largely written by Raymond Unwin – provided the first real attempt to get to grips with the design and provision of mass housing. It was a reaction to the monotony of bye-law housing but frequently itself led to its own form of monotony through the inter-war public sector neo-Georgian style estates and garden suburbs that it spawned. 'The failure of the tenement as a remedy [to the housing ills] led to a general belief (never yet corrected) that the only real cure was escape' (Ginsburg, 1973, p. 224). This escape led between the wars to a massive expansion in what the *Architectural Review* later derided as 'semidetsia' (the middle ground between centre and periphery) or what they saw as the worst excesses of suburbia – the arcadian dream of so many.

During the period, the 1932 Town and Country Planning Act represented a milestone in design control, allowing authorities to control size, height, design and the external appearance of buildings in areas where there was little likelihood of extensive development, in areas of natural interest or beauty, and in areas of historic or artistic interest. The Act thereby initiated an early two-tier system of design control, a system that also survives in conservation legislation through to today. The Ministry was still reluctant, however, to allow authorities full design control powers, warning instead in Circular 1305/33 that 'taste is not a matter for dogmatism' and that the powers were largely to be used for 'preventing outrages' (Ministry of Health, 1933). These instructions bowed to the concerns of the architectural profession as a developing anti-design control lobby, and severely limited the influence that local authorities could exert on design. Significantly, the circular advocated the use of design guidance and architectural panels, both of which have since played an important role in design control (Punter, 1986, p. 355).

In the case of the former (and as regards housing design), the role has been decisive; a role which began with the early rural housing design guides developed by the CPRE for areas such as the Peak District (Peak District Advisory Panel, 1934). Such guides showed a concern for issues of siting, urban form and composition and integration with the landscape, as well as with the intrinsic appearance of new housing development, this despite the growing hijack of the debate by the bugbear of all attempts to control design quality: the issue of aesthetics (see Fig. 2.1).

In the 1930s, design control, and residential design control in particular, became embroiled in the 'battle of the styles' that raged in the architectural press, as modernist houses built by architects for their clients, repeatedly fell foul of the 'conservative' planning committees. Architects denigrated the 'make believe domestic' and the 'factitious rusticity' of speculative housebuilders, while local councillors railed against 'alien intrusions' and European influences (Punter and Carmona, 1997a, p. 18). These debates revealed a yawning gap between the tastes of the design professionals and that of the lay public (see Chapter 3). The situation was compounded by an anti-suburban snobbery and lack of understanding of housing as a consumer good that again persists to the present day. Thus, neo-Georgian styles were promoted as approved taste by many in the design professions – including planners – but their widespread adoption in public sector housing schemes, as a result of the 1919 Housing Manual (inspired by the Tudor Walters Report), made them unsaleable to the public. The public conversely preferred the sham picturesque styles designed by the speculative housebuilders that clearly distinguished middle class housing from their social housing neighbours (Punter and Carmona, 1997a, p. 18). The venom of the argument is well illustrated by a quotation from *Housing in the Peak District*:

> The beauty of our English countryside is daily being disfigured, not only by the thoughtlessness of speculative builders, but also through the apathy and indifference of the public, for there are to-day great numbers of people, many in responsible positions, who think that the present has no obligations either to the past or the future, and that if a man wants to build a house he need consider only

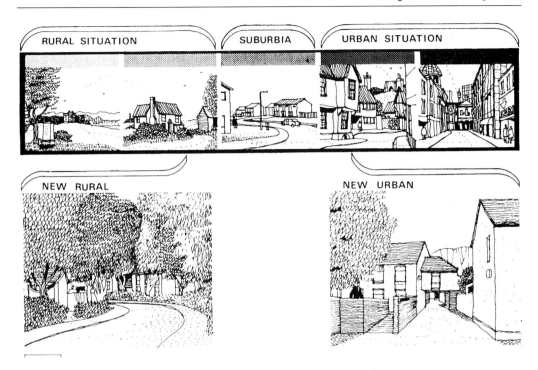

*Fig. 2.3 The Essex Design Guide visual spectrum of settlement patterns.*

numerous imitators it spawned, only a minority of which were based on a similar tailoring to locality. As Mel Dunbar (the assistant county planner for Essex largely responsible for the guide) warned: 'The guide was never intended to be a recipe or pattern book . . . it's a design tool'; an important distinction in light of the argument made in Circular 28/66 (Best, 1978, p. 950).

The guide recognised that there were three key aspects in the process of designing new housing. First, there was the client's requirements which related to the type of housing being provided and the market to which it was aimed. Second, there was the impact on design of the characteristics of the site itself, and third, there was what was referred to as the 'community brief'. It was argued that 'any new development forms part of and affects the community. Therefore, it is reasonable for its members to expect certain things from the development. The planning authority as the representative of the community in such matters provides this brief, [and] in respect of housing, the brief is the new policy and contents of this document'; in other words the guide (Essex County Council, 1973, p. 83).

The successful fusion of all these elements was considered a difficult task, a task requiring the involvement of an architect; a requirement recommended in the guide. Among the architectural profession, however, the reception given to the guide was less than favourable, and the letters pages of the *Architects' Journal* at the time were full of complaints that the planning profession was overstepping the bounds of its professional responsibilities and was consequently strangling creativity. Such comment was answered equally stridently by proponents of the guide who argued that it was intended as guidance only and would encourage more imaginative solutions rather than stifling them (Sim, 1993, pp. 123–30).

A survey of design guidance in 1976 testified to the success of the Essex guide, by charting the rapid spread of design guidance on residential design and layout across the country, particularly in the South East and in authorities with a high housing throughput. It also recorded the impression of planning officers that such guides – alongside design briefs – helped secure a better standard of development, particularly in urban and suburban authorities (DoE and HRF, 1976, pp. 1–4). 'For a while it did appear that the design of housing estates was to improve radically, and most planners held the view that the more "design guide" housing that was built the more that public perception would increase of the alternatives to the standard product of the past' (Holt, 1988, pp. 71–155).

The adoption of the new design guides confirmed a move away from the well established standards-based approach to residential design control, which, until that point, had been pursued by most authorities. This move reflected a deep-seated unease with the standard's approach to residential environments particularly among the architectural profession. The *Architectural Review* described residential design standards – in the same year that the Essex Design Guide was unveiled – as 'the cruellest straitjacket of rules and regulations which confine the designer to so narrow a tolerance of movement that inevitably the same depressing homescapes are spawned from one end of the country to the other' (Ginsburg, 1973, p. 228).

In 1976, a major piece of research sponsored by the DoE largely supported this view. 'The Value of Standards for the External Residential Environment' recorded that 'it is often felt that standards block initiative and innovation in environmental design [and] many designers think it futile to look beyond the "standard" solution when they feel that, even if they can improve on it, their design is likely to be rejected' (DoE, 1976, p. 23). Thus, the report concluded that standards frequently failed in their objective to improve design quality; largely because coverage was often patchy, because they only covered a limited number of environmental factors, and because when used, they were usually seen as the maximum rather than the minimum desirable qualities to be achieved in developments.

Consequently, the report recommended a far more critical and flexible use of standards, based on a wider range of indices and on a deference to context; suggesting in total thirteen key indicators against which to assess residential design (density, sunlight, daylight, privacy, view, air purity, shelter, quiet, access, provision for vehicles, accessibility of facilities, provision for recreation, safety from vehicles). Few local authorities were capable of developing such sophisticated indices however, while the few that did (in particular the London Boroughs) have since faced constant problems in defining the relationship of such standards to plan policy. Their value as control devices has consequently proved somewhat limited (Punter *et al.*, 1996, pp. 125–6).

In 1977 the DoE released 'Design Bulletin 32 (DB32): Residential Roads and Footpaths' (DoE and DoT, 1977). Influenced greatly by Essex and the other design guides it advocated: a hierarchy of access arrangements, ranging from mews courts and cul-de-sacs, to local distributor roads, and made an attempt to strike a better balance between the visual environment and the requirements of the car, for example through advocating shared road and footpath surfaces. All in all, it marked a further sea change in the control of residential environments. 'The aim was to help designers to create safer and more convenient surroundings for pedestrians; provide ready access to dwellings and parking spaces; ensure that land and other resources are used economically and with regard to maintenance requirements and improve the overall appearance of new housing schemes' (Housing Research Foundation, 1983).

In the circular accompanying the design bulletin, the Minister welcomed the initiative taken by the county and district authorities in producing the new forms of design guidance, stating that they strike 'a realistic balance between highways, planning, housing ... [and] ... public utilities' interests, and ... provide a flexible approach to the development and application of standards for local use' (DoE, 1977). It was expected, however, that many of the authorities would subsequently amend their advice to fall into line with DB32, thus encouraging a common approach and some consistency across the country. Most subsequently did and the worst prairie landscapes of suburbia were superseded by the more compact cul-de-sac layouts, road hierarchies and traditional styling advocated by the design guides (see Fig. 2.4).

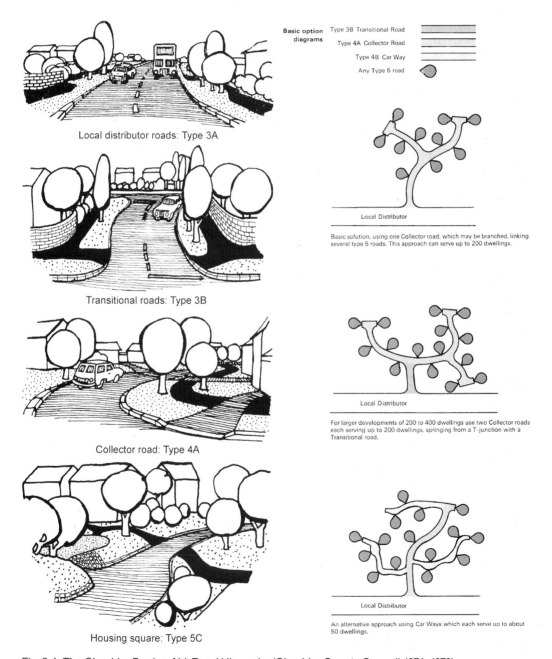

Fig. 2.4   The Cheshire Design Aid, Road Hierarchy (Cheshire County Council, 1974; 1976).

### Free market backlash

By now the private housebuilding sector was increasingly active and was (like the public sector) attracting much criticism. But attempts to find ways of improving design control constantly ran into counter measures to set the developer and the architect free (RFAC, 1990, p. 5). For example, the conclusions of the 1975 review of the development control system (Dobry Commission) – originally set up to find ways of streamlining development control – were effectively ignored when the commission came down in favour of tighter design control, in particular in designated areas (DoE, 1975, pp. 80–3). Subsequently, the 1977 expenditure committee of the House of Commons – under intense lobbying from the HBF and RIBA – noted: 'We accept that planning authorities should be able to exercise a degree of aesthetic control. However we think they must exercise restraint in this regard, since it would be most undesirable to stifle creativity and innovation' (House of Commons, 1977). The result of their deliberations was a call to central government for new advice on design control.

The subsequent Circular 22/80 (Fig. 2.5) – introduced by a new Conservative government committed to unfettering private enterprise – set the pattern for design control until the early 1990s. Many of the issues raised in the circular emanated directly from the deliberations of the House of Commons Expenditure Committee. Thus, the overriding emphasis was one of restricting design control to environmentally sensitive areas based on the argument that design is essentially subjective, that planning committees should not impose their views on developers, that there had to be good reason to control the external appearance of developments, and that design guidance was useful, but was to be 'used as guidance, and not as detailed rules' (DoE, 1980). This last comment, in particular, reflected the rough ride the 'Essex Design Guide' received at the hands of the expenditure committee.

Throughout the 1980s the essential thrust of Circular 22/80 remained in force, and was all but reiterated in 1985 in a new circular dealing exclusively with 'aesthetic control' (DoE, 1985). This despite a Royal Town Planning Institute (RTPI)/RIBA (1980) joint accord on design which conceded the legitimate interest of the planning system to consider design and context, and a draft circular in 1983 which was never adopted, but which in an annex went as far as to propose a checklist of legitimate concerns (with explanations) for the design deliberations of planning committees – scale, density, height, access, layout, landscaping, materials and other functional requirements such as parking, servicing and environment factors. One further interesting suggestion which the 1997 equivalent was to come back to (see pp. 70–6), was that 'The planning authority's requirements should be made explicit and should not be constantly changed or elaborated' (DoE, 1983, para. 5).

In 1988 the guidance was again reconfirmed in the first version of Planning Policy Guidance (PPG1): 'General Policy and Principles' (DoE, 1988a), which stated that 'matters of detailed design have long been an unnecessary source of contention and delay in the planning system'. It argued that 'Aesthetics is an extremely subjective matter', and that 'control of external appearance should only be exercised where there is a fully justified reason for doing so'. This largely negative stance was backed by the threat that 'where there are no reasonable objections to the external appearance proposed by the applicant and a refusal of permission is based simply on a preference for a different external appearance, there may be grounds for an award of costs in an inquiry appeal' (DoE, 1988a, paras. 27–29). This threat still stands in a moderated form in Circular 8/93 (DoE, 1993b, Para. 4 – see p 45).

With the 1988 version of PPG1, the free market – anti-design control – ideology reached its peak. However, Circular 22/80 (on which it was based) represented only half of a double blow for housing design when at roughly the same time Michael Heseltine – as Secretary of State

*Aesthetic Control*

18. The Secretary of State for the Environment's view on control of design was set out in his speech at York on 13 September 1979 to the Town and Country Planning Summer School. He said:

> 'Far too many of those involved in the system – whether the planning officer or the amateur on the planning committee – have tried to impose their standards quite unnecessarily on what individuals want to do ... Democracy as a system of government I will defend against all comers but as an arbiter of taste or as a judge of aesthetic or artistic standards it falls far short of a far less controlled system of individual, corporate or institutional patronage and initiative ...'

This view is endorsed by the Secretary of State for Wales.

19. Planning authorities should recognise that aesthetics is an extremely subjective matter. They should not therefore impose their tastes on developers simply because they believe them to be superior. Developers should not be compelled to conform to the fashion of the moment at the expense of individuality, originality or traditional styles. Nor should they be asked to adopt designs which are unpopular with their customers or clients.

20. Nevertheless control of external appearance can be important especially for instance in environmentally sensitive areas such as national parks, areas of outstanding natural beauty, conservation areas and areas where the quality of environment is of a particularly high standard. Local planning authorities should reject obviously poor designs which are out of scale or character with their surroundings. They should confine concern to those aspects of design which are significant for the aesthetic quality of the area. Only exceptionally should they control design details if the sensitive character of the area or the particular building justifies it. Even where such detailed control is exercised it should not be over-fastidious in such matters as, for example, the precise shade of colour of bricks. They should be closely guided in such matters by their professionally qualified advisers. This is especially important where a building has been designed by an architect for a particular site. Design guides may have a useful role to play provided they are used as guidance and not as detailed rules.

21. Control of external appearance should only be exercised where there is a fully justified reason for doing so. If local planning authorities take proper account of this policy there should be fewer instances of protracted negotiations over the design of projects and a reduction in the number of appeals to the Secretaries of State on matters of design. When such appeals are made the Secretaries of State will be very much guided by the policy advice set out in this circular in determining them.

*Fig. 2.5 Extract from Circular 22/80.*

for the Environment – also announced the abandoning of the Parker Morris standards, which, at least in the public sector, had increased space standards both inside and outside the dwelling (Anon., 1981). With this harsh regime for design control in place and with 'value for money' criteria also dictating the design of public sector housing, the government instigated the 'Time for Design' initiative (beginning in 1984/5) as an attempt to sweeten the pill. The idea was that various design-related initiatives in six chosen local authorities would highlight the importance of design. The most revealing initiatives examined the utility of design briefing and design guidance, but the overall effect of the experiment on design control practice in planning authorities, outside of those directly chosen, can best be described as marginal, particularly as no extra money was forthcoming for the initiative (DoE, 1990).

## A new deal

It was partially this harsh environment – which seemed to devalue the importance of good design – that drove the Prince of Wales to make a series of comments on the quality, or rather the lack of quality, in contemporary planning and design in the late 1980s. The Prince's comments once again brought the design debate to the fore, eventually spurring the government into action. The Prince's key arguments concerned the failure of much development to respect the context in which it was placed, leading him in his book *A Vision of Britain* (HRH The Prince of Wales, 1989) to suggest a set of ten commandments for harmonising development.

The Prince's speeches and book led to a series of further initiatives from other design commentators – most notably Francis Tibbalds (1988b) and John Delafons (1990) – both of whom supported a much broader range of issues defining environmental quality. The Royal Fine Art Commission (RFAC) also released an influential report at this time entitled 'Planning for Beauty', which advocated:

- the adoption by government of a more positive stance towards design control;
- that design should be recognised as a material consideration in all development; and
- that design guidelines should be much more widely used to emphasise context and the visual impact of buildings, as well as to articulate important public realm concerns (RFAC, 1990, p. 34).

In response to the renewed interest in design, Chris Patten – the then Secretary of State for the Environment – in a ground breaking speech to the RFAC, accepted the need to re-define government guidance on design, and that local authorities should examine the characteristics of valued local environments and the unwritten codes which had created them as a means of providing guidance to architects and developers in the future. The result of the speech was a second joint statement by the RTPI and RIBA which aimed to replace the advice in PPG1 (1988) as the official government statement on design (Tibbalds, 1991, p. 72). After minor amendments by the DoE, this time the statement was incorporated into government guidance as Annex A to a revised PPG1, released in March 1992 (DoE, 1992a – Fig. 2.6).

The Annex was markedly more positive about design control than its predecessor, although the decisively two-tier approach to design control remained firmly intact. The Annex recognised design as a material consideration and accepted a broader definition of design with an emphasis on the spaces between buildings. Most importantly, the statement recognised that authorities ought to enshrine their expectations of design in development plans and in supplementary design guidance, although this advice was tempered with warnings against excessive design interference and over-prescription in policy and guidance (DoE, 1992a, Annex A). The Annex also failed to embrace fully the new environmental imperative, which at the time of its publication was gaining momentum in the guise of the developing sustainability agenda.

Annex A to PPG1, and the newly revised Planning Policy Guidance Note (PPG) series as a whole, created a new framework within which decisions on design could be made, with (revised) PPG3: 'Housing', specifically relating and extending much of the design advice in PPG1 to residential development (DoE, 1992b). The publication of the revised PPG3 'indicated some mellowing of government's indulgence of the house building industry', through the increased emphasis on design, and through the withdrawal of the presumption in favour of releasing land for housing as allowed for in Circular 22/80 (Holt, 1992, pp. 071–000). However, in a departure from the general advice on design in PPG1, PPG3 drew directly from Circular 22/80 (DoE, 1980, para. 14) to emphasise the importance of the marketing judgement of housebuilders as the key basis for decisions on the functional requirements of residential development (DoE, 1992b, para. 6 – see pp. 39–41). DB32 was also revised and updated in 1992, supporting more innovative residential road layouts but prioritising a favoured

## ANNEX A: DESIGN CONSIDERATIONS   *Insert.*

A1. The appearance of proposed development and its relationship to its surroundings are material considerations, and those who determine planning applications and appeals should have regard to them in reaching their decisions.

A2. Good design should be the aim of all involved in the development process, but it is primarily the responsibility of designers and their clients. Applicants and planning authorities should recognise the benefits of engaging skilled advisers and encouraging high design standards. In considering a development proposal, authorities should recognise the design skills and advice of architects and consider carefully the advice of their own professionally qualified advisers, although the final decision remains that of the authority itself.

A3. Planning authorities should reject obviously poor designs which are out of scale or character with their surroundings. But aesthetic judgments are to some extent subjective and authorities should not impose their taste on applicants for planning permission simply because they believe it to be superior. Authorities should not seek to control the detailed design of buildings unless the sensitive character of the setting for the development justifies it.

A4. Applicants for planning permission should demonstrate wherever appropriate that they have considered the wider setting of buildings. New developments should respect but not necessarily mimic the character of their surroundings. Particular weight should be given to the impact of development on existing buildings and the landscape in environmentally sensitive areas such as National Parks, Areas of Outstanding Natural Beauty and Conservation Areas, where the scale of new development and the use of appropriate building materials will often be particularly important.

A5. The appearance and treatment of the spaces between and around buildings is also of great importance. Where these form part of an application site, the landscape design – whether hard or soft – will often be of comparable importance to the design of the buildings and should likewise be the subject of consideration, attention and expert advice. The aim should be for any development to result in a 'benefit' in environmental and landscape terms.

A6. Development plans and guidance for particular areas or sites should provide applicants with clear indications of planning authorities' design expectations. Such advice should avoid excessive prescription and detail and should concentrate on broad matters of scale, density, height, massing, layout, landscape and access. It should focus on encouraging good design rather than stifling experiment, originality or initiative. Indeed the design qualities of an exceptional scheme and its special contribution to the landscape or townscape may justify departing from local authorities' design guidance.

A7. Planning authorities should encourage applicants to consult them before formulating development proposals. Authorities' consideration of proposals will be assisted if applicants provide appropriate illustrative material, according to the circumstances, to show their proposals in context. It may sometimes be helpful for the applicant to submit a short written statement setting out the design principles of the proposal.

Fig. 2.6 PPGI Annex A.

'compromise' approach to road layout which aimed to balance housing, planning and highway objectives, thus failing to place the needs of the car behind those of the pedestrian or behind other urban design considerations (DoE and DoT, 1992).

    The new PPG1 and PPG3 were written to coincide with the fundamental changeover from an appeal-led planning system in the 1980s to a plan-led system in the 1990s. Brought about by a revision to the 1990 Town and Country Planning Act, Section 54A of the new legislation demanded that planning decisions 'be made in accordance with the plan unless material considerations indicate otherwise'. The result effectively enhanced the status of plan policy in an attempt to inject more certainty into a largely discretionary system, even though some have questioned the degree of certainty actually afforded by the change (Cronin, 1993; Blaney, 1993). Thus, with the new PPG1 encouraging planning authorities to indicate clearly their design requirements in development plans, and with Section 54A demanding that decisions be made in accordance with these plans, planning authorities across the country began to perceive a new climate for design control. In this, they possessed a stronger (although still highly constrained) hand, in which the development plan took on a far greater significance (Punter *et al.*, 1996, Ch. 9).

### A possible renaissance?

This at least partial conversion of central government to the benefits of good design was further emphasised through the instigation of two government initiatives. The first came through the commissioning of research, under pressure from the RTPI and RIBA (among others), aimed at producing a good practice guide on the writing of 'Design Policies in Local Plans'. The research resulted in the publication of a research report in 1996 (Punter *et al.*, 1996), while the core recommendations (summarised in Fig. 2.7) were influential in informing new government guidance on design (see Chapter 3). The good practice guide itself was soon overtaken by events and was never published, although the authors went on to develop the work in *The Design Dimension of Planning* (Punter and Carmona, 1997a) on which the current work builds.

Overtaking the 'Design Policies in Local Plans' work was the new Secretary of State – John Gummer's – 'Quality in Town and Country Initiative' (DoE, 1994c). At the heart of the discussion document that resulted was a commitment to the principles of sustainability in design, to the reuse of urban land, to bringing life back into urban centres and to reducing

- Development control experience must be utilised in policy writing, but enlightened plagiarism of policies has its place.
- Ensuring that development responds appropriately so its visual, social, functional and environmental context is a fundamental policy objective.
- Policies should be based on a broad concept of urban design, and integrate built and natural environmental concerns: sustainability should be a fundamental design objective.
- Each plan should develop a clear spatial design strategy at a district-wide scale.
- Analytical area appraisals should underpin policy formulation and be informed by pre-draft public consultation.
- Urban design policies embracing the scale of development, townscape and public realm impact should be the cornerstone of substantive policies.
- Policies should specifically respond to the most commonly encountered design problems and inadequacies.
- Policies should encourage the use of architectural skills and the development of contemporary designs that respect their surroundings.
- Considerations of landscape are important at all scales of design thinking and are an important element of sustainable development.
- Design criteria for conservation policies should be derived from conservation area assessments that emphasise design opportunities as well as constraints.
- Policies should encourage the preservation of listed buildings and pay special attention to the qualities identified in their listing, and to their setting.
- Design process policies can emphasise how best to approach key procedures in the control process such as application presentation, consultation and design briefing.
- Policies should be written with the means of implementation in mind, and amended in the light of monitoring experience.
- Consideration and criteria type policies are the most useful types of expression for design policies.
- Supplementary design guidance should be organised hierarchically, collated with design appraisals and assessments, and should be cross-referenced and published alongside the plan.

*Fig. 2.7 Design policies in local plans, core recommendations*

## Government guidance and advice on residential design in England – March 1992 to February 1997

### *The significance of government guidance*

The primary instruments of government advice on the control of residential design are widely spread across a number of sources, including in PPGs, circulars, and in a number of other government publications. Successive versions of PPG1 have confirmed that 'government statements of planning policy are material considerations which must be taken into account, where relevant, in decisions on planning applications'. As held in *E.C. Gransden and Co. Ltd* v *SSE and Gillingham BC* (1985) 'if decision-makers elect not to follow relevant statements of the government's planning policy they must give clear and convincing reasons' for the departure (DoE, 1992a, paras. 20–21). As such, government planning guidance provides the bedrock upon which the control of residential design rests.

Thus, PPG1 (1992) argued that 'development plans . . . should be consistent with national and regional planning policy . . . to provide a firm basis for rational and consistent decisions on planning applications and appeals' and that 'since the commencement of section 54A the secretaries of state have been examining development plans carefully to identify whether there appear to be conflicts with national . . . guidance' (DoE, 1992a, paras. 17 and 29). Hence the guidance clearly prioritised policy laid out in the PPGs and circulars above that in development plans, whilst recognising that development plans, complemented where necessary by supplementary guidance constitute the primary instruments through which government planning guidance should be implemented (DoE, 1992a, para. A6; DoE, 1997b, paras. 44 and 52). An examination of government planning guidance in relation to residential design is therefore necessary, as a means to understand the framework within which local authority residential design guidance is prepared, adopted and implemented.

### *Development plans and supplementary guidance*

PPG12: 'Development Plans and Regional Planning Guidance', sets the scene for any study of the English planning system. It is also of particular significance when examining design control as it establishes the framework within which plan policy is prepared, its legitimate content, and its relationship to the other forms of guidance provided by planning authorities. The 1992 version emphasised that plans should not be prescriptive but should offer a 'framework for sound and effective development control'. This, it suggested, must balance the needs of the market against the need to 'make adequate provision for development (the new homes and workplaces the nation needs)' and the need to safeguard the built and natural environments, thus ensuring that growth is sustainable (DoE, 1992c, para. 1.8).

A consistent message from central government has been that development plan policies should be clear, succinct and easy to understand, utilising brief and clearly presented explanations or reasoned justifications in order to facilitate maximum comprehension, and conviction in users. Within this broad framework 'the precise level of detail is [considered] a matter for local decision' (DoE, 1992c, paras. 5.3, 5.6 and 5.15). Events in the high court have also confirmed that the Secretary of State has effectively the last say on detail and content, through the wide ranging supervisory and directive powers granted in Section 17 of the 1990 Town and Country Planning Act (Anon., 1994).

In relation to supplementary planning guidance PPG12 clearly established that any 'policies and proposals that are likely to provide the basis for deciding planning applications, or for determining conditions to be attached to planning permissions, should be set out in the [development] plan', and that only these policies can have the special status provided by Section 54A. It also indicated that plan policies should not attempt to delegate decisions to supplementary guidance or to development briefs. Nevertheless, guidance which supplements the policies and proposals in the plan 'for example design guides for specified areas' were conceded by the Secretary of State to 'provide helpful guidance for those preparing planning applications', particularly when cross-referenced to plan policy and made publicly available. Supplementary guidance was therefore considered a 'material consideration', the weight accorded to which increased if prepared in consultation with the public and made the subject of council resolution (DoE, 1992c, paras. 3.18–3.19).[2]

### Sustainable development

The government white paper 'This Common Inheritance', set the scene for perhaps the most decisive switch in the emphasis of government planning policy during the 1990s; an emphasis on sustainability which more than any other factor led in time to a re-evaluation of the importance of planning and design. Two of its key objectives aimed to encourage the best location and design of new housing, and to foster good design in new buildings, particularly through supporting the use of design guidance and design briefs. Support was also given for the re-use of urban land for housing (HM government, 1990, pp. 20–22 and 89), an objective increasingly emphasised as the decade commenced.

In this regard, PPG3 underlined the important resource for housing development provided by the abundance of derelict and under-used land in many towns and cities. It indicated that development of these areas can reduce pressures elsewhere and make urban areas more pleasant places in which to live. The guidance conceded, however, the continuing need for greenfield sites, outside the bounds of existing urban areas, and suggested that in these areas sensitive relation to the 'existing pattern of development' would be imperative (DoE, 1992b, paras. 17–19). 'The Quality in Town and Country, Discussion Document' reiterated and supported this line, arguing in the introduction to the document that 'sustainable development means a war on waste – wasted land, wasted energy, wasted travel time'. It stressed that good quality also means good economics through building to last (DoE, 1994c, pp. 2–3).

PPG12 developed the new commitment from government to ensuring that development takes place in a sustainable manner, suggesting that this objective should underpin all aspects of planning policy. In this regard, the design and provision of housing was singled out for specific emphasis, alongside the safeguarding and improving of residential amenity, the maintenance of character and vitality in town and city centres, giving priority to good design in new development, and enhancing quality of life and public health through new development (DoE, 1992c, para. 1.8). Energy conservation was also highlighted in PPG12 as a legitimate concern of the planning system and one in which the design of residential areas, particularly on a strategic level, had a key role to play. Within the boundaries of a particular site, authorities could further legitimately influence energy efficiency 'through their influence on factors such as housing type, orientation and location' (DoE, 1992c, para. 6.14).

Most significant, however, was the revision of PPG13: 'Transport' in 1994. In line with the then government's sustainable development strategy (HM government, 1994), the note focused on the objective of 'planning for less [car] travel', through fostering forms of development that encourage walking, cycling and the use of public transport. In terms of

[2] The latest version of PPG12 (DETR, 2000b) is consistent with the 1992 version in all the essentials discussed above.

housing development, the guidance placed a priority on the development of housing within existing built up areas, and in areas well served by rail and other public transport. Such a strategy impacts on the design of housing at a strategic level, through an implied discouragement to unfettered suburban sprawl. It also impacts at the detailed level of individual developments by recommending (where appropriate) increased densities and the juxtaposition of employment and residential uses in new mixed-use areas (DoE, 1994a, paras. 1.1–3.3).

A concern for mixed-use areas is a relatively new phenomenon in government guidance, but one that increasingly gained currency throughout the period of the research. PPG13 highlighted the importance of planning at a 'neighbourhood scale' and argued that the juxtaposition of different uses in a locality effectively 'determines its attractiveness and vitality'. In particular, the guidance suggested that:

- by increasing the mix of uses in a locality, the need for car journeys will be reduced;
- that the streets will be made more lively; and
- that the opportunities for crime will be reduced.

Consequently, the note indirectly discouraged the planning of extensive mono-functional residential developments (DoE, 1994a, paras. 3.16–3.17). The 'Quality in Town and Country' initiative took up the theme and clearly supported the development of mixed-use areas, the importance of mixing uses for successful urban renewal, and the possibilities offered by the 'urban villages' concept in encouraging higher density, mixed use development in towns and cities (DoE, 1994c, pp. 6–7). Circular 5/94: 'Planning Out Crime', further emphasises the value of mixed-use areas, as a deterrent to crime (DoE, 1994b), while PPG4: 'Industrial and Commercial Development and Small Firms', states that 'it is now generally recognised that it may not be appropriate to separate industry and commerce . . . from residential communities for whom they are a source of employment and services', as long as such development does not adversely affect residential amenity (DoE, 1992e, paras. 14–15).

Stressing the relative attributes of mixed-use areas has thus become a major theme of recent government advice, although the choice of whether or not to designate such areas in local plans is left to the individual authority's discretion. Nevertheless, the attack on highly segregated land use development, particularly residential development, has become increasingly pronounced in government advice: the 'executive apartheid we see in far too many cul-de-sacs and closes' or the 'zoning madness that has gripped us for far too long', as John Gummer (1994, p. 9) characteristically described it.

Parking, a decisive factor in the layout of residential areas, was also dealt with briefly in PPG13, with the emphasis on reducing parking standards and on allowing flexibility in the provision of off street car parking spaces in residential developments. The guidance aimed to discourage car use and to release land which would formerly have been allocated to parking, therefore allowing development at higher densities (DoE, 1994a, paras. 4.3–4.6). The publication of PPG13 was of greatest significance in marking the change to a more sustainable approach to planning policy from central government. Residential-specific advice in PPG3 and DB32 was much slower to follow the lead.

### Design and housing

PPG3 indicated that it is for the development plan to show how the future requirements for housing can be met. It confirmed that such requirements need to have regard to market trends, including identification of the various types of housing required by the private sector in relation to likely user groups (DoE, 1992b, paras. 8–13). Like the other PPGs dealing with specific land use types or contexts, the 1992 version of PPG3 provided dedicated advice on the range of issues relating to a particular land use – the provision of housing. Significantly, however, unlike the other land use/context-specific PPGs at the time of its publication, PPG3 included advice on design. Although the general thrust of this advice was repeated directly from Annex A to PPG1 (see Fig. 2.6), its specific relation to residential development nevertheless confirmed the important emphasis government guidance has always placed on residential design over other forms of development – recreation, industrial/commercial, town centre/retail and rural (PPGs on the latter two subjects updated in 1996 and 1997 respectively to include specific design advice – see p. 42).

However, the special treatment given to housing in PPG3 had more to do with encouraging restraint in the control of residential design, than in encouraging better design quality. As revised in March 1992, PPG3 replaced an earlier version of the guidance which contained almost no advice on design (DoE, 1988b). The section on 'Good Design' (see Fig. 2.8) stated that 'developers should aim for a high quality of design and landscaping in all new housing developments ... [to] ... produce buildings which are well-designed for their purpose and for their surroundings'. It argued that such well-designed schemes, which respect the character of their local environment, are more likely to benefit from community support (DoE, 1992b, para. 4).

Authorities, however, were dissuaded from attempting to control the detailed design of residential developments, unless the quality of design was obviously very poor and out of scale or character with its surroundings. Within these restrictions a list of appropriate considerations was offered to guide local authorities in their deliberations, including the scale of development, its density, the height of buildings, the massing of their elements, the layout of a scheme, its landscaping, and its access and parking arrangements (DoE, 1992b, para. 5). All but the last of these concerns was derived from the seven point list of legitimate design considerations contained in Annex A to PPG1 (DoE, 1992a, para. A6). The final consideration reflects the ubiquitous concern for roads and parking (usually over other concerns) which had characterised government guidance on residential design from the 1970s onwards.

Out of these considerations density, physical scale, access and off street car parking were subsequently identified as issues particularly worthy of control, with authorities advised to include policies on these issues tailored to the different areas of residential development in their plan. Here, as throughout the guidance, over-detail and prescription was discouraged, while flexibility was considered the key, particularly 'in view of the different characteristics of particular sites and the need to provide a range of housing types at varying price levels' (DoE, 1992b, paras. 21 and 24).

The overall emphasis in PPG3 was therefore on 'fitting in' with the prevailing character and appearance of the neighbourhood in order to secure public acceptance of new housing development, tempered by warnings against unwarranted interference in design. PPG3 reinforced this interpretation by suggesting that the 'functional requirements within a development are for the most part a matter for the marketing judgement of developers, in the light of their assessment of their customers' requirements' – giving the examples of the provision of garages, internal space standards, and the size of private gardens. The same paragraph also warned against attempts by local authorities to prescribe rigid formulae when considering the location and relationship to one another of houses on a plot or when trying to regulate the mix of house types without specific planning reasons; again advocating deference to market considerations (DoE, 1992b, para. 6).

Good design

4 Developers should aim for a high quality of design and landscaping in all new housing developments. A well-designed scheme that respects the local environment can do much to make new housing more acceptable to the local community. A good scheme will produce buildings which are well-designed for their purpose and for their surroundings. Planning briefs can help developers by drawing attention to site characteristics, and to the importance of using appropriate materials in particularly sensitive areas.

5 Local planning authorities should consider development proposals in terms of their relationship to their setting, and by reference to the character and quality of the local environment, including any adjacent buildings. Relevant considerations are likely to include matters such as the overall scale and density of the development; the height and massing of its various elements; the layout of the scheme and its landscaping; and access and parking arrangements. While it will rarely be justifiable for local planning authorities to use the development control system to impose controls over detailed design, they should reject obviously poor designs which are out of scale or character with their surroundings. Authorities will wish to take account of the advice in DOE Design Bulletin 32 (*The Layout of Residential Roads and Footpaths*) in their assessment of development proposals.

6 Local planning authorities may need to control aspects of the design of new housing developments where these clearly have an impact on neighbouring development or on the general character of a neighbourhood. But functional requirements within a development are for the most part a matter for the marketing judgment of developers, in the light of their assessment of their customers' requirements. Such matters would include provision of garages, internal space standards, and the size of private gardens. In considering the location of houses on plots and their relationship to each other, local planning authorities should not attempt to prescribe rigid formulae. They should regulate the mix of house types only when there are specific planning reasons for such control, and in doing so they should take account of marketing considerations. Advice on the control of the design of buildings is given in Annex A to PPG1.

7 Developers should already be considering whether the internal design of housing, and access to it, can meet the needs of the disabled, whether as residents or visitors. To the extent that regulation is justified the Government looks to the Building Regulations and not the planning system to impose requirements. Access arrangements to all non-domestic buildings are already covered by the Regulations, and the Department is assessing the practicality of extending the requirement of Part M of the Building Regulations to new dwellings. However, where there is clear evidence of local need, a local planning authority could include in a local plan a policy indicating that it would seek to negotiate elements of housing, accessible tro the disabled, on suitable sites. Such sites would normally be located close to shops and public transport, and be in an area of level ground. The plan should not seek to impose detailed standards.

*Fig. 2.8. Extract from PPG3.*

## The design process

Much of the design advice contained within PPG3 was borrowed directly from Annex A to PPG1 (1992) and given a housing gloss. However, the general advice on design in PPG1 contained additional advice specifically related to the 'process of design'. Annex A made it clear that 'the appearance of proposed development and its relationship to its surroundings are material considerations' but warned that good design remained primarily the responsibility of designers and their clients, and that the subjective nature of aesthetic judgements should make authorities wary of trying to 'impose their taste on applicants ... simply because they believe it to be superior'. Instead, both applicants and authorities were encouraged to recognise the benefits of engaging skilled advisers, encourage good design, and recognise the design skills and advice of architects (DoE, 1992a, paras. A1–A3).

Like PPG3, PPG1 advanced a contextual approach to design, particularly in 'environmentally sensitive areas', but expressly warned applicants against mimicry of existing buildings, instead identifying experiment, originality and initiative as desirable attributes of design to be supported in policy (DoE, 1992a, paras. A4 and A6). To achieve their design aspirations, PPG1 encouraged planning authorities to provide clear indications of their 'design expectations' in development plans and guidance for particular areas or sites. Again, the guidance discouraged undue prescription and detail, but significantly emphasised the importance of the 'appearance and treatment of the spaces between and around buildings', and of both hard and soft landscape design (DoE, 1992a, paras. A5–A6). Annex A concluded by stressing a number of specific 'design process' concerns, namely, the value of pre-application consultation on design, the importance of appropriate presentation of applications – including showing proposals in context – and the potentially valuable role that written statements of design principle can play in helping authorities to assess the design merits of applications (DoE, 1992a, para. A7).

Little is said, however, about the need for area appraisal (or design analysis) in the pre-1997 PPGs. PPG12 referred to the need to 'keep all matters under review that are expected to affect the development of their area' and that to do this the 1990 Town and Country Planning Act empowers planning authorities to institute surveys of their areas including 'the principle physical and economic characteristics'. It went on to suggest that the results of such analysis should normally be made available to the public, and that authorities might consider the employment of consultants to gather such information (DoE, 1992c, paras. 4.1–4.3).

In relation to town centre environments, PPG6: 'Town Centres and Retail Development' began to indicate a change in emphasis on appraisal when published in 1996. It encourages planning authorities 'to undertake an urban design analysis, as part of their town centre strategy, to provide a framework for policies in their development plan and for guiding the preparation of development briefs for key sites' (DoE, 1996d, para. 2.33). In early 1997, PPG7: 'The Countryside – Environmental Quality and Economic and Social Development', extended this concern to the rural context. It highlights the value of engaging local populations in constructive debate about the nature of their environment, and in actively undertaking appraisals through two Countryside Commission-inspired appraisal techniques – Countryside Design Summaries and Village Design Statements (DoE, 1997c, para. 2.12 – see p. 147). Of the 'context-specific' government planning guidance – rural, town centres and residential (suburban) – only the latter, in the guise of PPG3, offered no advice at all on appraisal.

### Residential roads

DB32 is frequently mentioned in government planning advice as the primary source of detailed advice on the design and layout of residential areas. PPG3, for example, advised that 'authorities will wish to take account of . . . the advice in DoE Design Bulletin 32 in their assessment of development proposals' (DoE, 1992b, para. 5). Indeed, at the time of its publication the then Minister stated that, 'we expect local planning and highway authorities to take the advice contained in this edition into account when preparing local guidance and when specifying their requirements for adoption' (DoE and DoT, 1992, p. V). Thus, the considerations outlined in the bulletin underpin local authority powers to control the design and layout of residential development.

The advice recognises that the planning of roads and footpaths has a major impact on the character, quality and safety of residential areas, and affects the layout of houses, their gardens and the provision of children's play space. In addressing these issues, the bulletin aims to ensure 'a sensible balance ... [is] ... struck between planning, housing and highway considerations in the design of most new residential developments' (DoE and DoT, 1992, p. V).

Thus the responsibilities for capital and maintenance costs are effectively divided between local authorities, service providers and housing developers, and a 'corporate' approach to the preparation of guidance is advocated. This involves inputs from the different professional disciplines within local authorities, in consultation with the different service providers, housebuilders and other interested parties. The joint aim is to produce design guidance and 'highway standards that enable designers to create visually attractive, safe, convenient, nuisance free and secure surroundings that are economical to construct and maintain' (DoE and DoT, 1992, p. 63).

The bulletin argues that all requirements of the planning and highway authorities for the design of residential roads and footpaths – including any requirements for the provision and design of parking – should be fully integrated in guidance and expressed, first, through the 'framework' established by plan policy, and second, in supplementary guidance. Such guidance, it is recommended, should be framed in a manner that relates to local needs – '... standards may be set in a way that applies equally to a wide variety of design solutions to suit different kinds of urban, suburban and rural sites. Alternatively, standards may be related to the housing layouts most commonly submitted for approval, or to theoretical layouts in order to encourage innovation'. The guidance further advocates the use of supplementary news sheets or other methods to inform developers of schemes that the authority considers to be successful.

No attempt is made therefore to prescribe universal standards for the control of residential design. Thus, Section 1, which is devoted to the preparation of design briefs, argues that residential layouts promoted through briefs should, first and foremost, be based upon the requirements and preferences outlined in the development plan (DoE and DoT, 1992, pp. 3–16). Briefs should also have regard to:

- the physical and visual characteristics of the site and its surroundings;
- any road safety hazards or incidence of crime in the local area;
- the various functions performed by roads and footpaths;
- the size and directions of the main pedestrian, cycle and vehicular traffic flows;
- the proposed road speed limits;
- building density requirements, dwelling size and types;
- accessibility and parking requirements;
- private and common open space provision;
- considerations of daylight, sunlight, privacy and views; and
- finally, to landscaping and landscape maintenance.

From general principles, DB32 looks in progressively more detail at the practical requirements for road layouts, including issues of road hierarchy (see Fig. 2.9), the control of vehicle speeds and road alignment, the provision of parking, and an examination of the properties of, and relationships between, carriageways, junctions, turning circles, visibility, footways and parking bays (DoE and DoT, 1992, pp. 16–62).

DB32 includes much useful detailed guidance on the layout of residential areas. Nevertheless, overriding the suggested approaches, the government's (and housebuilders') desire for flexibility is obvious (DoE and DoT, 1992, pp. 64–6). A deeper reading of the advice even reveals an agenda for 'compromise' between the visual and social aspirations of urban design and the more functional concerns of highways design. Indeed, concern that authorities were placing 'a rather rigid interpretation' (Gummer, 1994, pp. 15–16) on the guidance, led to its further review during 1995/6, and the publication of a 'Companion Guide' to update its layout principles in 1998 (see Chapter 10).

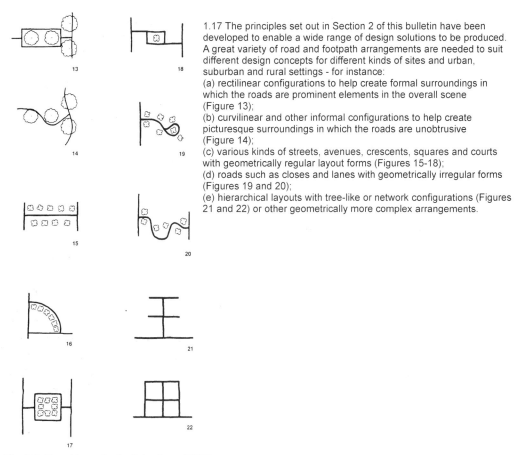

1.17 The principles set out in Section 2 of this bulletin have been developed to enable a wide range of design solutions to be produced. A great variety of road and footpath arrangements are needed to suit different design concepts for different kinds of sites and urban, suburban and rural settings - for instance:
(a) rectilinear configurations to help create formal surroundings in which the roads are prominent elements in the overall scene (Figure 13);
(b) curvilinear and other informal configurations to help create picturesque surroundings in which the roads are unobtrusive (Figure 14);
(c) various kinds of streets, avenues, crescents, squares and courts with geometrically regular layout forms (Figures 15-18);
(d) roads such as closes and lanes with geometrically irregular forms (Figures 19 and 20);
(e) hierarchical layouts with tree-like or network configurations (Figures 21 and 22) or other geometrically more complex arrangements.

*Fig. 2.9  Road layout principles from DB32.*

## Evaluation: government guidance to February 1997

In 1992 a new framework for controlling residential design was effectively established by the introduction of PPG1 Annex A, PPG3 and the second edition of DB32. The new guidance reflected a 'new deal' for design, one that finally recognised design as a material consideration, even if still cased in the restrictive language and hands-off philosophies of the 1980s, particularly regarding residential design. The historic inconsistencies apparent in central government's approach to design control were still very much apparent: on the one hand, proclaiming that the control of design was a legitimate role for planning authorities, while on the other, warning clearly against design interference. Nevertheless, the guidance suggested an important new direction for control, one that received further backing in later government statements and encompassed a new emphasis on urban rather than architectural design.

If seen in this regard, government guidance has given authorities a freer hand actively to pursue quality contextually appropriate design than some may have realised. Since 1992, this hand has been strengthened by the fact that most of the design principles raised as legitimate for control in PPG1 Annex A (1992) and in PPG3 (see Table 2.2) were urban design related – character, setting, appearance and treatment of spaces, landscape design (hard and soft), scale, density, height, massing, layout, and access, while most of those considered to be non-legitimate concerns related largely to matters of detailed design (see Table 2.3). This emphasis on issues urban was also gradually confirmed and extended, in design advice spread across government guidance.

Hence, by analysing government guidance, and by reading into the 'Quality in Town and Country' rhetoric at the time, a clearer and more legitimate role for urban design seemed to be emerging throughout the five-year period between March 1992 and February 1997. In other words, a new agenda for urban design and design control, moving away from the traditional conflation of design with external appearance. Nevertheless, throughout the 1990s, PPG3 – though its emphasis on the marketing judgement of developers – seemed to fly in the face of the new approach and may have been instrumental in restraining the development of more innovative approaches to design among local authorities. The situation was compounded by the overly rigid interpretations being placed on DB32.

A second piece of government guidance in the form of Circular 8/93: 'Awards of Costs Incurred in Planning and Other Proceedings' also seemed to back-pedal. The guidance articulates a threat that has dissuaded many authorities taking design considerations seriously. It states that 'If the degree of [design] control goes beyond what is appropriate for the circumstances of the location concerned, the authority's actions may be regarded as unreasonable' leading to the award of costs against the authority at appeal (DoE, 1993b, para. 14). Some commentators have argued that such limitations are both unreasonable and almost impossible to gauge (CPRE, 1995, p. 20). These views persist (see p. 184), despite concentration in the circular on detailed design and assurances from government that design would now be seen as a 'serious and significant' part of their judgement, and that authorities need no longer fear that arguments on design grounds might prove costly on appeal (Anon., 1995c).

At best, government guidance on residential design during this period can be described as consistently restrained in its prescriptions for improving private sector residential development. The key themes in government guidance in the period when 'a renaissance' in Government's attitude to design and the planning process was first hinted at in PPG1 (March 1992) to the time it was potentially delivered (February 1997) can be summarised as follows:

- government guidance on design continued to have the pivotal role in the creation of a framework for controlling residential design in England;
- the development plan has the key role in controlling development, including its design, and should include reference to all the design expectations of planning authorities;
- other design guidance has a supplementary role to the plan, but both design guides and briefs were supported for their value as positive guidance, elucidating that in the plan;
- 'compromise' approaches to housing layout had been implicitly supported that satisfy the needs of planning and highways authorities, service providers and housebuilders; if not always those of urban design;
- appraisal had been prioritised in town centre and rural contexts but remained undervalued in suburban contexts and in relation to residential design;
- sustainability had been an increasingly developed theme (at least superficially) in government guidance, with action prioritised to reduce wasted land, energy and travel time. In this, the agenda prescribed in PPG13 was at odds with that in PPG3;
- the value of mixing uses was also increasingly prioritised, although not in residential-specific guidance;

*Table 2.2 Legitimate design control concerns (normal areas) – to February 1997*

| Issue covered in guidance | Material status | Advisory status |
|---|---|---|
| access | PPG1, PPG3, PPG6 | DB32 |
| active frontages | PPG6 | PPG13 |
| Bio-diversity | TCI, RE | |
| building line | PPG6 | |
| bulk | TCI, PPG7 | |
| car park design | PPG6 | |
| character of place | PPG1, PPG3, PPG6, RE | DB32, SoS |
| colour | PPG7 | |
| context | PPG1, PPG3, TCI, PPG6, RE, PPG7 | DPG, SoS |
| crime prevention | PPG1, Circ' 5/94, PPG6 | DB32, PPG13 |
| daylight | CL | |
| defensible territory | Circ' 5/94 | |
| density | PPG1, PPG3, PPG13, PPG7 | DB32 |
| disabled access | | PPG6, Circ' 11/95 |
| energy efficiency | PPG12, PPG3 | |
| environmental quality | PPG3 | |
| external appearance | PPG1, PPG7 | |
| eyesores | PPG7 | |
| height | PPG1, PPG3 | |
| house size (if proven need) | PPG3 | DB32 |
| house type (if proven need) | PPG3 | PPG12, DB32, SoS |
| housing design | PPG3, PPG12, Circ' 5/94, TCI | |
| neighbourhood impact | PPG1 | |
| infrastructure availability | PPG1 | |
| interest (visual) | PPG6 | |
| landscape character | PPG7, RE | |
| landscape design | PPG1, PPG3, Circ' 36/78, PPG6, PPG7, Circ' 11/95 | Circ' 5/94 |
| landscape works/materials | Circ' 11/95 | |
| landscape, hard and soft | | Circ' 11/95 |
| landscape integration | PPG7 | |
| landscape management | | Circ' 11/95 |
| layout | PPG1, PPG3, Circ' 5/94 | DB32 |
| local distinctiveness | PPG6, PPG7 | |
| local style (rural areas) | RE | |
| massing | PPG1, PPG3, PPG7 | SoS |
| materials (rural areas) | RE, PPG7 | |
| materials (sensitive locations) | PPG1, PPG3, TCI | |
| mixed use | PPG7. PPG13, PPG6 | Circ' 5/94, QTC, SoS |
| number of units | PPG1 | |
| open space | PPG3 | DB32 |
| orientation | Circ' 5/94 | PPG12 |
| out-of-centre development design | PPG6 | |
| overlooking | PPG1, CL | |
| overshadowing | PPG3, CL | |
| parking | PPG1, PPG3, PPG13, PPG6 | DB32 |
| passive supervision | Circ' 5/94 | |
| paving | PPG6 | |
| perception of place | RE, PPG7 | SoS |
| privacy | PPG1 | |
| public/urban space | | PPG6 |
| quality of life and public health | PPG12 | |
| regional building traditions | PPG7 | |

| | | |
|---|---|---|
| relation to other buildings | *PPG3, TCI, PPG7* | |
| residential amenity | *PPG3, PPG12, TCI* | |
| residential road and footpath design | *PPG13, PPG7* | *DB32* |
| road hierarchy | | *DB32* |
| road safety | *PPG13* | *DB32* |
| scale | *PPG1, PPG3, PPG7* | |
| settlement pattern | *PPG3, PPG7* | *QTC, SoS* |
| shopfront design | | *PPG6* |
| siting | *PPG1, PPG3, Circ' 5/94, PPG7* | |
| size | *PPG1, PPG7* | |
| space between buildings | *PPG1, PPG3* | *SoS* |
| spatial design | *PPG13, PPG7* | |
| street frontage | *PPG6* | *PPG13* |
| street furniture/signs | *PPG6* | *Circ' 11/95* |
| sustainable development | *PPG12, PPG13, PPG6, RE, PPG7* | *QTC, SoS* |
| texture | *PPG7* | |
| town cramming | *PPG3, PPG12, TCI* | |
| traditional building styles | | *PPG7* |
| traffic calming | *PPG13* | |
| urban design | *PPG6* | |
| variety | *PPG6* | *Circ' 5/94, PPG13* |
| views & vistas | | *DB32, SoS* |
| vitality (in urban locations) | *PPG17, PPG6* | *PPG13* |

**Key: Tables 2.2–2.4**

- *CL* – Protected in Common Law
- *DPG* – Development Plans: (A Good Practice Guide)
- *DB32* – Design Bulletin 32
- *QTC* – Quality in Town and Country

- *RE* – Rural England (white paper)
- *SoS* – Secretary of State Speech 12.12. 94
- *TCI* – This Common Inheritance (white paper)

- *SDG* – Supplementary Design Guidance

- *SPG* – Supplementary Planning Guidance

Note: Tables complete up to release of PPG7 in February 1997, but do not include the subsequent release of PPG1 later that month.

Tables are differentiated to illustrate those issues which have material status given by government guidance – as legitimate areas for design control – from those which have advisory status only (due to the specific wording of the guidance or because of the status of the medium of guidance itself).

*Table 2.3 Non-legitimate design control concerns (normal areas) – to February 1997*

| Issue covered in guidance | Material status | Advisory status |
|---|---|---|
| detailed design (unless sensitive context) | *PPG1, PPG3* | *SoS* |
| disabled access | *PPG1, PPG3* | |
| functional requirements within a development | *PPG3* | |
| internal space standards | *PPG3* | |
| garages (provision or not) | *PPG3* | |
| gardens (size) | *PPG3* | |
| house type mix | *PPG3* | |
| location on plot (rigid formulae) | *PPG3* | |
| materials (in non-sensitive locations) | *PPG1, PPG3* | |
| mimicry of existing | *PPG1* | |
| outlook | *CL* | |
| rigid formulae (for house location) | | *PPG3* |
| style | *PPG3* | *SoS* |
| taste | *PPG1, Circ' 11/95* | |

Key: See Table 2.2.

- the powerful lobbying of the housebuilders had been evident in the advocacy of a particular restraint in the control of residential design. This had persisted, with the line between legitimate control and non-legitimate control still tightly drawn;
- a concern for residential roads and parking still dominated the DoE's conceptualisation of residential design concerns;
- overall, a limited conceptualisation of design was still apparent in government guidance on residential design, although broad urban design considerations (repeated in PPG3 from PPG1 Annex A) and design process concerns (see Table 2.4) were gradually coming to the fore.

*Table 2.4  Legitimate design/planning processes concerns (normal areas) – to February 1997*

| Process covered in guidance | Material status | Advisory status |
|---|---|---|
| appraisal valuable | PPG7 | DPG |
| area design guides supported | PPG1 | |
| avoid stifling originality/innovation | PPG1 | |
| briefs on layout and design of residential road and footpaths supported | DB32 | |
| briefs to aim for unified development | | TCI |
| briefs to identify goals/problems/opportunities | | TCI |
| briefs to identify site characteristics and appropriate materials in sensitive areas | PPG3 | |
| civic responsibility | | SoS |
| countryside design summaries and village design statements useful | | PPG7 |
| decision making criteria in policy not SPG | PPG12 | DPG |
| depart from policy for exceptional schemes | PPG1 | |
| design briefs supported | PPG1, PPG6 | DPG, SoS |
| design expectations to be in plan | PPG1, PPG6 | |
| economic viability | PPG7 | |
| encourage innovation | PPG1 | QTC, SoS |
| landscape character analysis valuable | PPG7 | |
| landscape implementation | Circ' 11/95 | |
| level of detail down to local decision | PPG12 | |
| over-detail and over-prescription in policy | PPG6 | PPG1, PPG3 |
| phasing of development | | Circ' 11/95 |
| phasing of landscape | Circ' 11/95 | |
| planning conditions/obligations useful for design | Circ 11/95 | |
| pre-application consultation | | PPG1 |
| presentation, importance of | | PPG1 |
| public consultation on design policy/SDG | | PPG6 |
| SDG on layout of residential areas supported | | DB32 |
| SDG on shopfront design supported | | PPG6 |
| secure public acceptance through design | | PPG3, PPG7 |
| show proposals in context | PPG1 | |
| skilled advice | | PPG1 |
| SPG is a material consideration | | DB32 |
| SPG and briefs useful, particularly when cross-referenced to policy | PPG12, PPG6 | TCI, SoS |
| standards on the design of residential road and footpaths supported | | DB32 |
| standards need flexibility | PPG13 | |
| survey of principal physical characteristics | PPG12 | |
| urban design analysis | | PPG6 |
| written statements of design principle | | PPG1 |

Key: See Table 2.2.

## Conclusions

A look back at the recent history of the planning system and its impact on residential design reveals two decisive trends. First, the gradual adoption of a wider design agenda, and second a continued reluctance to extend this agenda to the speculative residential sector. The wider agenda for design reflects, in part, the increasingly widespread acceptance by government – of both political persuasions – (Gummer, 1995, p. 7; Cabinet Office, 1997), planners (Griffiths, 1995, p. 6), and the development professions alike (HBF and RIBA, 1990, pp. 10–12), that control of urban design, rather than architecture, represents the most appropriate and effective means through which local authorities can influence the quality of new development, including development in residential areas. Acceptance of this crucial role for urban design has come slowly, however, with urban design mentioned for the first time in an official DoE publication as late as 1994 (DoE, 1994c, p. 2), and in actual planning guidance only in 1996 (DoE, 1996d, para. 2.33).

By February 1997, PPG6 and PPG7 had both been revised to ensure an appropriate high priority was given to design in town centres and in rural areas. Despite the impact of the housing projections (see Chapter 1), PPG3 had benefited from no such treatment, perhaps offering some indication of the priorities of central government and the continuing reluctance to be seen to interfere in the workings of the free market in private housing. Nevertheless, in the dying days of the last Conservative government a promise to revise PPG3 was made. The new administration also recognised the need to bring PPG3 into line with other guidance on design, and to abandon the 'compromise design' and 'marketing-led' philosophies of government guidance on residential design up to that point. The new version of PPG3 was released in draft form in March 1999 and, finally, officially extended the emerging themes of urban design, sustainability and local distinctiveness to residential development. The final version of this guidance is discussed in Chapter 10.

## INSET B: SUFFOLK COUNTY COUNCIL – A NEW GENERATION GUIDE

Following the government's updated thinking in the second edition of DB32, Suffolk County Council published new guidance aimed at encouraging quality housing development in Suffolk. The guidance was intended as a direct response to the rapidly growing population in the region and to the fact that most of the new housing required would be built on the edges of towns and larger villages as volume-built suburban development. In particular, the seven district authorities and the county council were greatly concerned about the overall quality of housing estate design, particularly during the boom period of the late 1980s.

The guide was prepared jointly by the county and districts as a multi-disciplinary team incorporating planners, highway engineers, and landscape and conservation architects. When published, the guide was heralded as the first of a new generation of guidance (Anon., 1992) encompassing all aspects of the planning process, from principles of road layout and landscaping through house design to providing cycleways and making adequate provision for those with disabilities. The authority saw a co-ordinated approach as a main ingredient in successful layout design, with attention given equally – and together – to all aspects of design and context. Thus, the introduction to the guide states that 'Mediocre layouts often arise when undue emphasis is placed upon one aspect of the design at the expense of other equally important factors, such as varied street-scene and landscaping' (p. 3).

A joint HBF and RIBA (1990) discussion paper seemed to offer a potential way forward to overcome the frequent contradictory objectives between housebuilders and the Suffolk authorities (see Fig. 4.1). The paper argued that there is a hierarchy of design importance, three factors which combine together to create good design, but which can nevertheless be separated and prioritised for the purposes of design control (see p. 133). The authorities adopted the logic.

Hence, the guide first prioritises the shape (layout) of development and the three dimensional spaces within it. It must be sufficiently distinctive to give a sense of character while responding positively to a particular setting, including to the landscape. Second, comes the materials with which the development is clothed. These again should be reflective of the character of the area and should offer a harmonious use of colour and texture that adds qualitative value to the development. Finally, comes the house itself, which, it is argued, is the least important factor on the basis that even ordinary houses, if placed in the right composition and related to a strong feature or theme, can look attractive.

In essence, the strategy prioritises urban design over architecture. The authorities argue that in the past, planners, architects and housebuilders have tended to spend too much time and thought on the design of individual dwellings and too little on urban design. Thus, the guide is intended to take designers through each of the three elements in turn in a logical thought process, before moving on to more detailed specification and adoption procedures.

The DB32 message that 'a road is more than a road' is supported and roads are viewed as important parts of the residential environment, rather than as mere traffic arteries. To achieve this, the concept of reducing traffic speeds within housing areas is accepted, which offers a more flexible application of road design standards and opportunity for the design of more creative spaces. Unlike the Essex approach (see Inset A), however, great faith is still placed in the use of a residential road hierarchy, which, it is argued, should be used with greater conviction to prevent monotonous road layouts. More flexibility is also offered in the layout of roads, and disconnected (cul-de-sac) and interconnected (grid) layouts are both promoted.

The guide starts from the premise that applicants should have regard to the precise location of the site in question and to the character of surrounding existing development. It suggests that the question should be 'What can the development do for the settlement?', rather than 'What can the site do for the development?', and that only a team approach can significantly raise design quality – architect, builder, highway engineer, landscape architect, and local planning authority. Thus, although the original drafts of the guide covered highways, planning and architectural concepts separately (Suffolk Planning Officers' Group, n.d), the final guide adopted a more integrated approach as a better means to direct the various disciplines to create sense of place.

The guide remains far less prescriptive than, for example, the new Essex approach, in an attempt to reflect government guidance but also to direct designers, developers and districts towards a site-specific rather than county-wide approach. Thus the chapters on materials and individual dwellings most explicitly offer 'Suffolk-specific' approaches to context, but with the emphasis on the variety of the Suffolk traditions. The aim is to re-establish and perpetuate the locally distinctive building characters of the different parts of Suffolk, both in building design and hard landscaping. The advice on building style borrows (and sensibly simplifies) another idea from the joint HBF/RIBA (1990, pp. 24–26) discussion paper. This argued that a range of approaches to style can be identified:

1. Progressive
2. Mainstream Traditional
3. Contextual
4. Decorative Revival
5. Historical References
6. Genuine Reproduction.

All of these the HBF/RIBA paper suggests are appropriate in their place because they are widely liked and show a good degree of care and effort in their design. The unacceptable style is the seventh category:

7. Could Do Better.

In Suffolk, just three alternatives are given: unashamedly modern, historically accurate reproduction and mainstream traditional. The last of these is considered to be the likely result of most development proposals.

The design guide has been adopted as supplementary planning guidance by all the Suffolk planning authorities, and is used by the Highway Authority as a basis for development control decision making. It offered the opportunity to establish in one place a set of robust design guidelines and a uniform set of design standards for the county – the highways engineer has been provided deliberately with a set of standards that allow greater creative variety. The guide is also referred to in all the district local plans to boost further its potential as a means to evaluate planning applications, and, where necessary, defend refusals at appeal.

At the district level, St Edmunsbury's plan, for example, also includes reference to the district's own design guidance (St. Edmundsbury Borough Council, 1993) and to a range of development frameworks prepared for major residential allocations in the district. The frameworks are given legitimacy in Policy 14 of the plan and are designed to establish the main principles under which development will proceed. The policy further promises the completion of more detailed planning and design briefs for significant residential sites and expects developers to produce master-plans setting out the basic form and layout of development as part of any planning application.

One such brief was produced for council owned land at Drovers Went (now Drovers Mead) on the edge of Bury St Edmunds. The brief took the design philosophy of the design guide and local plan frameworks to create a detailed design brief which sets out both a contextual and co-ordinated approach in which landscape and spaces rather than roads dominate (see Fig. B.1). Despite fears that good design would carry a land value penalty, the reverse has proved to be the case, with successive phases showing substantial gains in land value and house resale values over and above what would have been expected from more run-of-the-mill volume built developments (see Fig. B.2). In this case, the ability of the authority to deliver high quality housing was aided greatly by the land ownership, and by the determination of councillors to deliver something better (Birkbeck, 1997).

Since publication, the guide has been actively used by authorities and has been quoted in a variety of refusals of planning permission for residential estates that fail to co-ordinate adequately highways standards with wider issues relating to housing design, layout design, landscaping, materials and appropriate detailing of traditional built form (Chamberlain, 1994). Most recently the guide has been put through the definitive test as the means to defend successfully an appeal against planning refusal based on its road standards. The guide is proving influential in delivering a better standard of development from national housebuilders in greenfield (see Fig. B.2) and brownfield locations (see Fig. B.3).

Amenity society feedback on the guide has come from the CPRE who have promoted the guide as best practice. The co-operation between county and district authorities, most

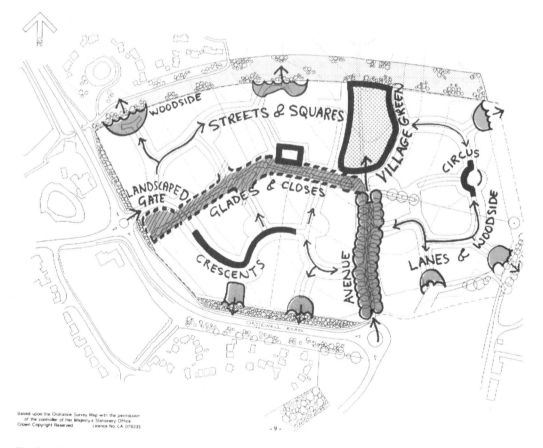

Fig. B1  Plan 5 – Themes, Drovers Went Development Brief (St Edmundsbury Borough Council, 1994).

*Fig. B2  Drovers Went, Bury St Edmunds.*

*Fig. B3  Saxon Gate, Bury St Edmunds by Redrow Homes.*

particularly between the district planning and county highways departments, is considered to be the most significant factor in the guide's early success. 'Other counties can only envy the unity of purpose which their Suffolk counterparts now share with the district authorities in the area' (CPRE, 1995, p. 14). This task has been eased by the fact that in 1974 some of the district authorities took over the highways design role from the county authority on an agency basis. In these districts (including St. Edmunsbury), the planning and highways functions have been combined to ensure due consideration is given to design at each stage of the planning process. In 2000, the guide is undergoing a major review.

# Chapter 3

# The design debate and a new framework for control

It has long been argued that the design quality of development in new and established environments represents the clearest outward expression of planning effort and the means through which local populations most readily evaluate the role and success of the planning and development process (Keeble, 1971, pp. 169–72). With support for local authorities to pursue more interventionist and proactive design agendas coming from central government in the UK (see Chapter 2), local authorities, and the populations they represent, may less readily stand for the laissez-faire approaches to design control (particularly residential design control) necessarily adopted in the past.

In this context, Chapter 3 explores the new framework for design control in England, post February 1997. It begins by identifying the established critiques of design control and the long established positions taken by the different stakeholders in the planning/development process. These critiques are subsequently used as a means to examine the significant changes in government advice introduced through the 1997 revision to PPG1 (DoE, 1997b). If read in conjunction with Chapter 10, it also brings the examination of government advice presented in Chapter 2 up to date.

Much has been written in numerous sources about the conflicting views of the different stakeholders in the design control process. No clear formulation of the UK discussions into a set of explicit themes has yet been offered however, of a type comparable to that developed by Case Scheer for 'design review' in the American context (Case Scheer and Preiser, 1994, pp. 1–10). It is this that Chapter 3 initially attempts to do; a re-formulation which subsequently provides a means to question the likely impact of the new government guidance on design following a detailed and critical examination of that advice in the second half of the chapter. The initial examination of PPG1 is itself largely based on a detailed review of the design paragraphs of the text in the light of earlier guidance on design discussed in Chapter 2 and the developing response of central government to increased pressures to recognise the value of quality design and the role of the public sector in helping to deliver it.

## The design debate

In an influential article, the late Francis Tibbalds wrote of the gap which had opened up between the established built environment professions in the UK. Tibbalds argued that seventy years ago the professions began to carve up urban concerns between them. Increasingly, planning became less physical in nature and more social science orientated,

*Fig. 3.1 'The Professional Conspiracy' (Hellman in Tibbalds, 1988a).*

abandoning its old civic design routes, while the rapid reduction in architect/planners that resulted prevented architecture from filling the gap. Thus, the 'great alibi' was created; an unintentional professional conspiracy which enabled the professions to blame each other for the declining urban quality (Tibbalds, 1988a – see Fig. 3.1).

The gap Tibbalds wrote of can most readily be observed between the architectural and planning professions. This, however, hides the true extent of the problem, in which the surveying, engineering (particularly highways), development and to a lesser extent landscape professions have also been guilty of sectorial interests and jealous ring fencing of professional activity. By the late 1960s an increasing number of professionals, from all camps, began to see that the split was contributing to a widespread urban deterioration. The result, Tibbalds argued, was the development of urban design as a discipline that attempts to build bridges and encourage multi-disciplinary co-operation with a focus on filling the gaps. Today, however, the urban gap is still all too apparent, particularly in new residential contexts (see pp. 89–96), and the wholesale acceptance of urban design action is still to be grasped. The former Secretary of State for the Environment, John Gummer, recognised the problem, writing that:

> ... the buildings which we construct and the space which we create have an impact on people's lives for centuries. [Yet] we are so determined not to choose that we leave it all to chance. So buildings are not seen or considered in context. The neighbourliness of architecture is not prized. And the urban scene is increasingly a mere clutter of construction (Gummer, 1995, p. 8).

With the breaking down of strict professional codes and remits during the 1980s – largely as a result of concerted government action to prioritise the free market and break professional restrictive practices – other breaches in the walls also became apparent. So, by the 1990s the design, construction management, and development roles of built environment professionals had become less clearly defined. The result was a partial acceptance of a new climate for design, with inter-professional team-working becoming more apparent (Cowan, 1995), but also a redoubling of efforts (by some) to protect those walls which remained intact. The highest remained the wall between the planning and design/development professions.

### The stakeholders

The lack of concern for urban design and the continued embrace of the 'great alibi' is nowhere more apparent than in the area of design control – the planning activity which since the evolution of planning action has most clearly crossed the no-man's-land, and which most frequently provokes inter-professional antagonism. The lack of a common cause between the different professions and between central government and local government over the years has therefore directly contributed to the sidelining of design as an area of planning action. Nevertheless, despite its treatment, design has remained a serious and significant part of the planning remit, with research on planning appeals confirming the continuing high emphasis on design in planning decision making. Thus design remains the determining factor in 32 per cent of appeals in England and a significant factor in over half of appeals (Punter in Anon., 1996b). Consequently, many authorities have continued to exercise their powers in the area, producing in the process copious design guidance to steer applicants in the production of better design solutions (Chapman and Larkham, 1992, p. 17).

Analysis of the full range of responses to the consultation exercise held on the (revised) PPG1[1] (discussed in Chapter 6 – DoE, 1996e) also confirms the broad interest in design. The exercise revealed that in a guidance note which provides a strategic commentary across the entire planning remit, over half of the 449 respondents dealt directly with the design-specific paragraphs in their responses, a number clearly in excess of interest in the wide range of other planning concerns addressed by the note.

It can be argued that the historic position of central government in the UK on design control has merely attempted to balance interests by reflecting the legitimate concerns of the range of key stakeholders in the control process. Nevertheless, as has been shown in Chapter 2, the development of design control practice has witnessed the alternating nature of government support for the role – from broadly agnostic to negative (and rarely positive) – reflecting the changing ideological positioning of successive governments and mirroring the associated rise and fall of influence wielded by the different stakeholders.

The range of stakeholders and their inter-relationships in the development and policy processes are complex (see pp. 87–9); nevertheless, in the design control debate, they can be simplistically divided into two groups. First, the development and design lobby represented particularly by the HBF and RIBA, whose successive presidents have derided local authority design control (Punter and Carmona, 1997a, p. 38), and who through consistent lobbying have shaped much of the evolution of a hands-off central government design policy agenda in England (Hubbard, 1994a, p. 311). The result has been that the equally legitimate concerns of the second major (usually pro-control) interest in the design control debate have been downplayed, for example in the series of largely negative – anti control – government circulars of the 1980s (DoE, 1980; DoE, 1985; DoE, 1988a). This position has most often been articulated by the planning profession closely allied to the 'amenity' lobby (local and national amenity and residents groups). To some extent the adoption of the 1992 version of PPG1 Annex A by central government (DoE, 1992a) went some way to restore the balance between these conflicting concerns. Nevertheless, dispute remained close to the surface, and erupted twice before the latest revision to PPG1 in 1997.

---

[1] Before formal revision of PPGs, the Department of the Environment (now Department for the Environment, Transport and the Regions) undertakes a consultation exercise during which interested parties are invited to comment on a draft version of the proposed note. These responses are used by the DETR to consider and, if necessary, further amend their proposed guidance. Subsequently, responses are collated and made available for public inspection in the DETR library in London.

clearly measurable – quantitative rather than qualitative – criteria as a basis for control (RIBA, 1995).

One of the few studies (the Gross Report – RIBA, 1965) to look in any depth at architects' perceptions of design control revealed that the problems perceived by the RIBA (albeit 30+ years ago) were largely illusory. The report confirmed that in actuality complaints about staff quality and delay in processing applications were far more common, with problems over aesthetic control affecting relatively few architects (Punter, 1987, p. 40).

For housebuilders, opposition to adapting their standard products and their historic opposition to design control is to a large extent driven by uncertainty. The housebuilders see the problem as caused by the case-by-case system of control operated in the UK, the difficulty of assessing a local authority's position on design in advance of making an application, and the consequential costs associated with protracted negotiations on design. The situation is compounded by the wide range of often inconsistent practice which exists between authorities, from detailed control of design, to little or no design control at all (Punter et al., 1996). Such inconsistency provides a major bone of contention between planning authorities and developers, for whom secure financial planning necessitates maximum certainty, and an awareness by authorities of the costs of indecision and delay and of the market in which developers operate (DoE and HRF, 1976).

*Design skills – the lack of design skills amongst planning (and design) professionals and the need for appropriate design skills to inform decision making*
A consistent bug bear of design professionals has been the lack of design skills among those evaluating design (Chapman and Larkham, 1992, p. 16). The charge has been that such a situation not only increases subjectivity and the exercise of personal taste and opinion, but also undermines the professional status and judgements of the trained designer (Hall, 1990, p. 4 – see Fig. 3.3). The situation has been exacerbated by the gradual move away from physical design in planning education since its evolution out of the architectural profession (Hubbard, 1994a, p. 312). The counterargument has emphasised

*Fig. 3.3  The architects' view of planning (Hellman in Carmona, 1996a).*

the gap between lay and professional tastes on design (Beer, 1983, p. 385; Hubbard, 1994b) and the legitimacy of lay councillors making judgements because they more readily reflect the tastes of wider society.

A 1982 study into design quality and development control concluded 'many new developments are going on the ground in England without anybody fully trained in design having been involved in their processing'. The study suggested this was a key factor in the general poor quality and monotony of many new environments – particularly residential environments – but was not an insoluble problem but one simply requiring long-term investment in design training for new (and existing) local authority staff (Beer, 1983, p. 403). Today, the design skills gap seemingly still remains to be filled (see pp. 189–97).

The argument has also been levelled against many trained design professionals. The lack of urban design education for architects in the UK and the low appreciation of context among architects have been the legitimate concerns of many commentators on design (Tugnutt and Robertson, 1987, p. 6), including (notably) HRH the Prince of Wales (1989). In part, the concern emanates from the different objectives of designer, client and planner, in that it is frequently in the interest of the designer and client for a development to stand out from its context and proclaim its presence, while for the planner – reflecting the views of local residents and a wider public – the objective is more often to ensure a development fits into its surroundings. Nevertheless, the poor quality of urban design education in many architecture schools and the misconceived substitution of urban design with 'big architecture' in others have undoubtedly spawned a generation of architects with a reduced sensitivity for wider urban context.

*Innovation in design – the value of creative expression in securing good design and the need for the planning process to recognise this*
A related concern has been the perception that design control stifles architectural expression and leads to the production of safe, unadventurous design solutions. Critics have argued that such processes prevent design that is appropriately expressive of its time, undermines a designer's basic right to freedom of expression and encourages poor copies of past vernacular styles (Case Scheer and Preiser, 1994, p. 8). In a notable intervention, the former President of the RIBA described planning committees as 'cultural pariahs operating out of their depth, with extraordinary arrogance, and frequently destroying the efforts of some . . . of the more imaginative architects' (Manser, 1980). The opposition of architects, in particular, to design control has largely developed as a reaction against the perceived deep-rooted public (and therefore planning committee) suspicion of modern design (Moro, 1958). In this context, committee members have often been castigated as 'architects' oppressors' even if those same commentators have been known to line up with councillors on a second battle front against 'the pastiche taste' of housebuilders and other developers (Scorpio, 1997).

Against such arguments, those supportive of design control highlight a basic mistrust of modern design within the wider population (Tugnutt and Robertson, 1987, pp. 6–7), which is also, appropriately or not, reflected in the tastes of planning committees. Received opinion now accepts that such conservatism has to be laid, at least in part, at the door of the design, development and planning professionals for the havoc wreaked to British towns and cities by the utopian 'modernist' planning, urban design and architecture of the 1960s (Gummer, 1994, p. 13).

Amenity interests further argue that the vast majority of planning applications in the UK are anyway made by those untrained in design (RFAC, 1990), and that prescription is necessary to bring the input of such stakeholders up to at least a minimum acceptable standard, rather than to stifle innovation from creative designers. With specific regard to the housing sector, the architectural input into this vast construction sector is severely limited, and so, although housing makes up the biggest sector of the architectural profession's workload – at about a quarter of an architect's total workload – only 15 per cent of private sector housing is certified by architects. Thus, although architects might legitimately complain about the poor quality of housing design, in this sector, at least, it is unlikely to be the dead hand of design control on architects' applications that undermines creativity; rather the failure of the housebuilders themselves to take architectural advice in the first place. As one architectural critic put it '. . . the power of architecture has had less impact on housing than on any other single sector of construction' (Rogers, 1994; 1997b).

Some commentators have countered, however, that the planning authorities also have much to answer for in stifling design expression, by simply failing to correct the perception that 'standard' solutions are more likely to gain planning permission without challenge. They argue, that while innovative design solutions continue to be the subject of greater scrutiny by planning committees – and therefore delay and increased costs – bland 'traditional' solutions go through on the nod, thus degrading the environment and discouraging developers from financing innovative approaches to design (English Partnerships, 1996, Sec. 6).

*Urban v. architectural design – the potential of urban design as an overarching framework moving beyond a concern with architectural detail and standards based design*
Much of the design control debate – and indeed the question posed to the four respondents (featured in Table 3.1) – has focused on architectural design, rather than on the broader concerns for urban design. Nevertheless, a range of commentators have consistently argued in favour of the deeper interpretation of design encapsulated in the concept 'urban design' (House of Commons, 1985b; Delafons, 1991; HBF and RIBA, 1990; Booth, 1982). In 1992 the then version of PPG1 began a move away from more restrictive conceptualisations of design towards a concern for wider urban quality – urban space, density, layout, landscape, access, and criteria defining the building envelope (see pp. 30–1). This move received widespread support among most of the key stakeholders including the design and planning professions. Once recognised, the consensus became the focus of the 'Quality in Town and Country Initiative' and a key tenet of the subsequent guidance on design in PPG1 (1997).

Despite the developing agenda, an ongoing feature of the debate has been the continuing conflation by architects of design control primarily with aesthetics, and thus with architectural design (RIBA, 1995). This preoccupation has ensured that the greatest opposition to urban design – as a focus for control – has come from the housebuilders by way of numerous objections to any extension of the most basic control of estate layout in the new generation of design policies in British local plans.[2] To the housebuilders, control of layout, in particular, makes further inroads into their marketing judgements; judgement, at the time of the research, still the subject of unequivocal support in the discrete government advice on the design of residential areas in PPG3.

Amenity and planning interests, on the other hand, have continued to support the legitimacy of detailed design control and the value of architecture that pays due homage to its surroundings – architectural, urban design and landscape. To amenity interests, specifically, the responsibility for poor quality development often lies equally with developers and local authorities; testimony, they argue, to the corporate identities of developers and

---

[2] The plan-led system in the UK now requires each local authority to produce a district wide development plan. This requirement (since 1991) has heralded a new generation of design policies in local plans, with many authorities writing such policies for the first time.

housebuilders, and to the unimaginative standardised road layouts of the highways engineers (CPRE, 1995, p. 9).

The highway engineer plays a particularly important role in controlling the layout of development, and has frequently been the butt of much criticism (from development and amenity interests) as regards their insistence on standardised, often uniform solutions to layout (POS *et al.*, 1998, pp. 7–8). The problem originates from the commercial necessity to build roads to adoptable standards, so that on completion of developments, highways authorities will be willing to take over responsibility for the maintenance of the new roads from the developer. By its nature, the discipline of the highway engineer is a largely technical one, and not one which lends itself easily to aesthetic concerns. The result has been a great frustration (at least since the 1950s) with the resulting road-dominated layouts of much new development (housing in particular); this despite long-established attempts both by local government – for example the Essex and Cheshire Design Guides (Essex County Council, 1973; Cheshire County Council, 1976) – and by central government – in successive Design Bulletins (DoE/DoT, 1977; DoE/DoT, 1992) – to introduce more scope for innovation in road layout design.

Consequently, there is still an often vented feeling that the requirements of the highway engineer receive too much prominence in the design of residential development, and that any improvements to standard road layouts and designs can only be achieved through prolonged negotiation. This negotiation, it is argued, largely covers the same ground time and time again, costs developers, architects and local authorities much time and money, and therefore promotes the selection of the easy and cost-effective option – the standard, road-dominated solution to layout design (HBF/RIBA, 1990, pp. 20–2; Gummer, 1994, pp. 15–16). Recent research appraising 'The Quality of London's Residential Environment' confirmed the critique of standards-based approaches, at least for residential design, arguing instead for a more creative and flexible interpretation of design standards, particularly those for roads, parking and density. Interestingly, however, the complete abandonment of standards was not sanctioned by the research because of their continued utility as effective 'backstop' controls (LPAC, 1994, p. 11).

Although not expressed in the 1992 version of PPG1 (or still recognised by many highways or planning authorities), the concern for urban design has witnessed an increasing movement away from a preoccupation with the visual 'townscape' dimension of urban design, and from standards-based functional approaches, to encompass broader social, perceptual and environmental conceptualisations as well (see pp. 132–6). Slowly these dimensions have been recognised by local authorities as legitimate for prescription in policy and by central government for articulation in government advice.

*Democracy v. individual rights – the public nature of all built environment interventions and the legitimacy of democracy as an arbiter of quality*

In 1979, the Secretary of State announced that democracy 'as an arbiter of taste or as a judge of aesthetic or artistic standards falls far short of a far less controlled system of individual corporate or institutional patronage and initiative' (DoE, 1980). In 1995 the then incumbent suggested 'The problem is not that we have had bad design, but that we have tried to avoid having urban design at all. We have been so concerned not to be prescriptive, so concerned not to impose a particular view, we have sometimes thought it better to have no view at all' (Gummer, 1995). Outwardly, at least, a shift is clear, reflecting a wider acceptance amongst government that planning can play a positive role in improving design quality and that this role is democratic (of sorts) because it incorporates the views of the public represented through their democratically elected, and thus accountable, representatives.

Among the key stakeholders, the design and development lobbies have consistently argued that the client and his/her designer must have the primary responsibility for design and that enhancing the powers of the public sector in controlling design merely leads to the unacceptably bland results of design by committee (Mallett, 1997a). This approach has been consistently advocated by government including in the 1992 version of PPG1 (DoE, 1992a, para. A2). The result has been that residents have all too often been the forgotten player in the debate, a factor abhorred by the Prince of Wales, who, with characteristic mistrust of professional expertise, suggested 'There must be one golden rule – we all need to be involved together – planning and architecture are much too important to be left to the professionals' (HRH The Prince of Wales, 1989, p. 97). Amenity and planning interests have accepted the argument that good design is unlikely without good designers, but have highlighted the inescapable impact of design interventions beyond the confines of their sites and the experience of their immediate users, as justifying the legitimacy of a public role in decisions made on design (Owen, 1995, pp. 144–5). The arguments are based on the incontrovertible fact that architecture and urban design are, by their nature, public arts, and that it is often the local population, rather than the designer, developer, or investor who are required to live with the day-to-day impact of completed developments on the locality.

The case made by architects develops out of the powerful argument for freedom of expression and against interference in the property rights of owners. Although architects played a significant role in the inception and evolution of design control in the UK, there has always been a profound mistrust by elements of the profession of any regulations that effectively limit their design freedom. Consequently, at least since the 1950s, there has been a strongly felt antagonism by many architects towards design control. Led by the RIBA, these architects have consistently asserted that planners and councillors have consistently rejected proposals by architects, whilst applications by non-architects have not been so affected.

Perhaps more centrally, the case made by architects also reflects alternative professional priorities borne out in a recent study of architects' perceptions of their services. This revealed that the respect of the public for architects' efforts rated as the least significant consideration in their evaluation of success; with repeat business, client feedback, and earnings all of far greater consequence (Building Profile, 1997). The report elicited the headline 'Architects Don't Give a Damn for Public Opinion' in the architectural press and a revealing statement from the editor of the report (a former RIBA press officer), who said: 'Often the public don't understand the message behind the building. And who cares what your fellows think, that's not as important as what your clients think' (Thompson A. in Anon., 1997b). The statement illustrates the elitist attitudes among at least some in the built environment professions that have helped to keep the design debate alive and well between successive offerings from central government.

In the US, discussion of freedom of expression takes on the added significance imbued by a potential for constitutional conflict with the First Amendment rights guaranteeing free speech (and by implication freedom of architectural expression). Critics of American 'design review' processes have argued that review systems merely reinforce majority-based (i.e. historic, white, European) cultural bias on minorities and therefore conflict with First Amendment rights (Case Scheer and Preiser, 1994, p. 5). Conversely, the US courts have consistently supported the increased regulation of design, whilst those who support design review have maintained that prejudice and arbitrariness can anyway be avoided by preconceived prescription in the form of public policy or ordinance (Tseng-yu Lai in Case Scheer and Preiser, 1994, pp. 40–1). In the UK, the cultural dimension has featured less in the debate, but the charge of elitism has still been prevalent. The argument goes that design is anyway an elitist preoccupation, and that a concern for design – and particularly for conservation – merely perpetuates inconsistencies in the environment as those with greatest to gain inevitably reside in areas benefiting from more prescriptive design control regimes. Such situations have been criticised as inequitable (Townsend, 1995, p. 3).

*Established context – the appropriateness of response to context and conservation designations to secure it*

Government guidance on design has consistently demonstrated a concern for established context, and that design interventions and evaluations should be made against an assessment of their contribution – or detraction – from that context (MHLG, 1969, para. 4; DoE, 1980, para. 20; 1992a, para. A4). Within this general thrust, a two-tier system of contextual control has been developed, with the character of the few 'designated' areas – conservation areas and the like – prioritised over less blessed environments. A clear divide has also marked the debate here. Design and development interests have consistently argued that context – although important – should not be used as a blunt instrument to prevent contemporary development (Mallet, 1997a), and that designations have often been used as a means to increase development control powers, rather than because of any real concern for design quality. The arguments have logically reinforced an underlying call for less 'detailed' design control and a related concern that the large numbers of designated areas (and buildings) have devalued the 'conservation currency' (Manser and Adam, 1992).

Conversely, amenity interests have argued consistently that the value of context should be recognised and that designers should first and foremost ensure the contextual fit of developments (wherever built). Such arguments have been backed by widespread public preference for development that respects its context and for statutory designations to protect 'the familiar and cherished local scene' (Larkham, 1996, p. 7). Planners and planning committees have also tended to prioritise the importance of context, while the extent of designations in the UK helps to confirm both their effectiveness as control devices, and the desire of planning authorities to have greater control over design than government policy has often allowed. Regarding housing design, even architects have been able to set aside their critique of design control and have been strongly critical of the speculative, standardised product of the mass housebuilders. Ian Nairn, for example, in his famous paper 'Outrage', described the speculative product as 'anywhere type houses ... packaged together in a manner devoid of identity or a sense of place' (Nairn, 1955) – an assessment based on their failure to respect context or any of the then developing rules of townscape.

Influential support to back the planning profession's claims for design control and the value of decisions made with regard to context has consistently come from two pseudo-governmental bodies. First, from the RFAC who have steadfastly upheld the need for proper design control, arguing in its 1980 publication 'Building in Context' that the overall impact of design control has 'been to raise the general standard of layout and design' (RFAC, 1980). This basic sentiment was, moreover, upheld in two further RFAC publications, 'Planning for Beauty', which makes the case for design guidelines against which applications should be assessed (see p. 157), and 'What Makes a Good Building', which argues for objective design criteria against which to evaluate building quality (RFAC, 1990; 1994). The second influential body to take the same pro-control view has been the Countryside Commission, which, in its 1989 publication 'Planning for a Greener Countryside', argued that in the case of new housing in the countryside, more respect for local style and a higher standard of design is needed, and that 'the problem has been exacerbated by government advice ... which restricts local authority involvement in design matters' (Countryside Commission, 1989). This sentiment was also reflected in more recent Countryside Commission publications such as 'Design in the Countryside', which attempted to give authorities new tools to appraise the context into which new development (particularly housing) is to fit (Countryside Commission, 1993; see p. 147).

*Interpreting 'design' – the language of design and the complementary nature of urban and architectural design*

In its attempt to move authorities away from a concern for detailed design and towards wider environmental quality, the 1992 version of PPG1 prescribed a range of 'broad' design criteria suitable for control – scale, density, height, massing, layout, landscape and access. At the same time the guidance identified 'The appearance of development and its relationship to its surroundings' (DoE, 1992a) as material considerations. Unfortunately, in the desire to reach a professional compromise in its preparation, it soon became clear that the guidance was open to wide interpretation (Tugnutt, 1991). Consequently, the architectural profession read the guidance as a charter for less 'interference' in architectural design, and the planning profession largely as encouragement to greater intervention, in urban and architectural design.

The disparity in interpretation brought into focus the inextricably linked and overlapping nature of architecture and urban design, in that buildings both define and articulate the public realm. Thus, prescribed design criteria are invariably capable of interpretation at a variety of scales – in detailed as well as more fundamental ways – and as urban design and architectural concerns (Punter and Carmona, 1996a; 1996b). Evaluation of even the most recent government guidance on design reveals that scope for confusion still exists (Carmona, 1997a). Thus, if even the minutely considered wording of the PPGs offer potential for dual interpretation, then time-consuming and expensive conflict on the language and interpretation of design concepts in local authority guidance is likely to remain a feature of design control practice for some time to come.

Beer (1983, p. 385) has argued that communication between all the key stakeholders in making decisions on design is often a difficult process, with different stakeholders frequently speaking very different languages – the 'design-speak' of the architect, the 'commercial-speak' of the developer, the 'technical-speak' of the highways engineer, and the 'policy-speak' of the planner. Clearly, each profession has its own jargon and all can be incomprehensible to the range of lay people involved – the local councillors and residents. The problem of day-to-day communication is a simple one, but one that leads to misunderstandings during negotiation on design; if not to complete failure of different sides in a debate to understand and appreciate the goals and objectives of the others. The tendency for design jargon to be interpreted differently by different parties frequently reduces the exercise of design control to wrangling over terminology used in policy and guidance (national and local); wrangling which such preconceived guidance on design is intended to remove.

*The professional role – the multi-actor/professional nature of all design and development interventions*

The influence and power wielded by the different stakeholders in the design and development process are rarely equal (Hayward and McGlynn, 1993, pp. 5–7). For example, only relatively infrequently today are final decisions on whether to develop or not made by the public sector and with such decisions lie the real power to control quality. To that extent the planning system is inevitably largely reactive, and dependent on the willingness of developers and investors to pay for quality design. Without such investment the system of design control would be hard-pressed to produce anything other than mediocrity.

*Good*

Nevertheless, in a free market economy where the pressure on the development industry is primarily the profit motive, planners and amenity interests consistently argue the case for greater intervention to ensure the public interest is safeguarded and development of appropriate quality secured (Steel, 1995, p. 20).

Such arguments have become increasingly acceptable to at least a minority of development/finance interests. These interests see design control as a means to ensure lasting value for their investments, by increasing the certainty with which long-term financial planning can be made, in which the quality of both the immediate and wider environment represents a key component in safeguarding property value (Loew, 1997). Such approaches have been supported by the RFAC who argue that working within constraints of context and development process should be a positive (rather than negative) design discipline (RFAC, 1994, p. 69).

To the architectural profession (and other design professions) the pressures are clearly two-sided with constraints exercised by the private (or public) paymasters, as well as by the public guarantors in the form of planning authorities (Punter, 1990, p. 18). In such a context, the constraints represented by public sector policy may offer the architect some means to stand up to his/her client, who may often want only the cheapest building to sell on to the end user. Nevertheless, the constraints on an architect's design freedom can, and often are, intense.

Responses to the discussion document published as part of the 'Quality in Town and Country' initiative (see below; DoE, 1994c) revealed an overwhelming agreement that the use of non-professionals in the design process and development/finance processes – particularly the negative impact of design and build and compulsory competitive tendering (CCT) – are of greatest moment in reducing development quality. Interestingly, in a document reflecting views from across the professional spectrum on the issue of quality, planning controls – or more specifically, the production of design guidance and briefs – were identified as positive influences on design (DoE, 1996b, p. 59). Clearly, design is a multi-professional exercise in which the responsibility for failure is carried across all stakeholders in the process and in which the pursuit of quality as an objective should be shared by all. The encouragement of multi-professional approaches to design and an acceptance of the valued role of all the separate contributors in the design and development process, has become a recurring theme of the design control debate (Dean, 1997; Buxton, 1997; Hirst 1997).

## Evaluation: The Design Debate

The grievances held by architects and developers are based to a large extent on legitimate concerns resulting from shortcomings in the system. This is inevitable because whatever the context there will always be limitations to what any design control system can achieve. In the end, the system as it stands is dependent on the developer/client and his/her aspirations, vision and resources to deliver quality; their 'Civic Responsibility' as the DoE has entitled it (Gummer, 1994, p. 8). Despite this, the true value of the system should not discount what remains unseen, more particularly, what the system prevents rather than in what it allows. In this regard, the need for the essential checks and balances provided by design control are easier to justify, while those who advocate complete reliance on civic responsibility, the workings of the market and professional expertise, to some extent place faith before reason. Effectively, they wish to deny the public the voice in design matters provided by the planning system, and reject the undoubted strong public support for design control as attested by the spread of conservation areas across the country (Delaflons, 1997, p. 186). The disastrous results of withdrawing the essential crutch provided by design control – no matter how imperfect – are plain to see in areas of the world subject to the high development pressures (commensurate with Western living) but without the balance provided by design control (parts of the US, Middle East and Far East). In the UK, the London Docklands 'non-plan' (non-urban design) Isle of Dogs provides a case-in-point (Carmona, 1991, pp. 133–6).

The positions of the protagonists in the debate have been laid out frequently and with great force over the years and still the debate simmers on. Nevertheless, the arguments have never been as clearly two-sided as sometimes they may seem: 'This has not been a simple designer versus planner debate, nor a contest between market-led freedom versus planning control. Many planners would feel that their role is not that of acting as guardian of the public taste, and many architects would argue that some aesthetic co-ordination is desirable to enhance public places and the "townscape" of buildings and open spaces' (Donovan and Larkham, 1996, p. 303).

The evaluation of the ongoing design debate has revealed a number of clear themes and a series of positions adopted – almost without question – by the different sides of the debate. The analysis revealed:

- continued polarised approaches by the professions and other stakeholders to the issue of design and its treatment by the planning system, but some breaking down of restrictive professional remits and practices;
- that despite its sidelining by government, design has continued to be regarded as a serious and significant part of the planning remit by planners, other controllers of design, and by the various amenity bodies;
- that the RIBA and HBF have been most vociferous in their opposition to such control;
- that debate revolves – in the main – around a series of dogmatic interpretations and stances: intervention v. interference; process or product; objectivity v. subjectivity; creativity v. standardisation; urban v. architectural design; democracy v. individual rights; innovation v. contextual fit;
- that the issue of design skills (or lack of them) crosses the professional divide; and
- that the failure to appreciate disparate professional roles and perspectives or even to communicate effectively, lies at the heart of intolerant professional stances and therefore the design control debate.

## A new framework for control

### *The potential for consensus*

In 1994 in an initial attempt to build consensus and break the professional impasse, the wide-ranging discussion document 'Quality in Town and County' challenged individuals in fields with an influence on the built environment – as well as communities – to consider what could be done to deliver 'quality'. The introduction proclaimed that 'The quality of our surroundings depends not only on government and developers, but upon companies as owners and tenants, the professions, local authorities, and individuals. The responsibility for what is built, and where, is shared, as are the rewards which good quality bestows' (DoE, 1994c, p. 3).

The resulting analysis identified six main themes from the cross-professional responses received (DoE, 1996b, p. 4). The need for:

1. mixed use development to be pursued as a key contribution to sustainable development;
2. integration and co-ordination of land-use and transport planning;
3. greater local involvement in projects;
4. more effective design guidance to identify and reinforce local character;
5. greater environmental awareness and design training;
6. increased built densities, whilst paradoxically also increasing open space provision.

Whilst covering a much wider remit than that of design control, the main themes were interesting for their recognition of an explicit public sector involvement in securing quality (themes 2, 4, and 5); for the widespread concern for sustainable development patterns (themes 1, 2, 5, and 6); and for the recognition of the value of local context and local involvement in design (themes 3 and 4). Outwardly, at least, some consensus was emerging on the need for intervention to secure quality, and through the widespread welcome that the initiative received (Gummer, 1994, p. 1), of the need to strive for further consensus on securing quality and greater awareness of the value of good design (theme 5).

In a characteristic speech launching the 'Quality Initiative', the then Secretary of State railed against the despair many local populations feel about 'the relentless homogenisation which has eroded so much local colour', against 'monotonous building which is designed for nowhere in particular' and against the nature of urban design as 'a neglected profession, cast into the wilderness by a reaction against the abuses of the 1960s' (Gummer, 1994, pp. 8 and 13). If the 'Quality Initiative' heralded some potential for cross-professional consensus on design, then John Gummer's dramatic words heralded an imminent U-turn in government thinking on the value of design; in particular, the need for development that is responsive to place, and the role of the public sector in helping to deliver it.

The U-turn came in 1996 in the form of the consultation paper on a second revised version of PPG1 (DoE, 1996e). The resultant mould-breaking guidance (DoE, 1997b – see Fig. 3.4) is analysed in the remainder of the chapter before conclusions are drawn in the light of the critiques already established, about the impact of the new framework on the different stakeholder groups and on design control practice.

### The new framework

The 1995 'Quality in Town and Country, Urban Design Campaign' documentation announced that:

> Too much of our national debate about development focuses on architecture but ignores urban design. As a result, too much of that debate revolves around a handful of one-off landmark buildings which, by their nature, will never be repeated (DoE, 1995a)

This was an observation supported in the 'Design Policies in Local Plans' research (Punter and Carmona, 1997a). The research argued that outside of environmentally sensitive areas, planning authorities are more able to influence the quality of the built environment if they concentrate on defining and controlling those urban design qualities which give character and quality to the public realm and which determine the most equitable use of public space.

The new design advice published in (revised) PPG1 took this message to heart, alongside a general re-emphasis of the importance of design as a material consideration in planning decisions. The new PPG1 begins by identifying sustainable development, mixed use and design as three themes 'which underpin the government's approach to the planning system'

## INTRODUCTION

3. This Note begins by discussing sustainable development, mixed use and design, three themes which underpin the Government's approach to the planning system. It then provides a number of policy messages in relation to various particular land uses. More detailed guidance is given in the other Government planning policy notes and good practice guides listed in Annex B. Finally, it sets out the operational principles to be observed in the planning system.

## Design

13. New buildings and their curtilages have a significant effect on the character and quality of an area. They define public spaces, streets and vistas and inevitably create the context for future development. These effects will often be to the benefit of an area but they can be detrimental. They are matters of proper public interest. The appearance of proposed development and its relationship to its surroundings are therefore material considerations in determining planning applications and appeals. Such considerations relate to the design of buildings and to urban design. These are distinct, albeit closely interrelated subjects. Both are important. Both require an understanding of the context in which development takes place whether in urban or rural areas.

14. For the purposes of this Guidance, urban design should be taken to mean the relationship between different buildings; the relationship between buildings and the streets, squares, parks, waterways and other spaces which make up the public domain; the nature and quality of the public domain itself; the relationship of one part of a village, town or city with other parts; and the patterns of movement and activity which are thereby established: in short, the complex relationships between all the elements of built and unbuilt space. As the appearance and treatment of the spaces between and around buildings is often of comparable importance to the design of the buildings themselves, landscape design should be considered as an integral part of urban design.

15. Good design should be the aim of all those involved in the development process and should be encouraged everywhere. Good design can help promote sustainable development; improve the quality of the existing environment; attract business and investment; and reinforce civic pride and a sense of place. It can help to secure continued public acceptance of necessary new development.

16. Applicants for planning permission should be able to demonstrate how they have taken account of the need for good design in their development proposals and that they have had regard to relevant development plan policies and supplementary design guidance. This should be done in a manner appropriate to the nature and scale of the proposals.

17. Local planning authorities should reject poor designs, particularly where their decisions are supported by clear plan policies or supplementary design guidance which has been subjected to public consultation and adopted by the local planning authority. Poor designs may include those inappropriate to their context, for example those clearly out of scale or incompatible with their surroundings.

18. Local planning authorities should not attempt to impose a particular architectural taste or style arbitrarily. It is, however, proper to seek to promote or reinforce local distinctiveness particularly where this is supported by clear plan policies or supplementary design guidance. Local planning authorities should not concern themselves with matters of detailed design except where such matters have a significant effect on the character or quality of the area, including neighbouring buildings. Particular weight should be given to the impact of development on existing buildings and on the character of areas recognised for their landscape or townscape value, such as National Parks, Areas of Outstanding Natural Beauty and Conservation Areas.

19. When the design of proposed development is consistent with relevant design policies and supplementary design guidance, planning permission should not be refused on design grounds unless there are exceptional circumstances. Design policies and guidance should avoid stifling responsible innovation, originality or initiative. Such policies and guidance should recognise that the qualities of an outstanding scheme may exceptionally justify departing from them.

20. Further guidance on the expression of design policies in development plans and supplementary design guidance, and on the information relating to design which should be submitted with planning applications, is contained in Annex A.

## Annex A:
## Handling of design issues

A1. Development plans should set out design policies against which development proposals are to be considered. Policies should be based on a proper assessment of the character of the surrounding built and natural environment, and should take account of the defining characteristics of each local area, for example local or regional building traditions and materials. The fact that a design or layout is appropriate for one area does not mean it is appropriate everywhere. Plan policies should avoid unnecessary prescription or detail and should concentrate on guiding the overall scale, density, massing, height, landscape, layout and access of new development in relation to neighbouring buildings and the local area more generally.

A2. Development plans may refer to supplementary design guidance, including local design guides and site-specific development briefs, which can usefully elucidate and exemplify plan policies, thereby giving greater certainty to all those involved in the design and development process. Where appropriate, such guidance should also explain how relevant general advice, including that relating to the design of roads and footways, is to be interpreted and applied at a local level in order to take account of the character of each area. Supplementary design guidance may usefully include advice about matters such as lighting and materials, where these are likely to have a significant impact on the character or quality of the existing environment.

A3. The weight accorded to supplementary design guidance in planning decisions will be expected to increase where it has been prepared in consultation with the public and with those whose work it may affect, and has been formally adopted by the local planning authority. Local planning authorities should include with such guidance a statement of the consultation undertaken and their response to representations made.

A4. Applicants for planning permission should, as a minimum, provide a short written statement setting out the design principles adopted as well as illustrative material in plan and elevation. This material should show the wider context and not just the development site and its immediately adjacent buildings. Inclusion of relevant perspective views can also be of value. Such material will be particularly important in relation to complex or large-scale development proposals, and those involving sensitive sites. For straightforward or small-scale proposals, this level of detail is unlikely to be necessary. Instead, illustrative material might simply comprise photographs of the development site and its surroundings, drawings of the proposed design itself and, where appropriate, plans of the proposed layout in relation to neighbouring development and uses.

A5. Applicants are encouraged to consult at an early stage with those, including local planning authorities, who may be expected to have a relevant and legitimate interest in the design aspects of their development proposals. Where applicants do so, local planning authorities should respond constructively by giving clear indications of their design expectations. Careful and early consideration of design issues can speed up the planning process by helping to make proposals for development acceptable to local planning authorities and local communities, thereby helping to avoid costly delay later.

A6. The use of conditions or planning obligations can be helpful in securing a high quality of design. Where design aspects of an approved development proposal are subject to conditions consistent with the advice in DOE Circular 11/95, or are subject to planning obligations consistent with the advice in DOE Circular 1.97, development which results from the grant of planning permission must comply with the approved design, unless subsequent changes to the design are justified, and are authorised by the local planning authority.

A7. In considering the design of proposed new development, local planning authorities, developers and designers should take into account the advice contained in DOE Circular 5/94, 'Planning out Crime'. In doing so, the approach adopted should be sufficiently flexible to allow solutions to remain sensitive to local circumstances.

*Fig. 3.4  Design-specific paragraphs from PPG1 (DoE, 1997b).*

(para. 3). Merely by examining the extent of the new design advice users now have fifteen paragraphs on design, with a further five on mixed uses and two on access (both key urban design considerations); as opposed to the seven in the old Annex A to PPG1 (DoE, 1992a). The range of issues covered has also been dramatically extended, as part of a new expanded agenda for design (see Table 3.2).[3]

### Prioritising urban design

The new emphasis invites the question: Has central government finally overcome its historical misgivings now to prioritise public sector intervention aimed at improving design quality? Immediate evidence is provided in the clear statement that 'Good design should be the aim of all those involved in the development process and should be encouraged everywhere' (para. 15). On the face of it, the statement – added after the consultation version of the note – represents a significant departure from the more obviously two-tier approaches advocated in the past. The move is far from total, however, and in another significant addition during the consultation period, the statement from the 1992 note was resurrected, that 'particular weight should be given to the impact of development . . . on the character of areas recognised for their landscape or townscape value' (para. 18).

The key innovation of the guidance is undoubtedly the emphasis placed on urban design. Thus, issues of spatial design, public domain, public spaces, vistas, civic pride, sense of place, and movement and activity patterns are addressed for the first time (paras. 13–14). In addition, the ubiquitous respect for context and the old seven-point DoE agenda – scale, density, massing, height, landscape, layout and access – continue to be prioritised (para. A1). Urban design is even usefully defined in the guidance – a definition that largely repeats that first seen in the 'Quality in Town and Country, Urban Design Campaign' (see p. 133), with some minor, but significant, amendments that make reference to the important social dimension of design – public domain and patterns of movement and activity.

In a further departure from the consultation draft, an explicit recognition is made that 'Good design can help promote sustainable development' (para. 15) – perhaps a hint towards the gradual acceptance of 'local distinctiveness' as a key indicator of sustainable development. The new urban design 'creed' of mixed use also receives substantial coverage on the grounds that mixed-use development 'can help create vitality and diversity and reduce the need to travel' – if contextually appropriate (paras. 8–12). As one means to achieve this, authorities are invited to consider promoting – through the planning system – opportunities for high quality mixed-use schemes such as 'urban villages' (para. 12).

Little heed is given, however, to the long-term campaign of the Landscape Institute (amongst others) for more explicit advice on landscape design, and particularly for a dedicated PPG on the issue (Anon., 1995b). If anything, the advice on this important concern for securing sustainable development is watered down from the 1992 note, with the removal of the key phrase 'The aim should be for any development to result in a "benefit" in environmental and landscape terms' (DoE, 1992a, para. A5). The distinction between hard and soft landscaping is also dropped (para. 14).

With this exception, the emphasis on urban design represents a significant extension of the limiting preoccupation with building design that characterised previous guidance. So, although the 1992 version of the note began to consider urban design concerns more comprehensively, it was not until 1996 that a guidance note – PPG6 (DoE, 1996d, para. 2.33) – actually mentioned the term 'urban design', and until 1997 that the subject was dealt with in any detail.

---

[3] Compare with Tables 2.2 and 2.3.

requires high standards of design, and therefore more detailed prescription in the plan (the plan extends to nine volumes, with village by village analysis and design policies relating to individual villages, or sites within them).

Nine years after work began, the plan was formally adopted (Cotswold District Council, 1999). In its first letter to the local authority commenting on the consultation draft of the plan, the DoE commented that the policies seem 'unnecessarily detailed, restrictive and negative' and lacked flexibility (quoted in Cooper, 1993). In subsequent meetings, the DoE warned against over-elaborate plan making, stressing the cost and time involved in public local inquiries (the Inquiry lasted six months). Clearly, in terms of time and resources the DoE has been proved correct. In terms of its advice on the over-detailed nature of the design policy it

*The Cotswold*
# DESIGN CODE

The Cotswold Design Code
is essential reading for
developers, architects
and builders in Cotswold
District. It covers in detail: –

♦ *The Cotswold Style*

♦ *Setting*

♦ *Harmony
and Street Scene*

♦ *Proportion*

♦ *Simplicity, Detail
and Decoration*

♦ *Materials*

♦ *Craftsmanship*

Cotswold District Council
*Caring for The Cotswolds*

MARCH 2000

*Fig. C.2 The Cotswold Design Code (Cotswold District Council, 2000).*

may have been proved wrong, however, with developments in government guidance coming more into line with the Cotswold approach rather than the other way around.

The officers have been particularly sensitive to criticism from local architectural interests. The District's Architects Panel carefully reviewed the chapter on design with varying and sometimes contradictory reactions, although in general supporting the initiative. The role of the Architects Panel was also inscribed into the plan, a body which the authority believes has a valued role in offering advice on important and contentious schemes, and in providing a point of contact between the Council and the architectural profession. Since its publication, the code has been widely accepted by designers in the district.

With a fiercely proud local population, the NIMBY factor is extremely strong and well organised in the district, and the design of new residential development is always a key local concern. During the consultation exercise, for example, the design policy attracted more detailed comment than any other; a measure of the sensitivity of the issue. In particular, there was strong support for high standards of design (including from the CPRE), but also a concern (from the HBF) that the approach would raise costs and reduce flexibility.

Officers concede that the code is imperfect and includes statements that are open to interpretation in individual cases. They argue, nevertheless, that this allows flexibility and is therefore a strength rather than a weakness. In 1996 the Inspector's report was received in which he concluded that 'all of this guidance may be extremely helpful but it should not have policy status' (Cotswold District Council, 1996). Instead, he recommended that the code should be published as supplementary design guidance, but should be mentioned in reworded policy. The recommendation was accepted, and in early 2000 the code was published as stand-alone supplementary design guidance (Cotswold District Council, 2000 – see Fig. C.2). Thus, although no longer part of the plan, reference in the reworded and

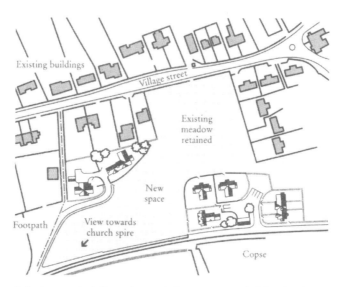

A development site in Down Ampney is shown above. New buildings have been positioned to keep the meadow, which is an important, pleasant break in the existing village street. This creates a new open space and, importantly, protects views towards the church spire. More information about the layout and design of this site can be found in the *Down Ampney Village Design Statement.*

*Fig. C.3  A development site in Down Ampney (Cotswold District Council, 2000, p. 5).*

dramatically shortened Policy 40 that 'The Council will consider applications with reference to the Cotswold Design Code, which has been published separately as Supplementary Design Guidance' will give it considerable status – a move at odds with the earlier DoE comments that the plan policies should stand alone and not depend on other documents, but supported in the latest guidance in PPG1 (DoE, 1997b, para. A2).

The Cotswold experience illustrates a carefully thought out and balanced approach to architectural design, demonstrating the strong desire of many authorities to control detailed design. The experience also illustrates the sometimes difficult distinction between policy and guidance, which eventually, in contrast to other experiences (see Inset D), forced the authority to remove the code from the plan. Finally, the approach illustrates how a positive approach to design can, despite the sensitive nature of the district, actually deliver more housing (Owen, 1995, pp. 155–6). Thus the plan allocated more land for housing than required by the structure plan on the basis that through sensitive appraisal and regard to the district's design aspirations, new housing could be successfully integrated into the historic fabric of most Cotswold settlements (see Fig. C.3).

# Chapter 4

# The speculative house: product and process

Booth has argued that as long as there has been a housebuilding industry promoting housing as a commodity, there have been critics who have claimed, with varying degrees of ferocity, that the product was sub-standard. Yet, he suggests, 'those who have criticised have only sometimes done so in the name of the eventual users', and rarely on the basis of objective studies of residents' attitudes to their environments (Booth, 1982, p. 21). Thus, as regards residential layout, Booth has observed a cycle of criticism, leading to reform and new standards that in turn provoke new criticism. Hence, the slums of the nineteenth century provoked an attempt to ensure more spacious standards for housing, yet, against these standards, Raymond Unwin argued in 1918 in favour of layouts which offered scope for more imaginative layout and building groupings. By the 1950s these new residential standards (in diluted form), were themselves under attack in the 'Architectural Review' by the advocates of the new townscape theories. In the 1960s the modernist credo of higher density living infused public sector housing development (and to a much more limited extent its private sector equivalents), but wasteful standards-based design still predominated before a concerted attack was mounted in the design guides of the 1970s to achieve a more rational use of space. In the 1990s the shift moved back once more to the promotion of higher density living, this time in the pursuit of the new objective of sustainability.

Still the debate remains to be settled, and perhaps it never will be. It may, however, offer some justification for the predominantly negative – or at least agnostic – attitude taken by government throughout the evolution of a comprehensive planning system in the UK to attempts to prescribe private sector residential quality. Thus, based on evidence that the predominance of public sector driven attempts to improve residential design quality have attempted – and failed – to produce significant improvements in the design of planned new residential developments, government may legitimately ask can such attempts ever work. Nevertheless, ample evidence now exists from the 1980s and 1990s that market-led approaches to delivering new housing environments are equally unable to deliver housing environments of a quality approaching that to which the public interest should rightly aspire (see pp. 89–96). The evidence also suggests that despite the lack of governmental support, the more sophisticated local authority-led approaches to controlling design have had at least some beneficial impact on the ground (Gupta, 1989).

Nevertheless, the key to any long-term improvement in residential design is likely to lie in the processes of delivering new residential development – in the structuring of the housing market, in the process of land allocation through the planning system, in the motivations of the different stakeholders involved in delivering new housing, and in the different perceptions about the product actually delivered. In this chapter, the speculative product and process are examined as a means to understand how and why the wider debate arises. The first part of the chapter examines the nature of the contemporary speculative house and housing estate and briefly presents the range of perspectives on that product. An example is included to illustrate the norm in speculative residential design now at the turn of the century. The second part of the chapter focuses in greater depth on the process inherent in delivering that product and in particular on the role and nature of the volume housebuilders and their customers.

## Perspectives on the speculative residential product

### The views of the different stakeholders

Criticism of the standard product of the housebuilding industry has been both wide-ranging and vehement. The Council for the Protection of Rural England (CPRE) have been perhaps most consistent and outspoken in their criticism of what they see as 'dreary suburbia', their President decrying the 'tragedy that the housebuilding boom during the 1980s saw almost universally low design standards' (Dimbleby, 1995). A recent CPRE publication describing the state of English housing development suggested that: 'in place of distinctiveness we have ubiquity – row upon row of near-identical brick-built family units, screened with larch-lap fencing and ranked behind concrete kerbs in an avenue of lights. It is the victory of uniformity over distinctiveness; the victory of suburbia over all', testimony – it says – to the corporate identities of the housebuilding companies and to the unimaginative, standardised road layouts of the highways engineers (CPRE, 1995, pp. 3–4 and 9).

Criticism of the housebuilders' product has not been restricted to the amenity groups, however, as even development-led organisations such as English Partnerships have bemoaned the 'could be anywhere' visually monotonous designs of much new housing. In their view, the blame is shared by planning authorities for not correcting the perception that 'standard' solutions are more likely to gain planning permission without delay (English Partnerships, 1998, Sec. 6).[1]

In 1995, in an about-turn in policy since the HBF-led agenda of the 1980s, the then Secretary of State also came out strongly against the homogenisation of the 'executive cul-de-sac; the zoning madness, and the creeping standardisation' of housing; declaring it 'an insult to our sense of place to offer precisely the same house in Warrington as in Wallingford, Wadebridge or Wolverhampton'. Instead, he argued the case for (although never delivered) a twin-track approach to residential development, encompassing 'both the need for more housing and the need for higher quality and better design' (Gummer, 1995, pp. 4–5).

It seems that the majority of the public also lament the lack of quality in housing design; in so doing, dismissing the frequent charge against those campaigning for better housing design that such concerns are essentially elitist in nature. In one of the few publicly available opinion surveys on the products of the housebuilders more than 60% of the active house-buying market dismissed the design of new homes as unappealing, 70% found the idea of living in a new-build home undesirable and 90% wished that housebuilders would be more adventurous in their designs (Rogers, 1994). More recent work has in large part confirmed these findings (Popular Housing Forum, 1998).

---

[1] English Partnerships is the national urban regeneration agency for England.

### The rebuttal

Against the chorus of criticism of much new housing, housebuilders convincingly argue that they know the market and only build what the market wants, and that their houses would not sell if they were disliked by the public (Davison, 1989; Osborne, 1991; Bateman, 1995). Strongly confirming their view is the fact that for those choosing to move into a new-build speculative residential property, levels of owner satisfaction with their home are likely to be very high (90 per cent plus according to research carried out in the late 1990s – Forrest *et al.*, 1997, p. 33). The housebuilders further argue that real improvements in quality cost money, something for which purchasers are not willing to pay. The result is that in an environment of tight profit margins the extra money can only come from one place – the price paid for land – something which the current land market and planning system both militate against (Davison, 1991).

In-depth historical reviews of design control confirm that the key stakeholders in the residential development process often display such entrenched positions (Punter *et al.*, 1996). This is partly due to the fact that changes to residential environments affect a wide range of interests, including the public (whether they like it or not), and consequently have the potential to stir up considerable passion. Furthermore, the interests of, and powers wielded by, the different stakeholders in the process are rarely equal. For example, architects (where used) often have an interest in producing distinctive developments which stand out, housebuilders in producing developments with marketable appeal (Manley and Guise, 1995, p. 35), while planners and amenity groups are more concerned to ensure that development blends into its surroundings (Hall, 1990, p. 6). Third parties, such as local residents, will frequently favour the status quo, but are often the least equipped to object to development and run the unfair risk of being branded NIMBYs when they do. For them, design is the easiest target against which to vent their frustrations.

Recent research for the Royal Institution of Chartered Surveyors (RICS) has confirmed this state of affairs, establishing that the volume housebuilders pay great attention to the design of the individual dwelling at the expense of its setting and any urban design principles. The research argues that housebuilders have little incentive to take a long-term view as house-buyers are constrained by considerations of location and price much more than design. Consequently, they aim to achieve only 'appropriate quality' urban design (appropriate to market circumstances), rather than the 'sustainable quality' provided by a minority of more enlightened developers (Rowley, 1996, pp. 6–7).

With large proportions of the country's houses being built by very few firms – the 'volume housebuilders' – who in turn set the standards which other smaller developers follow (Madden, 1982, p. 26), it is likely that the standard products of the housebuilders will constitute many, if not the majority, of the projected homes in England, whether on greenfield or brownfield land. Where there is evidence that better design sells houses however, housebuilders have often been willing to adapt their standard designs. For example, they have often shown themselves only too ready to follow the dictates of design guides – where they exist – in part as a reaction to evidence that this type of intervention by authorities creates a product with enhanced sales values and achieves development at higher densities (Hall, 1990, p. 8). Such prescription has also potentially offered an increased certainty for housebuilders in their exercise of financial judgements on design.

The RICS research also confirmed the need for more certainty over planning authority expectations of design, highlighting a desire for less confrontational approaches to design and the need to reduce housebuilders' risk, so freeing more resources for better quality development. Interestingly, the developments which performed best in design quality terms as part of the RICS research were also those where local authority ambitions and action to secure quality development were most explicit (Rowley, 1996, pp. 8–9).

### Contradictory objectives

Problems more often than not persist and relate both to contradictory objectives among the major stakeholders in the process, and to the particular idiosyncrasies of the speculative housing market (see Fig. 4.1). Nevertheless, the range of stakeholders involved in delivering and consuming any new residential environment will often be more complex than might at first sight be apparent. Significantly, the design of the contemporary residential environment is largely shaped by the combined inputs of each, while the final output of this process is determined by the power relationships between, and influence of, the different stakeholders.

- *Housebuilders* are driven by the profit motive and by the requirements of their shareholders and funders. Their concern for design stretches only so far as their marketing strategies allow; or as far as better design either results in higher sales values for their products, or products which receive all the necessary approvals without delay (Booth, 1982, p. 21). For them, the product is the individual house, and only to a lesser extent the context it defines, while the simplest way to judge what will sell is to repeat what sold before (Davison, 1989, p. 38).
- *House buyers* are in turn concerned that their investment in a new house will be a good one, at least until it is time for them to sell (frequently not very long). Such decisions are driven by cost, value for money, the functionality of the house and its size; by its location,

*Fig. 4.1 Contradictory objectives (Suffolk Planning Officer's Group, 1993).*

and only after that by intrinsic design (RICS, 1996, pp. 33–4; Popular Housing Forum, 1998, pp. 27–31). Innovation in house design is rarely a desirable feature for the house buyer, in large part because resale is often foremost in the buyer's mind and universality helps to guarantee a ready market (Cowburn, 1967, p. 398).

- *Funders* are the 'unseen hand' in the process (Punter, 1990, p. 19). Funders of both the housebuilders and the house buyers care little about the product, except that in the case of the former, it offers a good return on their investment over the short term – at little risk – and in the case of the latter, that over the medium term (usually up to 25 years – the length of a standard mortgage) the property will hold its value and adequately secure the loan in the case of default. Traditional construction is often a prerequisite.

- *Planning authorities* (planners and councillors) are concerned for the wider public (and political) interest, including protection of the environment, but are also under pressure from both housebuilders and central government to find and release enough land for housing as smoothly and efficiently as possible. Design is a concern, but one which can be swept aside for bureaucratic convenience and in the pursuit of other planning demands such as economic development, or the sometimes over-simplistic achievement (and preservation) of basic residential 'amenity' – light, space, privacy, etc. (POS *et al.*, 1998, pp. 10–11). Nevertheless, design is clearly on the planning agenda, as is the need to reduce any financial exposure to the public sector by ensuring the delivery of necessary infrastructure through planning gain.

- *Highways authorities* are primarily concerned with the functional operation of the roads and footpaths that they will be required to adopt; in particular, that they function safely and efficiently (maximising vehicle flow) and that they will not represent a greater financial liability on the authority than is strictly necessary (Adam, 1997). Through their Section 38 (of the Highways Act) powers to adopt roads, highways authority requirements carry considerable weight for developers anxious to avoid the financial penalties associated with non-adoption. Often the quickest and easiest way to achieve this is to follow any published standards to the letter, making this aspect of design a mathematical rather than a creative process. The highways authorities are the first of a series of public agencies whose primary concern is limited to a single issue and for whom intrinsic environmental quality is only of marginal importance.

- *Fire and emergency services* are concerned that new developments are designed to be accessible quickly and without hindrance as a means to guarantee (as far as possible) public and personal safety. For these services, direct and ready access to individual dwellings and efficient movement through an estate constitute their only concern.

- *Crime Prevention Officers* value the better design of housing areas because of the contribution a well designed physical environment can make to social well being and therefore to levels of crime. Most police forces subscribe to the view that levels of crime can be directly influenced by the design of the physical environment, largely by reducing the circumstances for opportunistic crime to occur, and by ensuring public and private space is clearly distinguished and overlooked (SERSCPOC, n.d.). In pursuing these ends, the argument has often been dogmatic and proposed solutions not always clearly grounded in empirical research (Steventon, 1996; Fairs, 1998).

- *Building controllers* have a significant impact on the design of the individual home and on the relationship of buildings to each other with regard to fire prevention. Therefore in policing the national building regulations, particularly those for energy efficiency, fire spread and disabled access, the building controller has an indirect impact on aesthetics, choice of materials, accessibility and layout. Like the crime prevention, fire and highways officers, this control is largely based on standard rules and is often inflexible in its implementation.

- *Established residential communities and amenity groups* will generally favour no development, but, if development is to be allowed, will favour development that respects the existing environment and which impacts as little as possible on the surroundings (for established residents, usually traditional, unconnected and owner occupied). Amenity groups (residents and conservation) will also favour the status quo, but when faced locally with the stark realities of housing demand will (like the established residents) have little direct power to influence design outcomes (CPRE, 1995).
- *Design professionals* (particularly architects) continue to deplore the state of British speculative housing design and particularly the fake mimicry of historic vernacular styles. However, because of their own enthusiasm in the recent past to force 'utopian' design agendas on residential development, they have been – in part – instrumental in ensuring their own exclusion from the mainstream residential market. Today, the industrialisation of the housing market (Bazlinton and Bartlett, 1997) and the continued dominance of standard house types and layout formulae effectively perpetuate designer (architect) exclusion from most of the speculative residential market (Black, 1997, p. 81).
- *The landowners* have most to gain and therefore also most to lose from the market provision of residential development (HBF and RIBA, 1990, p. 28). To them, maximum profit necessitates minimum interference (including in design) by the statutory authorities, particularly where each requirement laid down in advance by the planning system potentially cuts into the vastly increased value secured on the sale of their land. For landowners, profits of up to 10,000 per cent on the allocation of agricultural land to residential use have not been unusual (Adam, 1997).
- *Central government*, finally, like local government, will need to balance the conflicting objectives, to ensure the successful operation of the market that provides the housing the nation needs, while at the same time limiting environmental damage and opposition at the local level to new residential development. In achieving these latter objectives, the value of good design has been recognised for a while as a significant boon (DoE, 1992b, para. 4). But in achieving the former, the free market in speculative housing development received a free rein throughout the 1980s and 1990s, with attendant environmental damage and established community alienation the inevitable result.

### The product 1999/2000 – an example in Thamesmead

As the design of the speculative residential house and its environs has adapted and changed during the course of the twentieth century (see Fig. 1.2), and as different public sector attempts to influence its quality have come and gone, the positions of the various stakeholders have remained relatively consistent. Despite the high levels of satisfaction recorded by many of the actual purchasers of new build homes, at the end of the century the critiques of such homes also remain fairly consistent, and regularly include:

- *context*: a failure to respect or respond to urban and landscape context;
- *sense of place*: a failure to define adequately an identifiable sense of place;
- *community*: a failure through design to encourage a sense of community;
- *urban space*: a failure to create coherent urban spaces and visually interesting layouts;
- *legibility*: a failure to create legible environments;
- *connectivity*: a failure to create connected, permeable environments;
- *movement*: a failure to consider the pedestrian experience;
- *car dominance*: a failure to integrate successfully the needs of the car;
- *security*: a failure to create secure environments;

- *innovation*: a failure to deliver architectural quality or innovation;
- *flexibility*: a failure to create flexible, adaptable houses and environments;
- *choice*: a failure to offer real variety and choice;
- *landscape*: a failure to consider landscape (hard and soft) and to integrate open space;
- *sustainability*: a failure to respond to the sustainable agenda;
- *mixing uses*: a failure to move beyond the strict zoning philosophy.

With 170,000 volume built houses produced each year, such perceptions inevitably represent generalisations. Nevertheless, the widely held nature of all such perceptions (including among many of the practitioners involved in the research reported here – see pp. 262–9 – and among potential home buyers – see pp. 117–23), helps to give such perceptions a basis in fact. An example encompassing the work of six national housebuilders helps to demonstrate how and why such perceptions persist.

Thamesmead in South East London was masterplanned in the 1960s as a new residential district for 60,000 persons inside the ring of London's green belt. Initially planned at 35 per cent private to 65 per cent public sector housing, throughout the late 1960s and early 1970s, development of a series of undistinguished concrete low rise and deck access developments marked the emergence of this new community. By the 1990s, the original masterplan in many of its essentials had been abandoned, the projected population had been reduced to nearer 50,000 (with accompanying falls in density), the public sector promoter (the GLC) had given way to a community-led non-profit distributing company – Thamesmead Town Limited – and the proportion of private to public sector housing neared 50/50 (Wigfall, 1997).

Although the long-term vision of Thamesmead as a balanced community with an integrated built and natural environment still persists, since the discredited public sector interventions in the 1960s and 70s, development of the town has been characterised by a paucity of design guidance at either the local or strategic scales or by any real concern for design quality. In the late 1990s the design of residential development in Thamesmead was guided by four documents.

The first two – and also the most significant – were the Unitary Development Plans (UDPs) of Greenwich and Bexley (Thamesmead being bisected by the Borough Boundary). The Greenwich UDP, with a chapter specifically on Thamesmead was the most sophisticated – if still basic – with an updated masterplan for the town including basic guidelines on the allocation of uses within the town's different sub-areas. This was supplemented by density standards and 'motherhood'[2] type policies on housing standards in the 'Housing' chapter of the plan and by a basic range of policies on aesthetics, townscape and landscape, views, and safety and security in the 'Design and Conservation' chapter (London Borough of Greenwich, 1994). Bexley's UDP contained little more than 'motherhood' aspirations on context and crime in the 'Environment' chapter of the plan, more specific, yet unsophisticated policies on layout, landscape, architectural design, and infrastructure in the housing chapter, and a range of functional standards in the 'Design and Development Control Guidelines' section of the plan (London Borough of Bexley, 1996). Supplementing these documents were the non-statutory 'Thamesmead Residential Development Guidelines' (London Borough of Greenwich, 1989) for the Greenwich sector of the development, offering a range of standards on layout, highways design, infrastructure, density, landscape and space between dwellings, and the 1996 'Greenwich Waterfront Strategy' (London Borough of Greenwich, 1995), offering little more than generalised urban design aspirations for the area, of little obvious value.

---

[2] Motherhood forms of expression offer little more than 'the most general of objectives, i.e. "there shall be a high standard of design" with no elaboration or explanation of how this might be achieved or assessed' (Punter and Carmona, 1997a, p. 101).

In sum, throughout much of the 1990s the public authorities responsible for the long-term realisation of Thamesmead were guided by a disjointed, partial and unsophisticated policy-base, that left them largely abstaining from any serious attempt to influence residential design for the better, and, at best, negotiating on an application-by-application basis. Nevertheless, in national terms, Thamesmead offered certain advantages to delivering better quality residential design, including:

- a high quality physical context derived from its position on the river Thames and well developed green network;
- an acceptance that higher density development might be appropriate, especially in Thames-side locations (some argue that higher density solutions lead to more imaginative design solutions – Gupta, 1989);
- a greater acceptance by housebuilders that non-standard solutions are necessary in the South East (Biddulph, 1996, p. 161);
- ownership of the land by the community through Thamesmead Town Limited (public ownership or partnership will often lead to more considered design solutions – Black, 1997);[3]
- major infrastructure already in place to support new development;
- that, by 1999, Thamesmead also sat at the heart of London's major regeneration opportunity – the Thames Gateway – whilst in Thamesmead itself a buoyant – if still cheap by London standards – private market existed.

In 1999 five developments marked the major outputs of the private sector in Thamesmead. 620 new homes in the 'Thamesview' development by Wilcon Homes (the UK's 7th largest housebuilder);[4] 379 homes in the 'Quayside Point' development by Wimpey Homes (UK no. 4); and 1,500 homes in the 'Gallions Reach' development by Barratt Homes (UK no. 1), Beazer Homes (UK no. 2), Persimmon Homes (UK no. 3) and Fairclough Homes (UK no. 19). Barratt were also responsible for developments at Watersmeet Place and Hawksmore Place, the former of 168 homes and the latter of 24 (a late addition to a much larger development). The different outputs provide interesting examples of the speculative housing product, not only because they offer examples of the volume housebuilders building on reclaimed brownfield land (reclaimed from the former military uses that dominated the area), but also because of the contrasting approach taken in Gallions Reach to the other developments.

None of the smaller developments at Thamesview in the Borough of Bexley and Quayside Point, Watersmeet Place and Hawksmore Place all in the Borough of Greenwich, benefited from any form of development or design brief. Each therefore represents examples of their respective housebuilder's standard product, built to higher (London) density standards (up to 250 HRH[5]) and guided only by the respective authority's highways and planning standards (see Figs 4.2 and 4.3). Unsurprisingly, therefore, they reflect many of the frequent critiques of residential design (see pp. 89–90). Thus the developments:

- integrate poorly with their surroundings – most are inward looking and turn their backs on the major feeder roads;
- are exclusively mono-use;

---

[3] Unpublished work by the Urban Design Alliance (UDAL) in 1998 aiming to identify examples of where urban design had contributed to the delivery of successful regeneration through housing also revealed that public sector ownership of the land offered one of the key levers to delivering better quality design.
[4] Housebuilder rankings from Birkbeck (1999).
[5] HRH (habitable rooms per hectare).

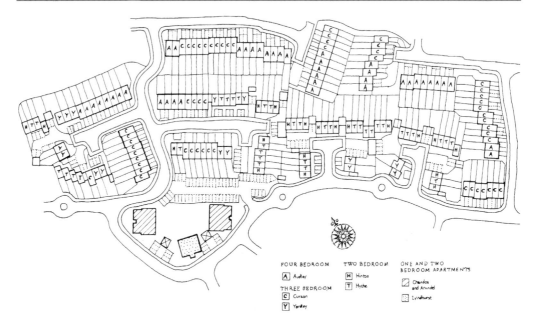

*Fig. 4.2  Speculative residential development at Thamesmead 1999 – typical layout.*

*Fig. 4.3  Speculative residential development at Thamesmead 1999 – realisation.*

- add up to little more than the sum of their parts, with individual houses failing to create coherent, positive streets and spaces;
- are dominated by the needs of the car, by roads and private parking;
- are also dominated by hard surfaces, with little space for private or public planting.

Gallions Reach, on the other hand, was promoted from its inception by Thamesmead Town Limited as an integrated planned whole, subject to its own masterplan drawn up by consultants PRP Architects and envisaging a permeable, perimeter block street pattern,

## Evaluation: the speculative product

Although it encompasses the work of five national housebuilders and two local authorities, Thamesmead is just one example, in one place, with its own unique context and political environment and represents neither the best, nor the worst of contemporary speculative housing development. Nevertheless, careful analysis of 52 schemes from a single volume housebuilder active throughout England supports the findings (Biddulph, 1996). In that analysis, the housebuilder purported to value the benefits of good design, going so far as to produce their own in-house design guide to improve practice across their 16 UK subsidiaries. Analysis revealed, however, that despite these efforts, only 40 per cent of the design principles promoted through the guide, were actually achieved. Among other factors, this failure was put down to the varying attitudes of the company subsidiaries to the guidance and to their varying ability and concern for design, as well as to local variations in the land and housing market which influenced the financial feasibility and demand for better design. The work graphically confirmed the widespread consistency of the outcomes so obvious in Thamesmead – in this case despite the housebuilder's own awareness that significant design improvements could be made – and the tremendous variation in practice locally, even in individual housebuilding companies.

The review of attitudes to, and the realities of, the speculative product has revealed:

- that widespread cross-interest group dissatisfaction continues to exist over the design quality of private sector residential development;
- that housebuilders convincingly argue that they know the market and deliver what the market wants;
- new build owner occupiers confirm this view recording high levels of satisfaction with their homes;
- evidence that design guides, where used, have improved the quality of housing and that housebuilders can be persuaded of their value;
- that a diversity of stakeholders are involved in the delivery and shaping of contemporary residential environments; stakeholders whose objections are often limited and frequently contradictory;
- that critiques of speculative residential environments remain fairly consistent and wide ranging across urban design, landscape, architectural and sustainable concerns;
- that left to their own devices, the volume builders will deliver the minimum standard of development acceptable to the market;
- that local authority attempts to improve the situation, if poorly conceived, can be as much part of the problem as part of the solution; and
- that guidance needs to combine a two-dimensional vision with a coherent view of realisation in the third dimension.

## The speculative residential process – housebuilders and buyers

### *Housebuilding and planning processes*

Although the influence of the RIBA has been significant throughout the evolution of design control, it was the influence of the development industry and especially the housebuilders (represented by the HBF) which most influenced the change in government thinking in the

1980s towards a more relaxed system of design control. This process fitted neatly into the free market philosophy of successive Conservative governments in the 1980s, and, as titles of white papers on planning in the period show, also fitted into the notion that planning control represented little more than an economic 'burden' on development (House of Commons, 1985a). For their part, housebuilders have consistently shared many of the same concerns as architects regarding design control, in particular, that control stifles design freedom, causes delays (DoE and HRF, 1976, pp. 49–53) and interferes with the proper operation of a free market (see Chapter 3). The animosities are well summed up by a statement from the Chief Planner of Bryant Homes:

> Some Planning Authorities appear to see the developer as some form of evil entity, dressed in a grey suit. He is to be tied down, everything he wants to do must be shackled and, at all costs, he must be prevented from utilising his expertise on what development would be best for a site (Bateman, 1995, p. 26).

In a study commissioned by the HBF specifically to address the issue of planning delay, delay was perceived by housebuilders to be the most severe constraint to production, exceeding market demand and land price (Roger Tym and Partners, 1989, pp. 63–4). The research ranked the causes of such delay as:

1. Density/design negotiations
2. Local authority staffing (numbers and calibre of staff)
3. Legal agreements
4. Planning committees (over-turning officers' recommendations)
5. The appeals process (where initial reasons for refusal were not confined to planning matters)
6. Statutory consultees.

Planning officers interviewed as part of the research agreed that negotiations over design standards were the most common cause of delay, although in their view after staff shortages (Roger Tym and Partners, 1989, p. 63). Interestingly, the housebuilders themselves conceded that the eight-week period for determining most planning applications was for the most part too short, and that fuller site appraisals would solve some of the problems along with greater use of pre-application negotiations on design.

Delays caused by the planning system represent a cyclical grievance of the housebuilding industry, and in 1996 the HBF's National Planning Officer went so far as to blame delays in planning permission for slowing down a recovery in the housing market – 'The DoE has no effective sanction against planning authorities breaking the eight-week rule on applications' (David Coates in Anon., 1996c). With the emergence of the plan-led system in the 1990s such criticisms from housebuilders extended beyond the development control process to the time taken in plan making, in so doing emphasising the complexities and inter-linked nature of the development and planning processes (see Fig. 4.6). In a plan-led context, it is at the plan making stage – when the land is first allocated – that much of the risk and potential gain for the developer (and landowner) lies in bringing land forward for development. At that stage delays can be measured in years rather than weeks or months (Bateman, 1995, p. 27).

Housebuilders maintain that despite its tendency to cause delays, design is an important concern for them also, but that a concern for better design should be driven by market demand for better living environments, rather than by planners who they observe for the most part as not being educated in design. Indeed, it is the market demand that some housebuilders argue has resulted in the 1990s in 'current and proposed schemes . . . [which]

DEVELOPMENT PROCESS                                    PLANNING PROCESS

```
┌─────────────────────────────┐          ┌──────────────────────────────────────┐
│ DEVELOPMENT PROSPECTS        │          │ FORWARD PLANNING                     │
│   Demand (demography,        │- - - - - │  ┌────────────────────────────────┐  │
│   economy, etc.)             │          │  │ Regional Guidance    (DOE)     │  │
│   Opportunities              │- - - - - │  │ Structure Plans     (County)   │  │
├─────────────────────────────┤          │  └────────────────────────────────┘  │
│ SITE IDENTIFICATION          │          │     Infrastructure planning          │
│   Developers/agents search   │ - - - ► Lobbying - - - ─┤ Local Plans  (District)│  │
│   Developer-landowner negot  │          │  └────────────────────────────────┘  │
│   Purchase of options        │          └──────────────────────────────────────┘
└─────────────────────────────┘

┌─────────────────────────────┐          ┌──────────────────────────────────────┐
│ DEVELOPMENT PROPOSAL         │          │ DEVELOPMENT CONTROL                  │
│   Assess feasibility      ───┼──► Outline application ──    (District)          │
├─────────────────────────────┤                     Outline consent (refusal)    │
│   Purchase site          ◄── │
│ DETAILED SCHEME           ───┼──► Negotiate planning agreements ◄──
│   Site surveys               │        & infrastructure
│   Design                     │
│   Financial appraisal     ───┼──► Detailed application
│                              │              Detailed consent (refusal)         │
│                    (Appeal) ◄─┤─ ─ ─ ─  (APPEALS PROCEDURE)                     │
├─────────────────────────────┤          │ Inquiry & report (Inspector)         │
│ IMPLEMENTATION               │          │ Decision (DOE)                       │
│   Legal agreements           │          └──────────────────────────────────────┘
│   Tenders                    │          ┌──────────────────────────────────────┐
│   Clear site                 │          │ BUILDING CONTROL                     │
│   Construction            ◄──│              Inspect/certify                     │
│   Marketing    - - - - - ─► Hand over social housing  - - - - - - - - - - - - ►│
│   Sales                      │              & community facilities             │
└─────────────────────────────┘
```

*Fig. 4.6  Model of development and the planning process (Bramley et al., 1995).*

are far superior to those proposed previously' (Bateman, 1995, p. 28). For Bryant Homes, for example, it is suggested that this concern reveals itself in more energy efficient buildings (driven by more demanding Building Regulations), by a landscape-led approach to masterplanning and by the design of attractive individual homes. The firm argues that:

> design should be left in the hands of the developers, with the help of constructive comments from the Local Authority. Developers spend significant amounts of money to design attractive buildings. ... Yet there are still a minority of planners who, on a straightforward site, consider that they 'are not appropriate' for absolutely no good planning reason, except that they dislike them or would 'like something different – but I couldn't tell you what' (Bateman, 1995, p. 28).

The freedom sought by the housebuilders and the indirect conservatism of their outputs is a long established feature of the speculative market, dating well before the twentieth century (Booth, 1982, p. 21). This conservatism, some argue, has only been bucked when the planning process through the production of design guides has forced improvement to the standard product, developments that have in turn released improved market potential (Hamilton, 1976).

Nevertheless, for housebuilders, design and profit are frequently seen as two quite separate areas of concern. Davison (1987a, p. 64), for example, has argued that generally 'The designer is thought to contribute to profitability only by achieving slight increases in density or by dressing up standard house types in a new fashion to boost sales'. He suggests,

'The industry still believes that good design costs money . . . [and that] the design impact, therefore is to reduce overall profit margin'.

To some, the planning strait-jacket enforced by central government since the evolution of comprehensive planning has effectively undermined meaningful efforts to intervene in and improve housing estate design. For them, the housebuilding sector is also different from most other sectors of the development industry, being characterised by (Black, 1997, p. 81):

- a build and walk away 'trading' ethos – closely linked to the rise in home ownership;
- commitment to a manufacturing, rather than a design process – geared to the production of large numbers of units on a production line principle;
- minimal design input or respect for local consultation or environment (social and physical).

Thus, unlike major town centre development – where partnerships between the public and private sectors are common and can result in a greater emphasis on design (see Fig. 4.7) – in major housing developments a more adversarial approach is more often the norm (see Fig. 4.8). The result is that local authorities are seen as just another regulatory and largely negative feed into the process, rather than as positive, contributing, partners.

In a system where more and more of the public realm is being handed over to the housebuilders to produce – roads, open spaces, schools, facilities and services, play areas, landscape, etc., and increasingly a social housing requirement – with only conditions to planning permissions and planning gain agreements to ensure its reluctant delivery, some commentators have argued that it is perhaps unsurprising that the results are so often widely perceived as unsatisfactory (Gardner, 1998, p. 2). Developers themselves have resisted this increasing tendency to 'piggyback' the delivery of social and public responsibilities on the backs of private residential development, the 'obligatory . . . basket of goodies' as one housebuilder referred to it, undermining, as they see it, their ability to deliver their core product (Bateman, 1995, p. 27).

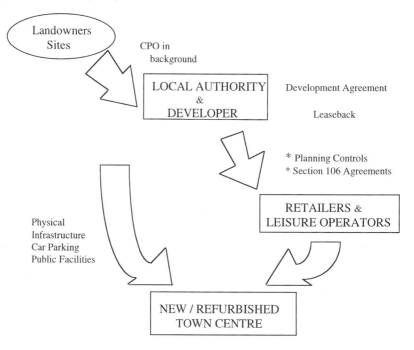

*Fig. 4.7 Traditional town centre development process (Black, 1997).*

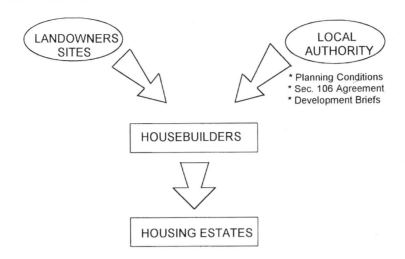

Fig. 4.8 *Traditional housing development process (for major sites) (Black, 1997).*

For the housebuilders, the arguments are clear and often put (HBF, 1996):

- given the choice, people want to live in peaceful and safe living environments with access to towns and cities but also to the countryside;
- the need is primarily for family homes of a traditional type with gardens, built to low densities and not crammed onto urban sites;
- that although urban housing will provide for some of the solutions to current housing demands, greenfield development on the edges of towns and cities should also make a major contribution.

Such housing they still view as their core product.

### The housebuilding sector

Because of the capital-intensive nature of the industry, to be among the top fifty a house-builder will typically need to be a public limited company. Most investors in that company will be institutional with a statutory responsibility to their own investors and a loyalty to the company only as strong as its performance. For understandable reasons, therefore, concern for design quality features poorly in most managers' priorities and financial performance and stock market profile much more highly (Davison, 1987a, pp. 65–7) – 'We are, after all in the business of making money, not houses' commented one national housebuilder (in Leopold and Bishop, 1983, p. 123).

Criticism from the housebuilders has understandably been consistently persuasive on successive governments, when, for example, the private housebuilding sector in 1993 (a depressed year) was worth £6.6 billion (28% of the entire construction industry). In that year the industry produced some 175,000 new homes (170,000 in 1998 – Birkbeck, 1999), of which 140,000 were for the private sector (81 per cent of dwelling completions in the 1990s, rising from just 55 per cent in 1980 – Hooper and Nicol, 1999, p. 793). Hence the stakes are huge, and the influence of the housebuilders on government is significant.

This situation is compounded by the fact that of the 20,000 builders registered with the National House Building Council (NHBC) in 1998, only ten were responsible for over 35 per cent of the combined UK output – 40 housebuilders for 60 per cent (Birkbeck, 1999) – and thus wield great influence and largely set the design standards of the sector (Madden, 1982). The situation contrasts with that in the 1950s when 90 per cent of private house building was built by local builders; builders with local connections, using local labour and capital and depending on local knowledge and reputation. By the 1970s most private housing was being built by firms that operated on a regional or national scale, and 'it was possible to buy a Wimpey House in every English county' (Couch, 1986, p. 1). Today, local housebuilders account for just 25 per cent of housing output and self-builders for about seven per cent.

As a result, Hall has argued that 'as far as design is concerned, the developer is rarely in a free market position, more often one of monopoly', and that 'In such circumstances the temptation is to maximise profit by reducing the quality of the product' (Hall, 1990, pp. 7–8). This is because the average homebuyer in search of a new property is not usually in a position to commission one from an architect, and therefore must accept whatever the builders provide (CPRE, 1995, p. 3). This view was confirmed in a deliberately provocative feature in the RIBA Journal which argued that traditionally the housing industry has been very good at producing market research which 'justifies the design status quo and minutely examines add-ons – white goods and frilly bits – that people will pay for', but is not so good at producing more generic research on what consumers want, rather than what they will accept. It is suggested that this has much to do with the fact that in the UK some 90,000 dwellings a year are taken out of circulation via demolition, so to at least maintain the existing levels of housing stock the market has a guaranteed underwritten potential of 90,000 units (over half of the total number of units built) of which – it is argued – in market terms it matters little what they look like, how they perform, and whether the public like them or not (Rogers, 1994, p. 10).

Although there may be some truth in this rather pessimistic assessment of the house-building market, it is also true that competition between the housebuilders has consistently remained strong, as expressed by the £9 million spent by the industry on advertising each year. Product innovation, however, has tended to come from the small (often local) housebuilders in their attempts to tap into niche markets (Rogers, 1994, p. 10) away from the volume housebuilders in what Welsh (1994, p. 5) has described as the 'stick 'em up, flog 'em, then bank 'em' mass produced sector.

For the housebuilder, the market is often clearly delineated and the industry has on many occasions been accused of concentrating on particular parts of the market to the exclusion of others. For example, most housebuilders have tended to concentrate on the lower end of the market and on starter homes to the exclusion of the upper end. Indeed, research undertaken in the late 1980s found that as house buyers moved up the housing ladder the aspiration was increasingly for an older house and decreasingly for a new home (Bishop and Davison, 1989).

The subtleties of the housing market contribute to distinguish housebuilding as a specialised sector of the construction industry significantly different from other sectors, with its own trends, requirements and development cycles (Black, 1997, pp. 81–2). Thus, although the construction aspect of what the housebuilders do is important, it is only one part of the whole. Their major objective is to 'find land and on it to create market value' (Madden, 1982), a process in many respects more akin to a marketing business than a building business. Therefore in the 1980s and early 1990s many of the companies with wide-ranging, unrelated activities that had also maintained a housebuilding division began to sell out to more specialised companies. Some of these specialist housebuilders were subsequently able to record substantial growth either by further specialising within the housebuilding market (e.g. McCarthy and Stone – in 1999 the UK's 24th largest housebuilder – grew by specialising in housing for the elderly), or by steadily acquiring other housebuilders (e.g. Beazer Homes – by 1999 the UK's second largest housebuilder) (Davison, 1987a, pp. 63–4).

By the late 1990s this pattern of specialisation and consolidation was continuing, but with two further patterns emerging (Birkbeck, 1999, p. 20). First the purchase of small 'boutique' operations by some of the major housebuilders (e.g. the purchase of the up-market Charles Church Homes by Beazer). These major quoted firms see a future as a string of individually focused and partially autonomous businesses, such as the Berkeley Group with its namesake Berkeley Homes alongside St George, Crosby Homes, and Beaufort Homes – links about which their buying public have little notion. Other housebuilders going down the same route have deliberately started up such individually focused subsidiaries from scratch (i.e. Harwood Homes set up by the Redrow Group).

The second and diametrically opposed pattern is the swallowing up of firms and their infusion into the corporate identity of the parent company. For these companies – such as Westbury – the belief is in the brand value of the national company. Therefore the assimilation of companies including Clarke Homes in 1996 or Maunders in 1998 continues until the original brand disappears without trace. Housebuilders like Westbury increasingly liken their activities to retailing with a concern to build 'critical mass' and build and retain 'market share', thus achieving economies of scale and allowing more business through the same fixed cost. Such groups are buying others to improve their presence in markets in which they are thinnest and to achieve a better strategic fit in all regions. Speaking after the acquisition of Maunders, the chief executive of Westbury argued that 'Like retailers, we're consolidating – and if you think back 10 years, nobody then imagined there'd be just four or five major chains today. There will be significantly fewer players in this industry in just a few years' (Martin Donohue in Birkbeck, 1999). Research has indicated that the processes of concentration observed since the 1970s are continuing at an ever accelerating pace (Nicol and Hooper, 1999).

The trend towards increasing concentration within the industry and arguably therefore to homogenisation can be partly laid at the door of the planning system. This is because the larger companies have been the major beneficiaries of restrictions caused by the planning system, because when land is scarce and land allocations and permissions are time-consuming and resource-intensive to secure, the companies with the greatest financial resources and technical skills have consistently been able to acquire the best sites (Baron, 1983, p. 19). The need for the public sector to lever any necessary infrastructure costs out of new development also favours increasing concentration, as planning authorities deliberately make larger land allocations to ensure delivery (Adam, 1997). Furthermore, the larger firms have been much more able to raise the vast sums of capital necessary to expand and build more homes either through retained earnings, rights issues or extra borrowings. Finally, the increased sophistication of the housebuilding industry favours the large builders, particularly the requirement for more sophisticated marketing techniques and a much wider range of in-house skills to ensure that large developments can be started and sold at acceptable rates. Significantly, however, the advantages of the volume builders begin to reduce as sites decrease in size, and as site on-costs[6] begin to increase as a proportion of the final sales value. This makes small housebuilders more competitive on small sites (Baron, 1983, p. 20) and offers one reason why the volume builders have been so hostile to the switch away from large greenfield developments.

---

[6] The fixed on-site costs that all sites carry regardless of size, i.e. the setting up costs and the running costs of a foreman, site huts, compound, small plant, rates and usually one or more labourers. These costs vary little with volume.

### Projecting a market image

Clearly, housebuilding is an industry, but an industry dealing with one of the biggest and most emotive decisions many people will ever have to make – choosing, buying and establishing their home – a decision torn by sometimes conflicting priorities to secure value for money as well as to satisfy a whole series of very personal perceptions and individual selection criteria. For these reasons the housebuilders are somewhat schizophrenic in their character. On the one hand they operate as multi-million-pound companies[7] in a cut-throat industry aiming to return significant profits to their investors. On the other hand, they attempt to present a friendly, locally responsive and concerned face to their customers in a sector where more conventional selling techniques are not always appropriate (research has indicated particular resistance to 'hard selling' and 'mass selling' techniques in the housebuilding market – Bishop and Davison, 1989, p. 41).

A review of web-sites from across the range of national housebuilders (see Table 4.2), for example, reveals the housebuilders give a very different message to their customers than to the corporate world and investors (often with separate web sites for these different purposes). So, in their 'public' sites, instead of stressing 'corporate' and 'national' they stress 'individual' and 'local', instead of stressing 'product' and 'profit' they stress 'home' and 'value', and instead of stressing 'market share' and 'turnover' they stress 'reliability', 'experience' and 'reputation'.

The need to build a public persona is obvious in the home page extracts. Also clear is a conscious attempt to respond to both the most frequent critiques of the new build market and to the common negative perceptions of potential new house buyers themselves (see pp. 117–23). Wimpey, for example, deal with one common perception head on, stating the obvious that 'Nobody wants to feel they are living in a row of boxes', and therefore intentionally attempt to lay to rest any perception that their products take such forms. In this regard most of the common themes stressed in the home pages directly concern perceived shortcomings of new houses, not least the need to respond to context and to deliver high quality design. They included:

- responsiveness to site and locality and careful choice of location (each mentioned by almost every housebuilder);
- development based on local knowledge;
- individuality of product;
- variety and choice;
- high quality design (quality landscaping, attractive and stylish buildings);
- high quality construction;
- the perception of 'home';
- creativity and innovation; and
- the spaciousness of internal layouts.

The web pages often stressed the size and pedigree of the individual companies and any awards they had won, the quality of their service and the value for money their product represented, including the internal features and white goods supplied with the house. The low maintenance character of new houses was also commonly stressed – a positive perception shared by most new house buyers (see p. 121).

---

[7] The sector records annual turnovers of up to £1 billion (plus) in the case of the combined companies owned by George Wimpey, or £800 million in the case of Barratts (Birkbeck, 1999, p. 21).

- fear of change (in the context of past innovation experiences) and the fact that traditional competitive strategies have largely served the industry well;
- low customer awareness about the potential of the product they are purchasing and low expectations about the benefits new housing can bring, thus failing to drive the change seen in other construction sectors.

To this list might be added the lack of real international competition in the market which has forced change in so many other industries (Raymond Young in Bazlinton and Bartlett, 1997, pp. 21–3). Nevertheless, although design innovation has been slow in the housebuilding industry, towards the end of the twentieth century significant pressures have been emerging which may yet force innovation. These include:

- the significant rise in output required if current housing projections are to be met;
- the changing demographic structure of the population with a rise in single person households as a result of an ageing and fragmenting population;
- increasing emphasis in government policy on re-using brownfield land, building at higher densities, and on promoting a much heralded – if still to emerge – urban renaissance;
- increasingly strict control over environmental standards which may require a movement away from traditional construction methods;
- increasing use of the planning process to deliver social and environmental objectives through planning gain;
- rising construction costs which are hitting housebuilder profit margins because of the shortage of labour with craft skills (Barlow, 1999, p. 27).

Responses mooted to address these pressures – if not yet widely adopted – include factory production, leaner production methodologies and mass customisation. Factory production has been attempted in the recent past, particularly in the public sector, with often disastrous results. Nevertheless, such processes are used extensively overseas, notably in Japan (David Gann in Bazlinton and Bartlett, 1997), and small-scale experiments in the UK continue to play a role. In one of the latest, the company concerned – Britspace Modular Building Systems – claims to offer 20 per cent savings on conventional housing costs with a production line aiming to turn out four new homes a day. No doubt responding to negative associations concerning modern technology in housing associated with the mistakes of the recent past, the prototypes hide their production line pedigree and instead feature panelled walls faced with 12 mm brick slips in a traditional style (Fairs, 1999).

Increasingly, some of the largest housebuilders in the business are also accepting the inevitability of the new prefabrication and modularisation technologies. Thus Wimpey Homes are hoping to reduce on-site construction time from 13 to four weeks per unit, through homes constructed of four to five factory-built modules for assembly on site. Wesbury Homes are investing in a factory with a projected capacity of 5,000 homes a year, based on prefabricated wall panels and floor cassettes, to form a structural envelope in two days when fitted together and roofed on site. In both cases the homes still exhibit traditional brick exteriors (Fairs, 2000a; 2000b).

Conversely, 'lean production' techniques seek to combine the advantages of craft work with those of mass production, by reducing assembly time and building according to customer demand, while at the same time avoiding the rigidities of factory systems and the high costs of craft work. The concept involves minimising stocks and ensuring continuous improvement in construction techniques, but requires a highly standardised range of products. 'Agile production' techniques are a variation on the theme, but adapt the concepts to a more tailor-made set of products. Agile techniques therefore offer the potential for 'mass customisation' – the production of highly customised products – at costs comparable with mass production by emphasising the need for continuous improvement of construction techniques and processes.

Research (Barlow, 1999) has revealed that these techniques are still in their infancy in the UK housebuilding sector and customisation, for example, is widely resisted as reducing the economic benefits of standardisation (Hooper and Nicol, 1999, p. 799). Nevertheless, some housebuilders have at least begun to introduce organisational changes 'seeking to erode functional barriers between design, production and marketing . . . as a way of improving information management and promoting internal discussion' about their product and its delivery (Barlow, 1999, p. 35).

Westbury, Wimpey and Bovis Homes, for example, were all identified by the Construction Task Force (led by Sir John Egan – DETR, 1998c), for their attempts to combine more responsive customisation strategies with standardisation. For the Construction Task Force, however, innovation was still more likely to come in the 1990s from the social housing sector – both in quality and construction – because most social housing is commissioned by a few major clients, who are more able to contemplate innovation than the myriad of individual private house buyers.

The reality of course is that there is very little wrong with standardisation per se, which in varying forms has been used as the primary construction method for housing in the UK since the (today) highly desirable Georgian and Victorian examples were constructed across the country. 'The problem with the pattern book is therefore not so much the principle but with the tired, limited range of designs so many pattern books contain', and particularly with the way they are related one to another and to the site on which they sit. Again, urban design would seem to be the key issue, while 'If it is treated as a positive tool standard house types could have an important role to play in reducing costs and allowing the dissemination of good practice without the need to constantly reinvent the wheel' (Rudlin and Falk, 1999, p. 119).

### The question of land

The powers of planning authorities derive directly from one source, control of the valuable commodity – land. In the UK, this control has had several consequences:

- it entrusts considerable powers to the hands of the planning authorities through their ability to give or deny planning permission – not least to influence design quality;
- it ensures these powers remain blunt instruments because they largely rely on private development coming forward, without which they have little significance;
- it restricts the availability of land for development and therefore – as a scarce resource – raises the value of land and consequently housing (Monk, 1991a);
- it ensures that as land is allocated for development its value increases dramatically; and
- it too often leads to the perception that once allocated for housing, blanket approval is given for any residential development proposed.

Two opposing views characterise these powers. First, that the planning system improves pure market outcomes because it can generate beneficial externalities that in turn generate higher land prices associated with the higher development values and lower risks through the process of plan making. Second, that the planning system acts as a constraint on the market, producing higher land costs without commensurate benefits, and notably with a less responsive land supply and increased time lags before development.

Undoubtedly the reality reflects something of both views and, as research has shown, the best outcomes might be ensured by a balance between certainty brought about by an effective planning process and avoidance of undue constraint brought about by an adequate supply of land. Without these characteristics, respectively, oversupply or over-development can result. As presently operated, however, the housing which is produced is frequently 'neither that which planners aim to produce nor that which a free market would prefer'. Thus policy can too easily impose a set of increased costs which result in higher land and house prices and a different (less desirable) built product in terms of quantity, quality and mix than is desired (Monk and Whitehead, 1999, p. 420).

Because of the scarcity of land for residential development, owners of housing land expect (and in the case of many public bodies are obliged by law) to secure the best return for their asset. The result is often the suppression of aspects of quality that reduce the land value. Therefore, because bad design can increase land values – over-development with uniform house types on minimum plots that ignores site characteristics and local identity – this is often the form proposals take. Such proposals come either from landowners themselves eager to secure outline permission before sale, or from housebuilders, forced by the market cost of the land to maximise their return and so make development viable (POS *et al.*, 1998, p. 12).

Landowners' expectations of value are understandably based on recent market activity and on development patterns that maximise return. Therefore expectations are conceived in a design vacuum, with – usually – no consideration given to the costs of delivering higher quality development. Aggravating such expectations are the processes of selling land, where land is sold to the highest bidder based on its residual value.[8] Therefore the landowner achieves the highest value for the land, while the housebuilder has often had strategically to ignore local authority design aspirations to make the bid (POS *et al.*, 1998, p. 14).

The result is developers on low profit margins, who risk their investors going elsewhere for a better return on their capital investment (20 per cent is required but rarely achieved), and who are vulnerable to delay and fluctuation in market value. Effectively they are left to pursue any means available to reduce delay and maximise the value of the land purchased (land which typically absorbs 40–50 per cent of their capital investments in order to maintain a two- to three-year land bank – Baron, 1983, p. 20). Consequently, many housebuilders will go to considerable lengths to persuade authorities that high land values do not permit higher quality design solutions, and that instead higher densities with larger units and smaller gardens are required to make development pay (Adam, 1997). Others will reduce the size of their land bank (particularly as land as a proportion of total house cost has dramatically increased – commonly up to 50 per cent in the South East), a risky strategy and one which leads to further land price inflation and reduces time for design in an effort to maintain outputs (Davison, 1987a, p. 66).

A categorisation of housebuilders based on their approaches to the planning process has been suggested (Short *et al.*, 1986, p. 111). Firms can be classified as:

- *cautious* – restricting their interest to safe sites with existing planning permissions;
- *naive* – often submitting unacceptable planning applications which are refused;
- *negotiators* – with a high success rate based on a willingness to engage with the planning process and test its limits;
- *aggressors* – with a tendency to go to appeal instead of negotiating, but also testing the limits of the planning system.

---

[8]  Residual value is calculated by estimating the number of units to be built on the land in question, the building costs per unit and hence for the site, infrastructure costs, and allowance for contingencies. The sum of these costs is then deducted from the total estimated selling price of the houses, and the residual is the land value, assuming a constant profit margin.

Like most private industries, speculative housebuilding depends for its survival on maintaining cash flow in the short run and profitability in the long run. In practice this means tightly controlling investment in land, and once on site, building as many houses as a volatile market can take as quickly as possible (Leopold and Bishop, 1983, p. 122). The natural tendency has therefore been for most housebuilders to act as 'aggressors', to take the planning system head on and to recourse to the appeals system to settle the inevitable disputes. It also means the very careful selection of sites with considerations of marketing, the chances of obtaining planning permission, the social context and the availability of servicing all weighing heavily on housebuilders' decisions (see Table 4.3).

In such a context, housebuilders are consistently critical of any regulatory attempts to alter their standard house types. Thus, housebuilders have been supportive of the increasing use of 'type approval' schemes by building control departments, where all houses of a standard type are approved en masse. However, they are equally dismissive of design guides, which, although they rarely impact on the all-important standard footprint of house types, frequently impose additional constraints on elevational design and layout. The variability of planning authority approaches in this regard continues to be the greatest bug bear (Hooper and Nicol, 1999, p. 802).

However purchased, the buying, holding and bringing forward of land for development represents one of the biggest risks for most housebuilders. The extent and nature of this risk depends on the nature of the housebuilder, and particularly on the extent to which they in turn rely on land price inflation for their profitability. For companies that maintain the minimum land bank of two to three years the major source of profit is derived from the construction and sale of houses, and crudely therefore, profit levels will relate directly to turnover. For others, such as Wimpey Homes whose long-term strategy has been to build up a considerable land bank – including non-designated agricultural land – profit is greatly enhanced by increases in land value (Bramley *et al.*, 1995, p. 93).

Research has indicated that only a fairly small proportion of land is purchased without planning permission, although because it is substantially cheaper the purchase of 'white land' has the potential to increase profits. Generally, however, only larger developers are able to take such risks, and when they do, are able to use substantial resources to get the land

Table 4.3  *Perceived importance of site selection criteria by housebuilders (Pacione, 1989)*

| Criteria in site selection | Ranking of importance |
|---|---|
| Market factors | 1 |
| Planning permission (availability or ease to get) | 2 |
| Basic services (existing and ease to supply) | 3 |
| Social class of neighbourhood | 4 |
| Condition of sub-soil | 5 |
| Access to schools | 5 |
| Site availability | 5 |
| Topographic conditions | 8 |
| The asking price of land | 8 |
| Size of site | 10 |
| Access to city centre | 10 |
| Proximity to local shops | 10 |
| Physical environmental quality | 13 |
| Access to employment | 14 |
| Availability of clearance grant | 15 |
| Existing ground cover | 16 |

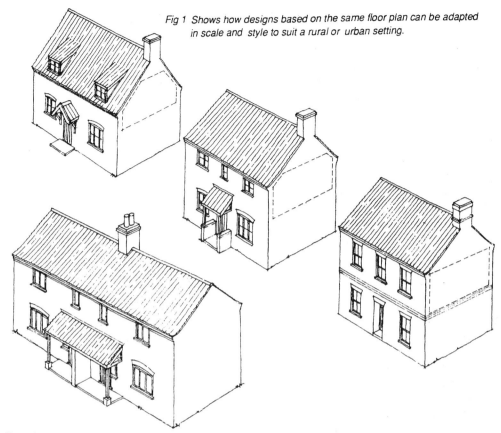

Fig 1 *Shows how designs based on the same floor plan can be adapted in scale and style to suit a rural or urban setting.*

Fig 2 *A simple vernacular style that can be used for detached, semi-detached or terraced properties.*

*Fig. D.2 Adaptability of the North Norfolk vernacular style (North Norfolk District Council, 1993).*

vernacular. In this context, basic examples are given of the use and adaptability of the local vernacular in the production of contemporary dwellings (see Fig. D.2). The guide is also used in conjunction with very occasional development briefs prepared for significant sites in the district, and with the Norfolk County Residential Design Guide which is complementary and focuses on layout concerns (Norfolk County Council, 1998) – although criticised by the district for the over-emphasis on cul-de-sac solutions.

The design guide has always been viewed as an essential means to objectively measure quality and get policy implemented. Since 1974, the guide has gradually developed drawing from three sources. First, refinements to the guide itself in the light of developing design experience and practice. Second, from the experience gained through development control practice; including the incorporation of justifications and robust expression. Third, and most importantly, from the inclusion of the guide as part of the North Norfolk Local Plan adding the weight inferred by Section 54A to the guidance. In this position the full guide made it through the public local inquiry into the adopted version of the plan in 1998 (a contrast to the Cotswold experience – see Inset C).

A Conservation and Design Manager has responsibility throughout the district for the conservation of historic buildings and areas and for the appropriate design of all new buildings. Thus, unlike most planning authorities where design negotiation is dominated by development control staff with little design training and with occasional and cursory reference to a (usually) lone designer for advice, in North Norfolk all proposals are submitted to a team of design professionals for consideration. Applications are viewed upon receipt and those failing to come up to the standard set by the guide are marked for later action. The design team is subsequently consulted on the applications identified using the same administrative process as that for other consultees. The development control team negotiate simple changes, with more complex negotiations handled direct by the design team. The design team is then involved at every stage of the development control process.

Wherever possible, prior informal discussions will also have taken place before an application is made. The intention is to provide a cost effective means to avoid protracted negotiation from entrenched positions once the eight-week clock is ticking (see p. 193). In all this, the relationship between the design and development control officer is a crucial one, with care taken to ensure that quality in the built environment remains a key objective shared by all. The role of the guide as an educative tool has proved significant in meeting this objective.

Statistical analysis of the rates of processing planning applications in the district has indicated that the design negotiations procedure does not prolong the process of the application overall (the authority maintains a respectable position in the eight week planning applications turnaround league table). This, it is thought, stems from the local understanding of agents and architects that informal consultations before registration of an application can speed its approval.

The authority clearly believes that the approach taken works because character has been preserved and local style continues to evolve (see Fig. D.3). The design guide's function is seen, at least in part, as a means to interpret this story for the lay person, developer or professional who may not have the time or knowledge to discover the local tradition for themselves. The guide is seen to be central to the success of the approach, offering a shared basis for deciding standards, with influence extending beyond the officers and elected members to the general public and their agents. Perhaps the most decisive test of the guide's success, however, is its association in the minds of local developers and the public with

*Fig. D.3  Housing at Sharrington, North Norfolk.*

quality, while the demand for houses which follow the guide is greater than for those which do not, offering higher resale values as well. Development control is now seen in the district as a value-adding activity (Anon.,1994b).

The system of control now harnessed in North Norfolk benefits from twenty-five years of experience and resources, with the controllers themselves admitting that progress has been slow – if constant – and that they have been less successful in influencing the quality of larger residential schemes. Nevertheless, developers on the whole have not been unwelcoming of the guide, although one major housebuilder did pull back from intended expansion in the area. Smaller housebuilders, in particular, have tended to see the advantages of building houses which fit the context and are more popular with their customers (CPRE,1995, p. 14).

Experience has shown that a system based on negotiation for achieving design quality takes time and trust to establish and requires commitment and support from elected members (both in resources and in backing officer decisions). Its survival has depended on a good track record in winning appeals; something in which the 'material status' of the guide plays a significant part (as the team refer to it – 'a guide with clout' – Brackenbury,1994, p. 72). Finally, and crucially, it has depended on no significantly greater costs to either authority or developers for the system than that associated with other systems which fail to add the same value.

# Chapter 5

# The fundamentals of controlling design

Discussion of the development of residential design control and government guidance in Chapters 2 and 3, revealed an agenda that shifts and evolves as political philosophy changes with successive governments (even with successive Secretaries of State), and as the resulting pressures on government from the different stakeholders in the process become more or less influential. Based on a review of the literature and an examination of practice in Glasgow, it has been argued elsewhere (Carmona M., in Greed and Roberts, 1998, Ch. 3) that a number of features distinguish the most sophisticated approaches to controlling design. Chapter 5 re-presents and develops the key findings of that work as a means to further inform the empirical research in Part II of the book. The thrust of the argument revealed that changes in government advice and the priority given to design by authorities becomes apparent in four main ways:

1. through the changing design criteria thought appropriate for control – the conceptualisation of design;
2. through the changing response to context, particularly the value placed on appraisal as the determining factor in that response;
3. through the value placed on the different mechanisms used to control design – the hierarchy of design guidance;
4. through the resources authorities are prepared to devote to design and to the process of securing better design.

When taken together, these four factors largely define an authority's approach to design control. Drawing from the literature they are presented as a four-part theoretical framework for controlling design.

**Theory, appraisal, hierarchy and resources**

*The need for a theoretical conceptualisation of design*

The absence of any clear definition of design in government guidance has been one of the key problems faced by planning authorities. Consequently, policies and guidance frequently fail to cover key areas, contain an inadequate range of considerations to ensure appropriate design control, and display a continuing bias towards architectural or external appearance issues at the expense of broader urban design concerns (Punter and Carmona, 1997a). To avoid this, it has been suggested in Chapter 3 that control practice as well as the debate about what constitutes well designed housing might beneficially focus on the urban design and landscape of residential areas before their architectural design is considered. The Chief Executive of the HBF, for example, has argued that the debate about good design has to start by looking at design 'in the widest possible sense ... It is not just about external design but about the impact of the mass of housing coming together on a site ... Perfectly nice standard portfolio house designs can look absolutely ghastly in the wrong place' (Roger Humber in Roskrow, 1997, p. 30). Research undertaken jointly for the HBF and RIBA (1990, pp. 10–12) confirmed this view, suggesting:

> There is a hierarchy of design importance, three key factors which, when combined create good design:
>
> - First, comes the shape of the development and the spaces within it, the scheme as it is seen in the landscape. ...
> - Second, comes the choice of materials and details that shape our response to the character and quality of the local built environment. ...
> - The last factor is the house itself. Planners, architects and developers spend too much time and thought on this, at the expense of the first two priorities. There is no point in having a beautifully designed house which uses the wrong materials and is laid out in an inappropriate form. A poorly designed house may become acceptable if it is built in the right materials and carefully sited.

Any new residential design guidance from government – like new local authority policies – might also logically reflect such a hierarchy – urban design, landscape design, architectural design – with careful thought given to the qualities sought at each level. Such thought will in turn beneficially reflect the full range of design concerns established in urban design theory.

Interestingly, and for the first time, central government attempted to define urban design as part of its 'Urban Design Campaign', in so doing effectively accepting that quality design consists of more than just buildings and that it is the underlying pattern of buildings, rather than the buildings themselves, that stand the test of time. Urban design was taken to mean:

> ... the relationship between different buildings; the relationship between buildings and the streets, squares, parks and other open spaces which make up the public domain; the relationship of one part of a village, town or city with other parts; and the interplay between our evolving environment of buildings and the values, expectations and resources of people: in short the complex inter-relationships between all the various elements of built and unbuilt space, and those responsible for them (DoE, 1995a, p. 2).

The definition was somewhat curious because it largely failed to move beyond the physical and perceptual aspects of urban design, although it did explicitly recognise the multi-layered nature of the discipline, its time dimension, and its spatial, morphological and contextual dimensions. Nevertheless, it provided a starting point for the more comprehensive government guidance on design to come in PPG1 (1997) (including a revised definition – see pp. 71–2).

The reviews of the development of residential design control and government guidance in Chapter 2 revealed that planning practice – until recently – has been dominated by the visual and contextual conceptualisations of the 'townscape' and conservation movements (external appearance, street scene, building height, views, etc.) and by the standards-based functional issues derived from a concern for residential amenity (privacy, sunlight, road layout, parking, etc.). Research has revealed, however, that local plans – and therefore presumably also planning practice – are slowly beginning to reflect social and sustainable issues as well, particularly a concern for accessibility and security, for the quality of public space, and for energy efficiency and ecological preservation (Punter *et al.*, 1996, paras. 6.2.1–6.7.4).

According to a number of theorists this shifting agenda is long overdue. Jarvis, for example, has long argued for the drawing of the artistic (visual) and social usage traditions '... into a closer and more positive relationship' (Jarvis, 1980, pp. 50–1). More recently, Rowley has identified urban design as a complex phenomenon which defies simple definition or explanation, but which encompasses '... the design, creation, and management of "good" urban spaces and places' as both an approach and a response to the processes of urban change and development. In other words, an ongoing evolutionary process of change, concerned with satisfying social and emotional needs as well as with the more prosaic requirements of a convenient, safe, healthy and efficient public realm (Rowley, 1994, p. 195).

Other theorists and organisations have been able to define similarly broad based definitions of urban design. Such definitions are, however, many and various; perhaps reflecting the essentially misleading nature of the term, in that those practising urban design frequently practise outside of urban locations and because design in this context is as much about technical problem solving and appropriate process as it is about any aesthetic or artistic interpretation (Gleave, 1990, p. 64). The Urban Design Group, for example, have defined an agenda for urban design that stresses the social and functional roles of urban design, as well as the process of urban procurement. Their agenda recognises the relationship between physical form and function, stewardship of resources, the process of space management and creation, the social role of public realm, equity concerns and the time dimension of urban design (Urban Design Group, 1994, p. 34).

Perhaps the best known of the recent theoretical frameworks for urban design – that from the 'Responsive Environments' team – also stresses a more social perception of design. This is encompassed in the four key principles of permeability, variety, legibility and robustness; while visual appropriateness, richness and personalisation encompass the more visual aspects of urban form – seen in the framework as relating primarily to the architectural, rather than the urban context (Bentley *et al.*, 1985, pp. 10–11). More recently, this framework has been supplemented with a range of sustainable concerns, which Bentley has termed 'Ecological Urban Design', thereby addressing one of the recognised omissions of the earlier work (Bentley, 1990). Tibbalds drew heavily on this work when devising his influential commandments for urban design in which he prioritised urban design over architecture. Alongside the key 'responsive' criteria, Tibbalds stressed the overriding value of context, the importance of mixing uses, designing to a human scale and incrementally, and the value of consultation (Tibbalds, 1988b).

Writing in the American context, but drawing from a wide range of theoretical contributions, Lang (1994) redefines the modernist functionalist agenda to encompass postmodern sociogenic and biogenic needs. He relates urban sociogenic design criteria to the basic human needs identified by Abraham Maslow – physiological, safety and security, affiliation, esteem and self-actualisation needs – and to the meeting of cognitive and aesthetic needs. The biogenic environment is related to the developing sustainable agenda.

Other contributors have produced a range of useful conceptualisations of urban design theory, mostly from an historical perspective, including Jarvis, 1980; Gosling and Maitland, 1984; Broadbent, 1990; Lloyd-Jones in Greed and Roberts, 1998; Madanipour, 1996, although perhaps the most systematic organisation of the literature into a coherent structure is the

'Epistemological Map for Urban Design' from Vernez Moudon (1992). In the map almost 200 separate texts are classified in a nine-part structure encompassing urban history studies, picturesque studies, image studies, environment-behaviour studies, place studies, material culture studies, typology-morphology studies, space-morphology studies and nature-ecology studies.

Taken together, and in the knowledge of the writings of many of the constituent theorists and practitioners used to generate the various definitions, principles and classifications (discussed in more detail in Punter and Carmona, 1996a, ch. 4), a simple framework can be derived within which the various conceptualisations of urban design can be accommodated. This encompasses an eight-part structure as represented in Fig. 5.1.

The intention is not to redefine urban design (too many definitions already exist), or to again systematically classify the major contributors to urban design theory, but merely to identify a working framework within which most theoretical contributions can fit and which can be simply and easily related to the design policy and control context. Using such a framework (or indeed any of the frameworks discussed above, or suggested elsewhere in design theory), authorities might structure the many design concepts currently found in government guidance (see Tables 2.2, 2.3, 3.2 and 10.1) and in use in local plans and supplementary guidance (see p. 213–21) – into a logical and usable form (see Table 5.1). Any such framework will need to be underpinned and informed by the local political, economic and environmental context but can clearly spell out the criteria against which development will be reviewed.

The failure of authorities to adopt any clear theoretical philosophy to underpin their design requirements has been a key finding of research directed towards the production of more equitable residential design guidance for the Borough of Kingswood. The researchers confirmed that the lack of theoretical underpinning in design guidance has frequently left authorities attempting to control the minutiae of design (particularly aesthetic considerations) at the expense of broader urban design concerns such as sustainability and equitability (Donovan and Larkham, 1996, p. 312). The result has been a continued marginalisation of the importance of design as its *raison d'être* was perceived to fall outside the core planning concern for environmental welfare.

The need for authorities to develop a theoretical framework to their design policies was also a key finding of the 'Design Policies in Local Plans' research (see Fig. 2.7 – Punter and Carmona, 1996b, p. 203). As regards residential design, where the conceptualisation of appropriate design considerations has been at its most impoverished, this recommendation would seem particularly relevant. In Chapter 7, the eight-part framework (identified above), is supplemented by design and planning process concerns – from the review of government guidance and the literature (see Table 2.4) – to provide a means to review critically the design advice contained in local authority guidance on residential design.

The framework is used in this book as a means to ensure that the evaluation of design principles remains consistent and comprehensive and relates back to a broader theoretical conceptualisation. For authorities, however, such a framework may be simplified by identifying for themselves the particular qualities they wish to secure in residential design, or problems they wish to avoid. In the case of the Borough of Kingswood, for example, the research offered – and prioritised – a list of design considerations as a means to establish more clearly the implications of development for the environmental welfare of its users: mobility and accessibility; personal security; pedestrian/vehicular bias; visual character; complement, copy or contrast?; and robustness. The resulting 'Design Guidance for Residential Development in Kingswood' (Kingswood Borough Council, 1996 – see Fig. 7.1) dealt with the considerations in some detail as a means to address the needs of future and present occupants in the Borough.

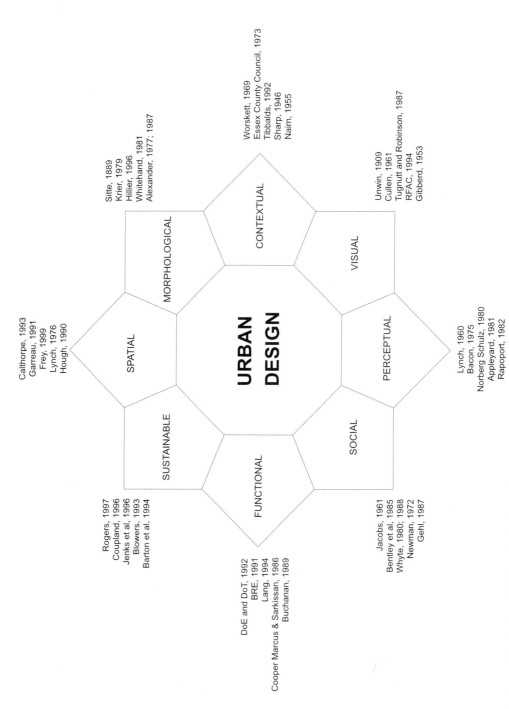

Calthorpe, 1993
Garreau, 1991
Frey, 1999
Lynch, 1976
Hough, 1990

Sitte, 1889
Krier, 1979
Hillier, 1996
Whitehand, 1981
Alexander, 1977; 1987

Worskett, 1969
Essex County Council, 1973
Tibbalds, 1992
Sharp, 1946
Nairn, 1955

Unwin, 1909
Cullen, 1961
Tugnutt and Robinson, 1987
RFAC, 1994
Gibberd, 1953

MORPHOLOGICAL

CONTEXTUAL

SPATIAL

VISUAL

**URBAN
DESIGN**

PERCEPTUAL

SUSTAINABLE

FUNCTIONAL

SOCIAL

Lynch, 1960
Bacon, 1975
Norberg Schulz, 1980
Appleyard, 1981
Rapoport, 1982

Rogers, 1997
Coupland, 1996
Jenks et al, 1996
Blowers, 1993
Barton et al, 1994

DoE and DoT, 1992
BRE, 1991
Lang, 1994
Cooper Marcus & Sarkissan, 1986
Buchanan, 1989

Jacobs, 1961
Bentley et al, 1985
Whyte, 1980; 1988
Newman, 1972
Gehl, 1987

*Fig. 5.1 Conceptualisation of urban design thought.*

- Public realm policies should embrace design-against-crime principles including considerations of defensible space, surveillance, visibility, lighting, and other security measures.
- Public realm policies should seek to promote walking and cycling as the most sustainable modes of transport, and enforce the quality of both through design controls and a network of enhancement schemes.
- Accessibility considerations will be important to the detailed design of public space and to ensuring that all groups can easily use public space.
- Local planning authorities can usefully adopt the 'per cent for art' scheme into policy in order to enhance the public realm, and link this with hard landscaping policies.

*Layout*
- Residential layouts should seek to maximise the level of local autonomy for local residents, structure development around energy efficient movement networks, and use landscape and open space to serve conservation, micro-climatic, and anti-pollution purposes.
- Road and parking layouts should prioritise safe, easy and direct pedestrian movement, and the creation of a network of attractive and legible public spaces, while being aware of the need for convenience for the private motorist.
- The provision of adequate and attractive private amenity space with a minimum of overlooking should be a key objective in all residential layouts.

*Policies for particular contexts, types and scales of development*
- Particular contexts within a borough/district may merit the development of specific policies and design strategies. These include countryside, urban fringe policies, town centres, residential areas, waterways and other areas with a strong identity. These will provide opportunities for tailoring landscape/townscape, urban form, and public realm policies to the nature of the locality.
- Policies for different scales of development provide a means of highlighting the different concerns of large, medium, and small scale developments and their relationship to site and surroundings.
- Policies for particular types of development offer a useful way of responding to recurrent design problems and expressing accumulated design experience.

Note: see Punter and Carmona (1997b) for further detailed recommendations on architecture, landscape and design process policies.

*Fig. 5.7 continued*

Comprehensive urban design policies therefore represent the keystone in the hierarchy, effectively implementing government guidance from above and forming a framework for the more detailed supplementary guidance below. These latter forms of guidance also have a potentially valuable role to play in policy elaboration and implementation by relating policies to neighbourhood strategies or to specific sites, and by calling attention to key problems associated with particular types of development. Such guidance potentially also provides an important source of advice to unskilled designers and should ensure a more efficient control process for all concerned (DoE, 1990, pp. 39–40). Furthermore, while central government is concerned to keep development plans thin and accessible to all (DoE, 1992d), other sources of advice on design issues seem inevitable, and indeed desirable, if authorities are to move design aspirations beyond the most basic urban design objectives. The full hierarchy of design guidance incorporates guidance from four distinct levels – national, strategic, district/city-wide and area/site-specific; and includes advice from central government, strategic and local authorities, and even from developers.

Various organising frameworks have been developed to classify design guidance. Chapman and Larkham (1992, pp. 33–5) have classified guidance in the form of a 'cascade', according to its level of operation (national to site-specific), its role in decision making – appraisal, encourage, guide, control – and its degree of prescription. Murray and Willie (1991, p. 22), on the other hand, have classified design guidance according to its relative scale of operation – district, neighbourhood, street, site, etc. Both frameworks represent

*Table 5.4  The hierarchy of urban design guidance*

| Guidance | Role and utility |
|---|---|
| *National guidance* | |
| 1. **Primary legislation (the planning acts)** | Provides the statutory basis for planning and conservation, and therefore also for development and design control. |
| 2. **Government guidance** PPGs NPPGs (in Scotland) | Sets out and elucidates government policy on planning matters, including design control and a new stress on urban design. Lays down the limits of design as a material consideration, thus limiting local choice. Such guidance is a paramount material consideration, but remains general and flexible in nature requiring interpretation in the light of local circumstances. |
| 3. **Government advice** Circulars PANs (in Scotland) Design Bulletins | Gives government advice on more detailed and technical design concerns such as crime or road layout. Criticism levelled over tendency to encourage copycat solutions, and lack of interpretation in the light of local circumstances, e.g. DB32. Can also be used successfully to illustrate good practice, e.g. PAN 44 (Scottish Office, 1994). |
| *Strategic guidance* | |
| 4. **Regional guidance (RPGs)** | Establishes broad regional emphasis on environment/design/ conservation in the light of competing claims on resources (economic, social, etc.). Tendency to ignore design as a detailed concern, and not a strategic issue, until recent guidance, e.g. RPG 3 (DoE, 1996g). |
| 5. **Structure plan/ UDP Part 1 policy** | Provides an important opportunity (usually missed) to set out a spatial design/environmental framework to guide local plan policies, and ensure consistent emphasis across districts. |
| 6. **Landscape character assessment** | Ensures emphasis is given to landscape concerns and helps ensure proper regard is had to natural design issues as well as to those concerning the built environment. Such appraisals are of maximum value if able to inform policy (prescriptive rather than descriptive). |
| 7. **County design guidance** | Influential over the years particularly for residential development, e.g. Essex, Cheshire, Kent, Sussex guides. Ensures a consistent approach to design across districts. Tend to focus on county matters such as road hierarchy and broad vernacular, but opportunity to establish broad urban design principles, e.g. Essex. General at best, and no substitute for district policy. |
| *District or City-wide Guidance* | |
| 8. **Local plan/ UDP Part 2 policy** | Provides the most potent tool in the planning authorities armoury, benefiting from the full force of section 54A. Should be used to lay down a contextually relevant framework for design control, prioritising urban design and landscape over architectural concerns. Closely scrutinised by central government to prevent over-prescription (see Punter *et al.*, 1996) |
| 9. **Development control guidelines** (in plan) | Used by authorities to place standards and guidance in the plan, i.e. the London Boroughs development standards appendices, but status unclear. Well suited to those key rules of thumb construed to be too detailed for policy, but which constitute an important basis for control, e.g. space around dwellings criteria. Tend to be quantitative rather than qualitative. |

10. **Design guides**
    (SDG)

A material consideration, which should relate clearly to plan policy and through which design advice can be elucidated and disseminated. Well suited to single design issues, or to different development types and contexts. Can encourage copycat solutions and suffer from a lack of weight. Nevertheless they possess great under-utilised potential to develop urban design policy.

11. **Design standards**

Largely relate to residential amenity considerations (health and safety concerns). Such quantitative measures rarely secure good design by themselves and need to be operated flexibly and with skill, alongside other urban form policy to avoid over-regimented solutions.

12. **Design strategies**
    (usually for established contexts)

Give spatial expression to urban design policy, and provide a mechanism through which detailed briefs and frameworks can be generated e.g. the Birmingham Urban Design Study (Tibbalds, Colbourne, Karski and Williams, 1990). A proactive form of guidance, best suited to expressing broad urban design issues. They represent a major resource investment in urban design and require an agreed vision of future form.

13. **Landscape strategies**

Focus on managing and enhancing, as well as protecting landscape (urban and rural). Such strategies help integrate natural and built environment concerns, ensuring a more sustainable approach to urban design concerns (e.g. Bath City Council, 1993). Require a great skills investment.

*Area or site-specific guidance*

14. **Area appraisal**
    Design Appraisal
    CA Assessments

Although resource intensive, such appraisal should form an essential part of the design policy writing process, ensuring that proper regard is given to the visual, social, functional and environmental context (e.g. Dacorum Borough Council, 1995b). It is vital to make appraisal prescriptive rather than descriptive, and to publish it alongside the plan as a material consideration.

15. **Design codes**
    (usually for new build)

Area related (but not site-specific) urban design codes or principles, usually used to structure areas of comprehensive development over long periods, but without two-dimensional masterplan. Can borrow cues from surrounding context or define anew, but no certainty over eventual form. Require long-term will to implement (e.g. Hulme Regeneration Ltd and Manchester City Council, 1994).

16. **Development frameworks**

A proactive approach to encouraging an appropriate two/three-dimensional form (capital web) on large, long-term sites. Offers maximum value if placed in the statutory plan and used to co-ordinate individual briefs. Allows flexibility for designers to design within a co-ordinated controlling framework.

17. **Design briefs**

Proactive, readily adaptable, resource efficient guidance well suited to defining the urban design, development and planning (not architectural) requirements of individual sites. Can be used to aid policy implementation, consultation, marketing and to lever planning gain. In practice often ignored and lacking design content, but nevertheless material considerations, capable of ensuring the best possible use of land and promoting design quality.

18. **Master plans**

Three-dimensional vision of future form (allowing some architectural freedom within limits of defined form). Maximise certainty, but minimise flexibility. Rarely used by local authorities as too resource intensive and considered too prescriptive.

useful synopses of the relationships between the different forms of design guidance in the hierarchy. Neither, however, include the full range of guidance currently in use, and therefore fail to illustrate the potential range of tools available to government and planning authorities in controlling design. In fact, an eighteen-level classification can be identified within the hierarchy, although it is likely that very few areas will be subject to more than eight of these (Table 5.4).

Below the level of district, scepticism over the true value of design guidance has been persistent in some quarters (Gummer, 1994, p. 15), particularly when considered alongside the resource implications involved in their preparation, implementation and review. Nevertheless, when interviewed, authorities have generally revealed a strong faith in the utility of supplementary design guidance, particularly when closely related to plan policy and made the subject of public consultation (Punter *et al.*, 1996). This faith is demonstrated by, first, the high priority given by many authorities to the preparation of such guidance as part of an ongoing programme – as and when time and resources permit – and, second, by the substantial body of supplementary guidance already in use by the majority of authorities (see pp. 225–7).

These perceptions have generally been confirmed by studies examining the utility of supplementary design guidance. The 'Time for Design' study, for example, revealed that 55 per cent of authorities believed supplementary guidance had a 'moderate' or 'considerable' effect in improving applications, 75 per cent thought such guidance had a 'significant' effect in improving the operation of development control and 54 per cent rated guidance as having a 'significant effect' when dealing with appeals. The general feeling appeared to be that guidance was most effective as a back-up to pre-application negotiations; for providing a consistent approach to design within planning departments; and as an educative tool leading to a gradual improvement in the public's perception of good design. The research concluded that the production of design guidance was the most successful type of initiative in achieving the aim of the study, the aim being to improve the quality of design (DoE, 1990, pp. 39–40 and p. 9).

A later study also concluded that the attitudes of local authority planning departments towards design guidance and its potential benefits are generally positive, although legislative advice and resource constraints seemed to be inhibiting factors. Other inhibiting factors revealed included that authorities frequently failed to make the relationship between plan policy and design guidance clear and that adopted design policies and published design guides represented only a small proportion of the total amount of design guidance available, much of which is still provided on an informal, advisory or ad hoc basis (Chapman and Larkham, 1992, p. 36). This practice flew in the face of advice given at the time in PPG 12 that the use of informal or 'bottom drawer' policies was '... unsatisfactory and incompatible with the requirements of ...' a plan-led system (DoE 1992c, para. 3.20). It also fails to gain advantage from the potential benefits of a fully integrated hierarchy of design guidance.

Good practice pointers on the preparation of supplementary design guidance in order to maximise its effectiveness can be drawn from the work. They include:

- the need to make the relationship between policy and guidance explicit;
- the need to publish all design guidance and any informal policies;
- the need to tie guidance preparation into a fully informed overview, or assessment, of priority rather than as knee-jerk reactions to topical issues;
- the need to target guidance to the perceived audience, be that applicants, the public or inspectors (in minority languages if necessary);
- the need to avoid unnecessary description and over-prescription;
- the need for appropriate methodologies to inform area appraisals and assessments;

- the encouragement of guidance to reflect wider urban design priorities and not always detailed design concerns;
- the need to make design briefs as attractive and easy to use as design guidance usually is; and
- the need to update or disregard the large quantity of obviously outdated guidance still in use (after Chapman and Larkham, 1992, pp. 23–5).

To these can be added a further suggestion made in this and in the earlier 'Time for Design' study:

- There is considerable scope for standardised guidance, particularly in non-contentious areas, to be formulated on a national or regional basis. Typical subjects might include crime prevention, mobility provision for people with disabilities, and so forth.

A further major study – 'Planning for Beauty' – carried out for the RFAC (1990), also backed the largely positive view of supplementary design guidance. Among other recommendations, it suggested that government should 'Encourage planning authorities to draw up local design guidelines . . . and then use them as a checklist, not a straitjacket', either supplementing or as part of the local plan itself. General headings, it argued, could include:

- *planning and context* – including, density, site coverage, bulk, height, street alignment, landscape, protection of views, climate including rights to sunlight and wind protection;
- *community impact* – including, mixed use, grain, public realm including types of space such as squares or alleys, the need for doors or entrances, fitness for purpose;
- *visual effect* – including, materials, colour, silhouette, scale, proportion, rhythm, ornament, works of art and fenestration.

Such a system of design guidelines is already used both in the US (e.g. Portland and San Francisco) and in Continental Europe (e.g. Paris, Siena and Bologna). These guidelines, the study argued, could potentially be developed in the UK as a method of reducing subjectivity and increasing contextual compatibility.

Although addressing the problem from a very different perspective, this approach has much in common with the 'design constraints' approach briefly advocated by the RIBA (1995 – see p. 74). Based on nationally defined standard guidelines, it was argued that compliance with such guidelines by applicants should lead to 'deemed planning permission'. The crucial and telling difference, however, is that such guidelines would be locally rather than nationally determined in the RFAC's proposals and consequently contextually based and demo- cratically derived.

The process of policy writing for development plans or design guides is part of the wider design process and is in itself a creative problem-solving process. Nevertheless most design policies are abstract in nature because they relate to future development proposals, which, at the time of writing, are invariably unknown. The design policies in British local plans, for example, are written to guide development over a projected ten-year period. Therefore, beyond broad spatial design strategies indicating how an authority's plan area will develop over the long term, the process of development plan writing is unlikely to indicate actual physical design solutions.

Nevertheless, to ensure that design principles are appropriately reflected at the site- specific level, many public authorities promote design solutions for particular sites through the use of design briefs, frameworks or codes. These types of guidance form the final stage in the hierarchy of design guidance and interpret the broad design policies to the level of the individual development. Consequently, such guidance is resource intensive to prepare, but also widely regarded as extremely effective in making public design aspirations explicit and therefore in securing better design (see p. 265).

In the UK, design briefs are the most common forms of site-specific design guidance. Depending on the local circumstances briefs may emphasise design concerns, broad planning issues, or development/management issues and so 'development briefs' are the more common generic term for design briefs, planning briefs and developer's briefs. Nevertheless, design briefs are potentially of value for a wide variety of reasons:

- to clarify policy higher up the hierarchy and thereby clearly establish the authority's design expectations;
- as a clearly positive approach to planning and design;
- to ensure that all important design issues are considered systematically;
- to offer a basis from which to promote sites and negotiate solutions;
- to encourage collaborative approaches to design;
- to ensure that the public interest is considered alongside private interests (particularly the levering of public amenities out of developments); and
- to offer a quick and easy means to provide more certainty and transparency in the design decision-making process.

In common with all design policy instruments, the more sophisticated briefs, frameworks and codes are promotional and comprehensive, providing a ready means of moving broad policy objectives closer to realisation. In this role they combine policy-based information, with indicative or actual design solutions for development. The skill for the urban designer would seem to be to write such documents in a form that prioritises the requirements of an authority over guidance – the latter to which the designer need only have regard – and combines firmness in the wording of the former with flexibility in the wording of the latter.

Significantly, however, recent good practice guidance sponsored by central government has revealed that design briefs, if poorly conceived, can too often have a negative rather than positive impact on design quality (DETR, 1998d, pp. 8–11). The guidance concluded that briefs have value in improving the efficiency of the planning and development process, and in improving the quality of development, but should not be used where:

- the development plan and any other supplementary guidance already provides an adequate basis for determining planning applications;
- the local authority has no firm requirements for a site;
- acceptable proposals are already being prepared;
- authorities do not possess the necessary skills base to encourage appropriate design solutions or to recognise the market limitations acting on a site.

In an unduly negative report, going somewhat against the grain of other government guidance at the time of its publication, the research warned that: 'The cost and time involved in preparing a planning brief should always be compared against the likely cost and time of securing acceptable development without it', and that, 'Site-specific design guidance should only be necessary where there are grounds for modifying general policies or standards, or where there are resources on or around the site which require specific attention or protection' (DETR, 1998d, pp. 8 and 18). The negative tone of the guidance in part reflected the generally poor quality of the briefs revealed by the research. It also down-played their potentially positive role if, and only if, their writing and implementation benefited from the resources utilised to prepare the best practice briefs identified by the work.

The issue of resources (or the lack of them) relates to the next key dimension discussed in this chapter and provides a salutary warning that any policy mechanism is unlikely to be effective unless backed by appropriately skilled and dedicated human resources throughout its production and during its implementation. Bringing the point home, with specific regard to residential design, the guidance found that 'despite the existence of design briefs, housing schemes were being developed to largely standardised layouts throughout England and Wales', and, in particular, that urban design and road layout requirements were poorly conceived. It suggested that 'Realistically achievable higher standards could have been set in planning briefs with the help of expert advice' (DETR, 1998d, p. 18), and without such advice briefs were best not produced at all.

### The need for resource efficient partnership approaches

The issue of resources dominates discussion of design control and is, for example, a recurring theme in this book. The greatest need, and the greatest drain on resources is inevitably the skilled manpower necessary to successfully operate any system for reviewing design; an investment which in turn unlocks the potential for design appraisal, for the preparation of appropriately sophisticated policy tools, and for the implementation of design objectives through negotiation based on those policies through the operation of development control.

In the previous section, the development of a policy base was identified as one type of end product of the process of planning for better design. However, the same design stages inherent in the production of policy also inform the delivery of the final end product, the realisation of actual development on the ground, appropriately informed by design policy and/or guidance. So, taking the notion of design process a stage further, there is also need for investment in the processes of development control as a means to deliver policy objectives, in other words, better design outcomes. These processes include formal procedures of application presentation and public consultation, but also (usually) informal procedures of site survey, consultation with specialists, and negotiation with applicants. Hence, for any application for new development, those charged with its administration would ideally:

- Before an application for planning permission is received:
  1. offer the means for potential developers to consult the authority about design proposals;
  2. if necessary, instigate design briefing procedures;
  3. if appropriate, instigate collaborative arrangements.

- After an application for planning permission is received:
  1. review the application to ensure design aspects have been clearly and appropriately presented (drawings including context, photomontage, models, design statements);
  2. instigate public consultation procedures;
  3. appraise the site and its surroundings to establish the design context;
  4. review established design policies for the site (existing sources of design policy and guidance – national/strategic/district-wide/site-specific);
  5. obtain skilled/specialist advice (i.e. design panel procedures, historic building specialist, landscape specialists, etc.);
  6. on the basis of information gathered/received negotiate design improvements;
  7. consider and negotiate implementation requirements (phasing, planning gain requirements, reserved matters, etc.);
  8. on the basis of information gathered/received make a reasoned recommendation or decision (grant permission, refuse permission, grant permission with conditions).

- After a negative decision has been made:
  1. where necessary use the information gathered/received to fight any appeal;
  2. use the appeal decision to monitor review procedures, but also, where necessary, to revise design policy and guidance.

- After a positive decision has been made (or an appeal successfully made):
  1. monitor carefully the implementation of all aspects of the design (and if necessary enforce decisions/conditions);
  2. evaluate the final design outcomes on the ground;
  3. use the information to monitor review procedures, but also, where necessary, to revise design policy and guidance.

Of course the role of local authorities in securing quality environments can, and should, represent much more than their role in controlling design. Indeed, authorities have the potential to influence urban quality through a much wider range of their statutory functions, for example, through: urban management and maintenance; town centre management; conservation work; land use allocation (zoning); urban regeneration; transport planning; local environmental action, e.g. Local Agenda 21; crime prevention and control; through education, culture, image building and promotion; and above all by being proactive about facilitating development and urban quality. For this reason, it is useful to touch briefly on a successful approach (already well covered in the literature) where a number of key elements have come together – alongside other proactive approaches and a political and professional will to create a better urban environment – to facilitate a dramatic transformation in the urban environment.

Although not primarily residential in nature, the example of Birmingham City Centre is included because of the comprehensive approach taken, and because of the stark contrast it offers against the standards-based control of design in the residential areas of many towns and cities (including in Birmingham – Birmingham City Council, n.d.). The example illustrates a framework that incorporates: an overriding concern for urban design over architecture; the use of urban design theory to underpin policy and guidance; recognition of the value and utility of thorough-going area appraisal; and based on the above, the adoption of a comprehensive hierarchy of design policies and guidance; all implemented through a resource efficient, partnership approach, to the control of design.

*Birmingham City Centre: An Example*
Influenced by best practice abroad – particularly in the US – and by a more enlightened environment for control at home, authorities such as Birmingham have concentrated their design efforts (and limited resources) in their central areas in an attempt to gain a momentum towards a wider urban quality. For many years Birmingham was associated with little more than its 'concrete collar' motorway ring road system, its impenetrable and forbidding system of underpasses and with a number of particularly insensitive 1960s and 1970s re-developments – including the notorious Bull Ring Shopping Centre. By the late 1980s, however, a concerted effort was put in place to break out of the city's self-imposed collar and give the streets back to the pedestrians (Birmingham City Council, 1993a). The aim was to end the association between Birmingham and poor design, and between Birmingham and (as the home of the British motor industry) a destructive love affair with the motor car. The approach adopted involved investment in a new design strategy for the city centre as part of the City's wider regeneration strategy (Sparks, 1997, p. 24).

The 1987 'City Centre Strategy' (Birmingham City Council, 1987) was the first tangible output from this new concern and aimed to encourage a new mix of activities and provide a

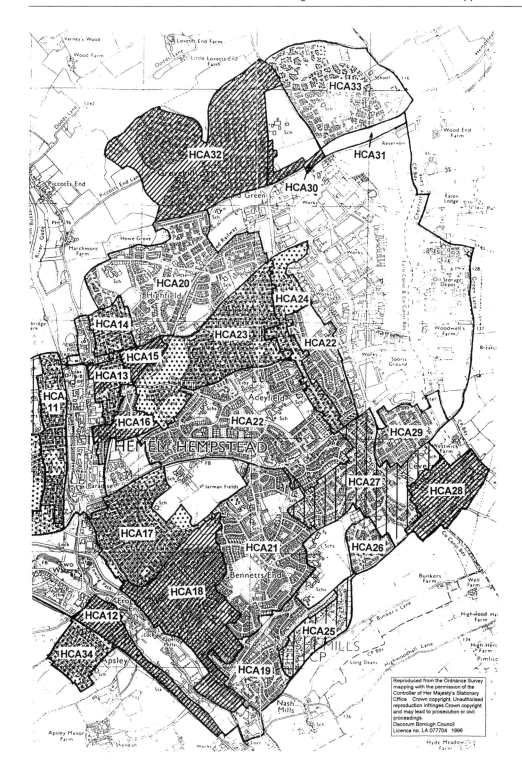

Reproduced from the Ordnance Survey mapping with the permission of the Controller of Her Majesty's Stationary Office  Crown copyright. Unauthorised reproduction infringes Crown copyright and may lead to prosecution or civil proceedings.
Dacorum Borough Council
Licence no. LA 077704  1996

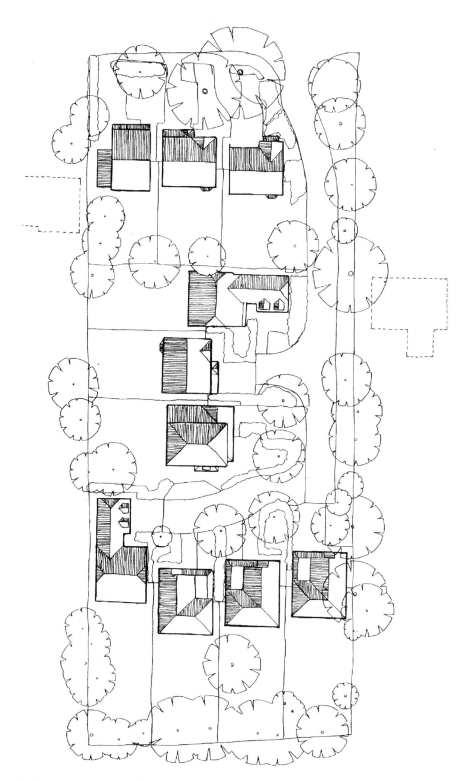

*Fig. E.2  Proposed housing at Covert Road, Berkhamsted – rejected scheme.*

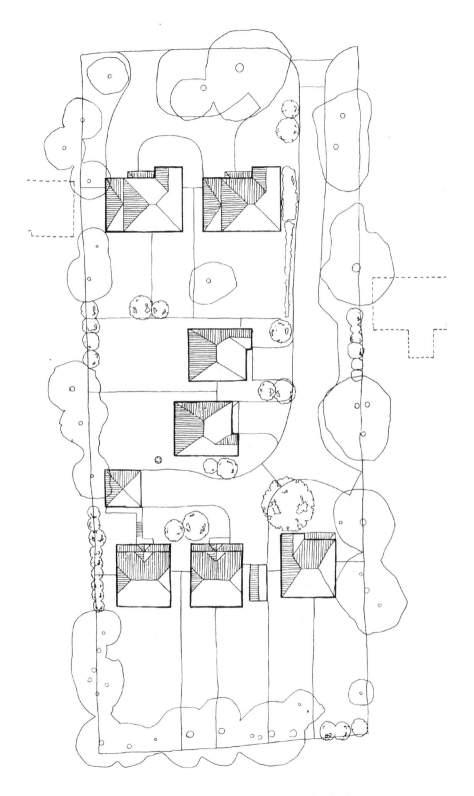

Fig. E.3  Proposed housing at Covert Road, Berkhamsted – revised scheme.

of plots; amalgamation of plots to create development sites; and straightforward infilling – and policy on development within the plot – extensions and so forth. The outcomes were considered during an extensive consultation exercise mounted on the RACS.

In 1996, the review of the Hertfordshire Structure Plan placed particular emphasis on the concept of (urban) planned regeneration to deliver the county housing targets. Dacorum viewed the RACs work as a means to address directly opportunities for new housing within the borough's urban areas. Therefore, during 1997, a further analysis was undertaken on the design areas (now relabelled 'character areas'), to look at the scope for delivering housing through infill. Some refinements were made and the areas were re-categorised as 'opportunity', 'limited opportunity', 'very limited opportunity' and 'minimal change' areas. Council approved the revised RACs in 1998 which was subsequently adopted as supplementary planning guidance (Dacorum Borough Council, 1998a).

The character areas and policies were also included in the first revision of the Dacorum Borough Local Plan (Dacorum Borough Council, 1998b) as a separately published but integral volume and underwent a further round of consultation with the rest of the plan. No objections were received from the government Regional Office or, surprisingly, from developers, although a number of residents objected because their areas had been designated 'areas of opportunity'.

Because of a lack of staff resources, RACS has been a long time in the making (five years to consultation stage), but is now in regular use in the development control process. It is accepted that as part of the process of officers reviewing applications, a site inspection and area assessment will still always be required. Nevertheless, having an agreed and published appraisal is intended to strengthen the judgement of officers. It also provides a ready source for other interested parties – principally housebuilders – who may not have the benefit of detailed local knowledge. Officers also argue that the degree to which the study has been useful to assist in the negotiation is significant, although difficult to measure.

Currently, no refusal of planning permission has yet been issued by the council that cites its policies as the primary reason, and it is too early to attribute clearly any appeal successes to the application of RACS. Nevertheless, the study has been cited by Planning Inspectors as a contributory factor in a number of appeal decisions. A key example concerns a proposed development in the Northchurch character area of Berkhamsted. There, in 1997, a small development of ten houses by volume housebuilder Crest Homes was refused planning permission on the grounds of density (see Fig. E.2). Quoting the RACS, the Inspector observed: 'The study indicated the character of Northchurch as being that of a residential area of medium-sized dwellings set in a mainly ordered, formal layout, with regular spaces and building lines with both suburban and semi-rural qualities. To my mind, this last phase applies particularly to Covert Road'. Consequently the appeal was dismissed and a new scheme submitted of seven units at a lower, less regimented, density which subsequently secured planning permission (see Fig. E.3). Larger floorplate standard units also reflected the larger homes characteristic of the area.

RACS necessitated a complete survey of the residential areas in the three towns, the completion of which took extensive time and resources. To reduce the expense, the authority used junior officers and students to complete the survey work and the study (and its future implementation) has been carried out without the involvement of specific design trained staff. Clearly, the approach is resource and labour intensive, while the length of time taken to prepare the study suggests that the approach is unlikely to be adopted by many other authorities. Its final impact is yet to be seen, although the early promising signs lead officers to be confident that the substantial investment will not be without worthwhile returns.

# Part Two:
# Current practice and innovation in control

# Chapter 6

# Bridging the professional divide

In Chapter 3 the framework for design control in England in the form of (revised) PPG1 was examined alongside a re-formulation of the established critiques of design control. From the analysis, the implications of the revised framework on the key stakeholders in the design control process were considered and the extent to which the guidance addresses the key themes of the design control debate reviewed. In Chapter 6 the rare opportunity is taken of reviewing a snapshot of opinion on design control from across the full range of stakeholders in the design/development process. Together, the linked Chapters 3 and 6 offer the means to address directly the first research objective: to explore the evolving framework for design control in England and the attitudes of the key stakeholders in the planning and development process to that new framework.

In a perceptive contribution to the design debate Ian Davison, the author of the joint HBF/ RIBA publication 'Good Design in Housing', suggested that most commentators may be approaching the problem from the wrong direction, and that rather than pursue an elusive agreement about what is good design, it might be easier to achieve some consensus about the nature of bad design. This he defines as 'design that is not responsive to the sense of place, the character of landscape or context, or design that offers contrast without logic'. He suggests that 'Most of us, developer, designer, Prince or public, could readily identify and agree on the inadequacy of mass produced, stereotypical design which is repeated without care or concern for its contribution to a sense of place' (HBF/RIBA, 1990, p. 12). In this chapter, the aim has been to adopt the positive approach advocated by Davison. So, instead of focusing on the perennial areas of disagreement (aired in Chapter 3), the research needed to draw out those cross-professional areas – if any – where agreement can be found on design and its treatment through the planning process will be covered.

## Research method

Publication of a consultation version of revised guidance on design (DoE, 1996e) during the period of research provided the ideal opportunity and means to undertake a detailed comparative review of the views of the key stakeholders on the developing agenda. The analysis was undertaken on the basis of responses provided to the consultation exercise in the period following the publication of the draft guidance – July to September 1996. An initial request for copies of responses to the consultation exercise was made directly (and speculatively) to five of the key stakeholders – the HBF, RTPI, RIBA, Urban Design Group

(UDG) and the CPRE – as a means to examine the effectiveness of the proposed analysis (largely by examining the comprehensiveness of the responses received).

Reflecting the significance of the new guidance on design, all the initial responses received were comprehensive in nature and represented responses both to the government's new framework and to forwarding each respondent's own particular agenda. Initial analysis of the five responses suggested that the line of research would be fruitful as a means to gauge key stakeholder opinion and that an extension of the effort to a wider range of respondents should be attempted.

To achieve this, a request was made directly to the DoE for a list of the full range of respondents to the consultation exercise. A list of responses was received (DoE, 1996f), and analysed, to gauge the overall pattern of responses to the consultation exercise and to select a range of further respondents to ensure good coverage from across key stakeholder groups. In total (including the five responses already received), twenty key responses were chosen. The full text of the remaining fifteen respondents not already secured was then obtained direct from the DoE library (London), where copies of all responses to DoE (now DETR) consultation exercises are stored and made available for public inspection.

To ensure comprehensive analysis of both their spirit and detailed content, responses were analysed in two ways: qualitatively and quantitatively. First, each was categorised into one of four stakeholder groups:

1.    the development lobby;
2.    the design professionals;
3.    the planners; and
4.    the amenity lobby.

Next, carefully chosen extracts were taken from each of the responses covering the key messages of the particular respondent. The extracts from each stakeholder group were then analysed together (see Figs 6.1–6.4). Second, a detailed issue by issue comparative analysis was made under groupings chosen to reflect coverage in the revised government guidance (Tables 3.2 and 3.3), but in a manner that allowed greater differentiation of the design criteria and process coverage of that advice. Thus, the responses of the twenty respondents were categorised; according to whether each respondent supported or rejected the concerns outlined in the consultation version of revised PPG1 and/or whether the criticisms made were taken on board (or not) in the final published guidance (DoE, 1997b). From the analysis a series of eight key consensus positions were identified; positions, it is argued, that provide a potential basis and starting point from which to bridge the cross-professional design divide.

As a further means to test the responses analysed, the theoretical critiques of design control established in Chapter 3 are revisited and used as a means to gauge whether the well-established positions of the key stakeholders in the design control process remained wedded to the dogmatic approaches of the past, or whether any flexibility and movement could be detected to offer some future scope for consensus on design control. Finally, some tentative conclusions are drawn on developing the broad consensus, with a particular focus on the issue of design skills – the major concern of the key stakeholders to avoid consideration in the new framework provided by (revised) PPG1.

### Analysis of responses

The opportunity of reviewing a snapshot of opinion across all groups of stakeholders in the design control debate is rare and offers the possibility of identifying any changes to

building design, and for the need to translate urban design concepts to
as well.

English Heritage focused their comments on the implications of c
environment, regretting the failure to assimilate fully conservation cc
planning issues such as design (EH1), and the relegation of the ubiq
harm' test to the 'operational' paragraphs of the note. Nevertheless, the
local distinctiveness and appraisal of context was welcomed, alth
misgivings as the Civic Trust, that, following years of largely negative
central government, the ability of local authorities to advise applicants
be seriously questioned (EH2). An investment in time and resources wa$
answer to filling the skills gap, while an argument for the use of statutory designations to
define and preserve local distinctiveness was forcefully made.

Like the 'professional' responses, the RFAC used the opportunity of the consultation
exercise to promote their function as the government's advisory body on design by arguing
the case for specific mention of that role in the guidance (RFAC1). The consistent
encouragement from the RFAC for planning authority involvement in design concerns was
also developed with specific support for the advice on mixing uses, urban design and the
role of design policies in encouraging good, innovative and original design. Finally, in this
balanced response, the need for skilled designers and professional staff was articulated,
alongside a call for authorities to reject unimaginative and incompetent design (RFAC2),
and for the promotion of residential developments that offer visual interest, vitality and good
urban design.

### Detailed comparative analysis

Initial examination of the responses confirmed many of the established positions of the key
stakeholders in the process (see Chapter 3), and that to some degree the majority of
responses are aimed at advancing the narrow sectorial interests of respondents rather than
in pursuit of environmental quality per se. Nevertheless, the only (almost) entirely negative
response came from the BPF with the majority of respondents making some positive
contribution to the consultation exercise and accepting the case for at least some public
sector intervention in the cause of better design.

By focusing on the areas of agreement – rather than on the many and ubiquitous areas of
disagreement between the different respondents – the research was able to reveal a
common agenda for improved design control (see p. 189). The next stage was the detailed
comparative analysis of the responses undertaken against six broad groupings to
complement the (overview) analysis of key messages (already undertaken):

1. Response to context
2. Design criteria
3. Mixed use and sustainable design
4. Design process
5. Design policy/guidance
6. Local authority design review.

The discussion that follows uses the data from the (overview) analysis of respondents
messages (above) and from the more detailed comparative analysis of responses as a
means to identify common ground between the different stakeholder groups. The detailed
comparative analysis – when complete – revealed over 200 separate design criteria/
processes (across the six groupings) against which responses were compared.

*nse to context*

importance of established context was widely accepted by development, design, planning and amenity interests alike, alongside the need for design to respond to that context. Only the expression of that concern varied from advocacy of a universal need for design to relate to context, to more conditional identifications of particular contexts for designers to have regard (residential, rural, landscape), to focused arguments to respect local distinctiveness, sense of place or to avoid town cramming.

The means and extent of that response marked the major point of departure. Broadly, a conservation approach to context found support from the HBF, RIBA, CPRE, Countryside Commission and English Heritage – in the case of the first two to preserve the two-tier system of design control (so ensuring less intervention in non-designated areas) and in the case of the others to ensure the continuing conservation of historic environments. At the same time more positive (less restrictive) responses to conservation were advocated by the BPF, RIBA, RTPI and RFAC; with the Landscape Institute, RTPI, DPOS and CPRE arguing the case for a philosophical break with the established two-tier system of design control, to prioritise the role of design as a means to enhance poor quality environments, and the need for good design 'everywhere'.

The advice to advocate good design 'everywhere' and the conceptually conflicting advice to prioritise high quality design in sensitive locations were both accepted by government in the final guidance (DoE, 1997b, paras. 15–16). Support for design review with regard to context can be identified as the first broad area of cross stakeholder group consensus.

*Design criteria*

Evidence for the support of landscape, planning and amenity interests for a more interventionist response to context came in the greater number of suggested design criteria (urban design, landscape and architectural) supported by these interests. The analysis also revealed support from planning and amenity interests for the control of building design and a range of more detailed design concerns (external appearance, local vernacular traditions, materials, visual interest), but a much more cautious approach to such matters from development and design interests (excluding the Landscape Institute). For such interests, control of building design was only considered legitimate when design is 'obviously' out of character with its surroundings – again emphasising context as the key test.

Support for the general increased emphasis on design/urban design was much more consistent with fourteen out of the twenty respondents recording explicit support for the emphasis on design and/or urban design, while five of the remaining respondents (BPF, CBI, UVF, ACA, ACE) expressed (almost) no preference – either positive or negative – on design criteria or the value of design. The final respondent – the RIBA – favoured a range of specific urban design criteria as the basis for control. Support for urban design therefore represents the second broad area of consensus between respondents.

Strong support for increased emphasis on landscape design came from the Landscape Institute, RTPI, DPOS and from the CPRE. The other sixteen respondents failed to mention landscape at all. Nevertheless, in the absence of comments – either positive or negative – general support for intervention to improve landscape as part of the broader concern for urban design can be assumed. Taken together, issues of access, access into buildings and disabled access were addressed by nine out of the twenty responses, but ranged from hands-off approaches advocated by the development interests (HBF, BPF, CBI), to mixed messages from the RIBA and DPOS concerned to encourage accessibility but prevent conflict with the building regulations, to almost evangelical support for the benefits of barrier free environments – internally and externally – from the ASI. In this area, therefore, agreement was less clearly apparent.

*Mixed use and sustainable design*

The priority given to urban design was complemented by broad – although not total – support for the related themes of mixed-used development and sustainable design. Intervention to encourage mixed-use development was explicitly supported by twelve out of the fifteen respondents who addressed the issue. The other three respondents (HBF, BPF and RIBA) – without discounting such developments – preferred to highlight the problems (economic, design, development process) in successfully implementing such schemes, concerns also widespread among the more explicitly supportive respondents. Although not an area benefiting from complete consensus, support for mixed-use development can nevertheless be identified as the third area benefiting from broad support across interest groups. The support comes with the proviso, however, that difficulties with implementation are widely accepted, alongside a general recognition that mixed use is no panacea for sustainability.

Support for specific sustainable design criteria was more patchy, with nine out of the twenty respondents highlighting at least one criterion or approach as worthy of control on sustainable grounds (design, conservation activity, energy efficiency, sustainable materials), and a further three supporting the emphasis on sustainable development more generally. Only the BPF castigated sustainable development – alongside mixed use and design – as subjective, while the encouragement from the ASI and Civic Trust for government explicitly to recognise the contribution of good design in securing sustainable development paid dividends through incorporation of their advice into the final guidance (DoE, 1997b, para. 15).

*Design process*

Design process concerns were addressed by fifteen out of the twenty respondents, indicating the importance attached to design and development process as a means to achieve good, or at least viable, design product. Broadly, development and design interests argued that design should be seen as part of the wider development process and should be first and foremost commercially appropriate. Such commercial considerations were also extended to the burden placed on developers in the production of illustrative material. For such material, it was suggested, no blanket rules should apply, but requirements should be appropriate to the development size (a viewpoint reflected in the final guidance – DoE, 1997b, para. A4), and should be determined by the applicant. Conversely, planning and amenity interests argued that quality pays – although over the longer term – and that applicants should show due regard to context and urban design principles in their illustrative material.

Broadest support (particularly among professional interests) and the fourth key area of consensus was found in the agreement that design policy and control, by itself, could not secure good design and that professional design skills were required to achieve such quality. The RIBA were strident in their advocacy of 'architectural' skills with the ACA, ACE, Landscape Institute, RTPI and RFAC less professionally partisan but equally strident in their advocacy of 'professional' design skills – architectural, urban design, landscape and engineering. Broad support was also found for the related concern of encouraging innovative design, particularly from the architectural respondents and from the RFAC and BPF, although in the latter case as a means to reduce prescription and increase developer freedom.

*Design policy/guidance*

All of the eighteen respondents that addressed design policy issues accepted either explicitly or implicitly that some form of design policy/guidance was required, so constituting the fifth key area of consensus. The means and nature of design guidance prioritised by different respondents, however, varied dramatically. The RICS, UDG and CPRE went furthest

LIVERPOOL JOHN MOORES UNIVERSITY
LEARNING SERVICES

in their support for comprehensive design guidance, with the RICS and UDG both supporting explicit hierarchies of design guidance – urban design strategies and urban design frameworks; complemented by design guides in the case of the RICS and by design briefs in the case of the UDG.

Support for design policy was given by seven respondents (HBF, RTPI, DPOS, CPRE, ASI, LI and RFAC), further support to design briefs by the first four of these, and support to other forms of unspecified supplementary design guidance by the RICS, UDG, ICE, DPOS and CPRE. Advocacy for other forms of guidance from respondents included: for Countryside Design Summaries and Village Design Statements (CT, CPRE and CC); for design guides on mixed-use (RTPI and DPOS), local distinctiveness (DPOS), and conservation areas (EH); and for further advice from central government in the form of a PPG on Landscaping (LI), a PPG on sustainability (DPOS), for good practice examples in an appendix to PPG1 (CT), for a good practice guide on design (ASI and DPOS), and most radically for model (nationally defined) design policies for adoption by local authorities (RIBA).

Design and development interests were coolest in their support for design policy and guidance, emphasising the need to avoid over-prescription and subsequent delay and for consultation on the economic viability of policy and guidance. Wider consultation was encouraged by the RTPI and DPOS, while appraisal as the basis of policy and guidance was supported explicitly by just five respondents (HBF, LI, ACO, CPRE and EH), and implicitly by an additional two (CT and CC). Nevertheless, taken together, twelve out of the eighteen respondents – across interest groups – emphasised the importance of at least some form of analysis (consultation or appraisal) as a means to understand context (including economic context) before policy/guidance prescription. The analytical basis of design policy and guidance therefore formed the sixth key area of broad consensus, and further complements the consensus on the importance of context.

*Local authority design review*
Analysis of the responses with regard to the process of local authority design review revealed two distinct camps. First, a largely negative view of the review process came from the RIBA and development interests, citing as problems: potential for delay, that design is difficult to measure and subjective, the dangers of design by committee, and inconsistency of local authority advice. Second, a more positive view of the review process from the Landscape Institute, DPOS and amenity interests advocating a greater commitment to design and a more proactive response to improving design quality from local authorities and central government. The need for authorities to devote greater time and resources to design was particularly stressed (UDG, LI, CT and EH).

The concern for greater resources relates closely to the seventh point of consensus, that authorities need also to invest in professional design skills and advice. In a variety of forms the lack of design skills in local authorities was lamented by eleven out of the sixteen respondents who addressed the design review process, across stakeholder groups. If considered alongside a concern for encouraging the use of professional design skills in the design process (see above), the general concern for recognising and utilising professional design skills proved to be one of the most consistent laments of the responses examined, and one unrecognised either in the draft version of PPG1, or, following the consultation exercise, in the final guidance. A range of approaches was highlighted by respondents to address the skills gap: authorities should be proactive; authorities should take external professional advice; professional design advisory panels should be used; design award schemes run; design training offered; and greater use of the RFAC (now CABE) made.

A  CHARACTERISTICS OF THE EXISTING
HOUSING STOCK
- age (Victorian, Edwardian, Inter-war, other)
- type (detached, semi-detached, terraced, other)

B  URBAN DESIGN
- interesting/unusual urban form, landmarks
- established streetscene/townscape
- scale, massing, disposition of buildings
- important views and vistas, the skyline
- continuity/uniformity of buildings
- squares and spaces of character
- unbuilt zones and natural corridors, gaps
- building quality
- problem sites and eyesores

C  RESIDENTS' AMENITY
- overlooking
- lack of daylight
- privacy

D  TRAFFIC AND HIGHWAY MATTERS
- car parking
- access
- type of road

E  LANDSCAPE AND AMENITY CRITERIA
- presence of trees and verges and their contribution to the streetscene
- public and private amenity space
- quality and greenness of forecourts
- size of private gardens
- flood plains and areas liable to flooding

F  EXISTENCE OF PROTECTIVE DESIGNATION
- listed building status
- conservation area status
- green belt
- metropolitan open land
- areas of special/local character
- tree preservation orders

*Fig. F.1  Principal characteristics surveyed (Munro and Lane, 1990, p. 15).*

A.  primarily older (pre-1910) properties (mainly terraces), essentially urban in character with above Borough average densities.
B.  mainly inter-war housing with a low to medium level of greenness (as seen from the street).
C.  mainly inter-war housing with a medium to high level of greenness (as seen from the street).
D.  exceptionally green areas with very low densities.

Although the study itself was never formally adopted as supplementary planning guidance, it has had a significant input into the development of new borough-wide policies in the form of more broad-brush policies than those typified in most design guides. The major concern over the nature and form of recent residential development meant the first priority was to write a key policy aimed at ensuring that new development maintained (and enhanced where appropriate) the established character of its locality. This extensive (four-page) policy included reference both to the quality of individual developments and to the cumulative impact of successive developments on the character of the borough as a whole.

The development of more detailed policies involved extensive debate about whether to develop area-specific policies for the areas of broadly distinct character, or policies for the individual (generic) characteristics identified. The debate focused on whether area-specific policies might, by their nature, fossilise the established character of areas, so reducing scope for the necessary new housing. Unlike in Dacorum (see Inset E), the decision was made to avoid area-specific policies and instead to develop a series of general environmental policies aimed at protecting and enhancing the character of the borough as a whole; including policies on protecting the structural elements identified by the survey (Munro and Lane, 1990, p. 18).

Extensive discussion also revolved around the role and value of density policy. Officers concluded that the role of density policies was of secondary importance when viewed against the main concern with protecting the established character of the borough. Nevertheless, as a second line of defence a residential density policy was included in the plan which indicated the council's intention to consider prevailing density levels in residential

*Fig. F.2  Map 8 environmental categorisation (Wootton Jeffreys, 1989).*

# Map 8

 A

 B

 C

D

 **Structural open land**

Blank spaces refer to district or local
centres or to areas of employment (E).

## Environmental Categorisation

(by street character)

Para 6.3.7 et seq.

Environmental Assessment of
Residential Areas in Harrow :   1989

North

0       1       2

Kilometres (approx.)

districts – without specifying maximum or minimum levels to be achieved. This policy (H8) – like all the new policies – drew heavily on, and referenced for its legitimacy, the analysis.

The new policies came through the adoption process largely unscathed (London Borough of Harrow, 1994), and have stood up well to the test of time and the rigours of the appeals system. Thus an era of more effective design control in Harrow has resulted. However, with forecast increases in household numbers in London, the challenge of accommodating new homes in the capital is leading to further intensification pressures. Design-led approaches to intensification, including the 'Sustainable Residential Quality' principles developed by Llewelyn-Davies (see p. 317) are seen to offer one possible way forward which may in the long run lead to significant changes in the character of London's 'suburban' boroughs (although officers observe that as yet no one would dare admit it). Now, at the turn of the century, this debate is being played out in Harrow and will need to be resolved as the plan comes forward for review. It may be that the renewed pressures bring with them the better quality development sought, but, as yet, rarely seen in Harrow. The concern is that this may be at the expense of the qualities greatly prized by existing residents.

Officers argue that the policies have enabled greater protection of the structural features (and therefore character) identified in the new policies. This, along with a reduction in backland schemes, has resulted in a consequential reduction in resident and councillor objections to new housing development. It is thought, however, that the inherent design quality of individual residential schemes over the same period has not improved (see Fig. F.3).

This failure to improve the inherent design of residential developments is put down to the perception among many housebuilders that building in already suburban environments does not necessitate 'anything special'. The lack of in-house design skills in the authority also makes negotiation on design difficult beyond the borough's conservation areas. The Harrow experience illustrates graphically the value of appraisal as the basis for design policy generation, but equally graphically how the failure to invest in design skills to implement the resulting detailed design policy may undermine an otherwise innovative approach. The Harrow experience further illustrates the vital importance placed by residents of suburban environments on the provision and protection of a high-quality green environment in new and established residential areas.

*Fig. F.3 Typical late 1990s higher density housing development in Harrow.*

# Chapter 7

# Residential design policy and guidance:

# a snapshot of practice in the 1990s

From a detailed analysis of the potential for consensus offered by the current 'general' government guidance on design in Chapter 6, the book focuses specifically in the remainder of Part 2, on residential design and its control as the means to address directly the key research aim. Thus, in Chapter 8, the research examines a range of innovative residential design control practice as a means to explore the preparation, use and types of residential design guidance. Before that, the results of a country-wide survey and content analysis of residential design guidance is presented, amounting to a snapshot of practice in the 1990s.

The chapter directly addresses research objectives 2 and 3: to review critically the prevalence and hierarchical structure of residential design policy and guidance – county and district/unitary – and how up-to-date the different forms of guidance are in practice; and to evaluate the content, prescription and analytical basis of residential design policy and guidance and the regional emphasis of authorities – county and district/unitary.

## Research method

### Country-wide survey of residential design guidance

The analysis was undertaken in two stages. First, a 100 per cent country-wide postal survey of all English local authorities – county, district, metropolitan and London boroughs – was undertaken to assess design policy and guidance prevalence and to request copies (from each authority) of the full hierarchy of design guidance in active use at that time for controlling residential design.[1]

The initial request for information was made in 1994 with a follow-up reminder in March of that year. Some county councils were also sent separate letters to their highways department if their planning department first advised that residential design and layout was considered primarily a highways matter. Subsequent requests for updates were made in 1995

---

[1] The local authority structure in England is divided between two-tier and single-tier areas. In two-tier areas 'county authorities' form the strategic planning and highways authority, although day-to-day control of development and local planning is undertaken by 'district authorities'. Other areas – mainly the metropolitan city areas and London boroughs – have a system of single-tier or 'unitary authorities'. In these areas, strategic, highways and local planning are all undertaken by the one authority. As such they produce Unitary Development Plans (UDPs) rather than local or structure plans which are produced respectively by district and county authorities in non-metropolitan areas. County authorities lost their responsibility for local planning and development control in 1972 in the local government act of that year.

and to selected authorities (previously unable to supply information) in 1996. The letter requested:

1. Any *Residential Design Guidance* or *Standards* published by the authority dealing with the design and/or layout of *private sector, new-build* residential development or with the *appraisal* of residential environments.
2. A photocopy of any *Policies, Guidance, Standards* or *Appraisal* that the authority uses to control residential design and layout in the *most recent Local Plan*, whether or not this has been adopted.[2]
3. Any recent site-specific residential *Design Briefs* produced by the authority, or by developers at the request of the authority.
4. Information on any *Research* or *Innovative Approaches* taken in this area by the authority.

To ensure as complete a picture as possible was obtained of the country-wide prevalence of residential design guidance, those authorities unwilling to supply copies of their design guidance, were sent a simple pro-forma and explanatory letter asking them to tick the types of guidance used by their authority. As returns were received from local authorities a database was updated to record the information.

### Content analysis

The second stage of this part of the research involved the detailed content analysis of the design policy and guidance collected from all of the responding authorities. The content analysis was a huge task, carried out over an eighteen-month period between April 1995 and October 1996. Because of the size of the task and the need to ensure consistency over an extended period of time, a pro-forma was devised as a means to record the data. Based on earlier experience of design policy analysis (Punter *et al.*, 1996), it was decided the pro-forma should be as detailed as possible to avoid (as far as possible) the inevitable variation in interpretation of design concepts as a consequence of the extensive, overlapping and consequently confusing jargon used to discuss design concerns. Hence, an extensive range of design concerns were selected for inclusion in the pro-forma from government advice, the literature review and wider design theory (see Table 5.1). These were listed alphabetically so that a simple tick could be placed against each if included in any of five forms of guidance: plan policy, design guides, design standards, design appraisal or site briefs. After dry-running the pro-forma with the first twenty authorities an 'others' category was added for the inevitable range of concepts not included in the pro-forma and extra notes were added to aid the consistent interpretation of concepts in overlapping categories.

The design concepts were listed against the five forms of residential design guidance received from local authorities as a means to gauge at which level in the guidance hierarchy the particular concept was addressed. In addition, the pro-forma required a number of judgements to be made about the guidance based on its coverage of the design concepts:

- *The overall emphasis placed on design* – a judgement based on the extent of coverage of design concerns, in any one type of guidance or across the full hierarchy.
- *The overall emphasis placed on sustainable design* – a judgement based on the extent of coverage of sustainable design concerns, in any one type of guidance or across the full hierarchy.

---

[2] Letters to county authorities were amended to request: A photocopy of any Council Resolutions or Structure Plan Policies which deal with residential design or are concerned with the legitimisation of design guidance or standards.

- *The consistency with government advice* – a judgement primarily made on the overall level of prescription, the expression of design concerns (whether expressed as matters for guidance or control), and the position of these concerns (whether in policy or supplementary guidance).[3] To help in making this judgement the design criteria were classified as: legitimate interests for local authority control; non-legitimate interests; or issues not covered in government guidance (from Tables 2.2 to 2.4).
- *Overall comments on the authority's approach to design* – most useful as a means to record innovative practice and therefore to identify subsequently the innovative case study authorities.

Finally, a further set of factual concerns were recorded concerning the position, status and analytical rigour of authorities and the residential design guidance they produce. For ease of pro-forma transcription the content analysis results were recorded directly on to pro-forma hard copies. Subsequently, the results were transcribed on to a database for computer manipulation of the results.

### Methodological problems

Some problems were inevitable with differential interpretation of the terminology used in the simple pro-forma sent to initially non-responding authorities. Thus, a small number of authorities failed to understand clearly the differences between, for example, residential layout standards published as supplementary design guidance and layout standards in the plan, the tendency being to tick both boxes rather than just one. Because of the confusion, data from the simple pro-forma distinguishing the types of guidance found in the plan was not used in the content analysis, only data on the broad types of guidance – design policy, design guides, design briefs, etc. – as part of the country-wide survey.

The decision was taken early on in the research project to restrict the work to examining the control of private sector, new-build, residential development and that the research would exclude explicit policy and guidance on:

- residential development in conservation areas or other designated areas;
- city centre residential development;
- housing in the open countryside;
- residential extensions and conversions (including of listed buildings); and
- social housing.

Rather than making requests for information to authorities unduly complex it was decided to distinguish between the different forms of guidance once received. Hence policy/guidance on forms of development outside the scope of the research was simply ignored when received.

Some minor confusion was obvious, however, between general local plan policies on design and specific policy on residential design. The letter to authorities specifically requested 'any policies, guidance, standards or appraisal that you use to control residential design and layout in your most recent local plan', with the intention that this would catch both 'general' and 'residential-specific' policies. From knowledge of previous research (Punter *et al.*, 1996) it soon became obvious that a small number of district/unitary authorities were

---

[3] Design concerns were marked on the pro-forma as legitimate or non-legitimate at the time of preparing the research instrument in April 1995 and data was subsequently recorded as such between then and October 1996. Judgements about whether guidance was consistent (or not) with government advice were consequently made before the latest revisions to PPG1 in 1997.

sending only their residential-specific policies and not their general design policies as well. For the purposes of the research it can be assumed that in these authorities the residential-specific policies take precedence over the general policies on matters of residential development and hence are the primary policies used to control residential design. Nevertheless, it should be noted that the content analysis does suffer from this potential flaw, which may devalue the contribution of local plan/UDP design policy. Alternatively, it may reflect no more than the inevitable variation in design control practice between authorities.

### Country-wide survey of residential design guidance

*Response rate*

To gauge a true picture of the country-wide prevalence, age and hierarchical relationships between different forms of residential design policy and guidance, the research required a good response rate from planning authorities.[4] Hence much time was spent in requesting information and chasing (by phone) promised information that had not arrived. The efforts paid off with very high response rates recorded for each authority type and a 93% response rate overall (see Table 7.1).[5]

It is difficult to draw conclusions about the 7% of authorities that did not reply to the survey. A small number wrote to indicate that lack of resources meant they were unable to respond to research requests, others may simply have had no guidance to send and hence felt that a response was unnecessary (despite the simple pro-forma requesting a response even in such circumstances). It may be appropriate to assume that residential design control practice – in most of the non-responding authorities – would be unlikely to fall among the best practice authorities, and that, in many, a low priority given to design may be reflected in their disinterest in the research. This observation is supported by a comparison between non-responding authorities and the best practice authorities identified in the earlier 'Design Policies in Local Plans' research (Punter *et al.*, 1996). None of the best practice authorities identified during that research are included in the list of non-responding authorities for the current work.

*Table 7.1  Survey response rates*

| Authority type | Total authority numbers | Full responses received | Pro-forma response only | Total response rate (%) |
|---|---|---|---|---|
| County councils | 39 | 38 | 1 | 100 |
| London boroughs | 33 | 30 | 0 | 91 |
| Metropolitan boroughs | 36 | 27 | 6 | 92 |
| District councils | 296 | 227 | 47 | 93 |
| Totals | 404 | 322 | 54 | 93 |

[4] The survey was begun before the 1995/1996 local government reorganisation. Hence response rates, survey results and content analysis relate to the pre-reorganisation authority structures.

[5] The particularly high response rate from the county councils (100%) may be partly explained by the separate letters sent to the planning and highways departments of some authorities.

*Prevalence*

Table 7.2 offers a summary of the survey returns. The historic divisions in responsibility for residential design were obvious in the relative emphasis placed on different control mechanisms by county and district authorities. Thus, county control of residential design, which originated from their highways responsibility, was in large part still expressed through design standards (59%). Nevertheless, a good proportion of counties over the years have developed these standards into more comprehensive design guides moving beyond the limiting concern for road layout. The important, and ongoing, role of the county authority in controlling residential design was obvious in the 41% of county councils that contain supplementary design guidance going well beyond road layout standards. The much lesser role (advisory only) of the county planning authorities – as opposed to highways authorities – in day-to-day design control decision making was also apparent in the almost complete absence of design briefs and in the low priority given to residential design in structure plan policy.

For district and unitary authorities, the importance of Section 54A of the 1990 Planning Act giving primacy to the development plan was also obvious in the very clear choice of the development plan as the key mechanism for controlling residential design. The almost complete coverage of residential design concerns in London borough UDPs (97%) reflects the long-established nature of design policy in London and also the well-established presence of borough-wide plans. The slightly lower coverage in metropolitan and district authorities (88 and 86%) reflects the less-established and still evolving nature of district-wide plans in these areas. In the London boroughs, plans have also been accompanied, historically, by a standards chapter or supplement (Gould, 1992, p. 13). This explains the high incidence of standards (67%) as opposed to design guides (33%) in the London boroughs and the corresponding high incidence of that guidance appearing as part of the local plan rather than as independently published planning guidance.

In metropolitan authorities the emphasis on design guides was strongest with 58% of authorities possessing some form of residential design guide. In district councils the figure fell to 30% with a correspondingly low level of design standards (20%). The lower incidence of such forms of guidance may merely reflect their existence at the higher, county, level in many districts. Thus, although some authorities clearly choose either to supplement the county guidance, or repeat it (often in a plan appendix), many refrain from the production of district or area-wide design guidance outside the plan.

Forms of explicit design appraisal were poorly represented in the survey across authority types with county authorities eliciting no appraisals, metropolitan boroughs just one, and

*Table 7.2  Residential design policy/guidance prevalence*

| Authority | Plan policies | Design guides | Design standards | Design appraisal | Site briefs |
|---|---|---|---|---|---|
| County councils | 23% | 41% | 59% | – | 3% |
| London boroughs | 97% | 33% | 67% | 10% | 47% |
| Metropolitan boroughs | 88% | 58% | 30% | 3% | 61% |
| District councils | 86% | 30% | 20% | 9% | 47% |

*Note:*
Figures include draft versions of guidance and guidance 'not sent' but referred to in the pro-forma. Percentages are calculated from the total returns received from each authority type, not as a percentage of the total number of each authority type.

London boroughs and district councils around 10% each. The figures may hide appraisal undertaken but unpublished and therefore not supplied by authorities, but despite extra attempts to secure appraisals identified during the literature review, evidence for systematic appraisal remained elusive.

Design briefs were used much more frequently (with the exception of county authorities) with 55% of district and unitary authorities actively using site-specific guidance to control residential design. Surprisingly, despite their short-term nature, 11% of these were found as part of emerging development plans, in varying degrees of detail. Other forms of supplementary guidance were also frequently included within or attached to local plans as appendices, with residential design standards proving the most popular; perhaps as a means to make previously 'bottom draw' policies more explicit as required by PPG12 (DoE, 1992c, para. 3.19). In many authorities, however, the tradition of standards and/or design guidance appearing as part of the plan, usually as 'development control guidelines' (see Table 5.4), was clearly long established.

In addition to the guidance already available, a number of authorities indicated their involvement in the production of new residential design guidance, or their intention to produce more guidance in the future (10% of county authorities; 9% of metropolitan authorities and 4% of districts). Although the information was not explicitly sought and is therefore unlikely to illustrate the full picture, it may nevertheless indicate some important trends, most notably the continued faith placed in residential design guidance at the county level. Continued faith in the value of residential design guidance of all types was also obvious in the responses of metropolitan and district authorities, while the much longer established tradition of design guidance in the London boroughs may explain their failure to highlight any new initiatives.

### Hierarchical use

A key objective of the research was to examine the hierarchical use of design guidance and to assess to what extent authorities rely on different forms of guidance working in combination to maximise the effectiveness of design control processes (see Table 7.3). The well-established nature of design guidance in the London boroughs was confirmed by the more sophisticated use of different forms of guidance – in hierarchical combination – to control residential design. Thus, no London boroughs exist without any form of guidance to control residential design, while the largest proportion of boroughs have three forms of

*Table 7.3  Residential design policy/guidance hierarchy*

| Authority | Authorities with 0 types of guidance | Authorities with 1 type of guidance | Authorities with 2 types of guidance | Authorities with 3 types of guidance | Authorities with 4 types of guidance | Authorities with 5 types of guidance |
|---|---|---|---|---|---|---|
| County councils | 5% | 64% | 31% | – | – | – |
| London boroughs | – | 10% | 37% | 47% | 7% | – |
| Metropolitan boroughs | 3% | 18% | 18% | 52% | 9% | – |
| District councils | 5% | 34% | 34% | 20% | 6% | 1% |

*Note:*
Percentages are calculated from the total returns received from each authority type, not as a percentage of the total number of each authority type. Percentages are rounded up or down and so totals in some tables in the Chapter may not always add up to exactly 100.

guidance to control design – most often policy, standards and briefs. A similar pattern was seen in metropolitan boroughs, although the combination was more often policy, design guides and briefs, and the proportion with none or just one form of guidance was higher (21% as opposed to 10%). In both types of authority, significant numbers (7 and 9%) use four types of guidance. A flatter curve was seen in district councils who exhibited much larger numbers of authorities using none or just one form of guidance (39%), but at the other end of the spectrum three authorities (1%) who professed to use all five forms.

The pattern may be partially explained by the tendency of many district authorities to look to the county level for more detailed residential design standards and guidance. At that level, by far the greatest number of county authorities (64%) produced only one form of guidance (usually a design guide or standards), and none produced more than two forms. Taken together, the pattern illustrates a considerable faith in the value of different forms of guidance working together from the different levels of the design guidance hierarchy – strategic, district-wide, site-specific (see Table 5.4). Thus, 50–60% of district and unitary authorities (London and metropolitan boroughs) benefit directly from three or more forms of design guidance; for district authorities usually county guides/standards, local plan policy and design briefs; and for unitary authorities usually UDP policy, design guides/standards and design briefs.

### Age/status

Government guidance determines that the age and status of plan policy – its prematurity – should determine the weight ascribed to it (DoE, 1997b, paras. 47–49). Thus, policy carries maximum weight immediately upon adoption, weight which tails off the older it gets and successively at each stage before adoption. Although not explicitly stated in government guidance, it is reasonable to suppose that the principle applies to other forms of supplementary guidance as well. In this context the out-of-date nature of many design guides and standards has been widely criticised, while design briefs are usually regarded as short-term guidance mechanisms only (Madanipour *et al.*, 1993, p. 32).

Plan policy and the small number of residential design appraisals were generally well up-to-date, although at the time of surveying a large proportion (81%) of the district and unitary authority plans were still at pre-adoption stages (see Table 7.4).[6] Nevertheless, the effect of changes in the 1990 Town and Country Planning Act requiring authorities to produce district-wide development plans was clear in the up-to-date coverage of residential design policy in local plans and UDPs – many produced for the first time. Design briefs were also fairly up-to-date; although for a mechanism generally considered to be short term in its operation, a significant minority in district (19%) and unitary (8%) authorities were older than five years.

*Table 7.4  Status of development plans*

| Authority | Adopted plan policies | Deposit plan policies | Consultation plan policies |
|---|---|---|---|
| County councils | 87% | 13% | – |
| District/unitary councils | 19% | 51% | 30% |

---

[6] Earlier research (Punter *et al.*, 1996) has indicated that the adoption process often affects the content of design policies little beyond minor adjustments to policy expression.

At a time of very gradual emergence from a severe recession in the housing market when the sample was taken, the continued use of briefs prepared in the boom housing market of the late 1980s may reveal a general lack of responsiveness to market conditions. Alternatively, the lack of activity in the housing market over the period may merely have acted to extend the life of briefs for sites which in normal circumstances, would have been developed more quickly.

Least up-to-date of the residential control mechanisms were the free-standing design guides and standards – except in the case of the London boroughs, where the practice of including standards and guidance in the plan has ensured continued up-dating of such guidance as successive plans are rolled forward. Significantly, 12% of county residential design guidance and 40% of county residential standards were older than ten years (6% of the former older than twenty years), 7% of metropolitan borough residential design guidance was over ten years and 9% of district council residential design guidance.

The out-of-date nature of much of the guidance received was recognised in accompanying 'apologetic' letters from authorities along with promises, in many cases, to update the guidance as soon as resources allowed. In particular, a large number of county authorities (planning and highways) were engaged at the time in updating their residential design guides and standards, including: Cheshire, Cornwall, Essex, Kent, Norfolk, Shropshire and Warwickshire. The research revealed that a largely new generation of county residential design guides was being put in place, continuing the now long-established – if somewhat against the grain – influence on residential design and layout at the county level. This faith in the value of residential design guides was also obvious in the large number of recent guides (five years old or less) from metropolitan and district authorities, each of which could boast 73% of their output within that period.

### Evaluation: country-wide survey

Two general but nevertheless significant findings became apparent on initially reviewing the survey results. First, that the pursuit of quality in housing design continues to occupy the agendas of authorities at both the strategic and local levels; and second, that this objective ensures that extensive residential design policy and guidance continues to be produced in a variety of forms: as design policies in local plans/UDPs, as design guides and standards outside the plan, and in the form of site-specific design briefs. A detailed analysis of the survey returns revealed that:

- county authorities continue to have an important and ongoing role in producing guidance to control the design and layout of residential development, and in large part, this role is still expressed through the highways department in the form of residential road standards;
- however, a significant proportion of county highways/planning authorities publish more comprehensive residential design guides, a role that seems to reduce the need for district authorities to produce their own guidance;
- local plan policy is the clear first choice mechanism for controlling residential design in district and unitary authorities;
- the new emphasis on the development plan has reduced none of the enthusiasm for other forms of design guidance, particularly residential design guides, which are

forms of guidance as a means to advertise their intention to prepare design briefs for important residential developments. Finally, a very small number of authorities used the opportunity provided by guidance to outline their presentational requirements, and, in just 1% of district/unitary authorities, to seek written design statements.

Design process concerns were dealt with little more comprehensively. Some form of pre-application consultation and/or wider character appraisal was required by less than 20% of authorities, and more limited site surveys by almost 30%. Phasing masterplans were required for large residential developments by almost a third of district/unitary authorities, while a similar proportion of county authorities conceded that development had to be commercially viable to succeed. Finally, the linked concerns for encouraging skilled design advice and innovative designs were dealt with, respectively, in 24% of counties and just 12% of district/unitary authorities and conversely in 21% and 31%. The latter guidance touched on a strong desire in a small number of authorities to avoid standardised housing designs, and, in an even smaller number, to promote explicitly contemporary design solutions.

Design and planning process concerns were not well represented in residential design guidance, but were more often found in county and district/unitary design guides than in standards, briefs or policy. In the case of design policy, such concerns may have been dealt with outside of the design/residential design policies specifically examined in the plan strategy or implementation section. Nevertheless, based on previous research (Punter *et al.*, 1996), it is unlikely that such concerns would have found widespread coverage elsewhere.

## Evaluation: design criteria and guidance hierarchy

The content analysis revealed extensive and wide ranging residential design control practice and a deep concern among authorities to influence, for the better, the design of private sector residential development. As part of this process, a rich (if potentially confusing) design language was revealed.

When examined across guidance mechanisms, coverage of residential design concerns revealed two clear patterns: the first, reflected across the range of different design issues (except spatial and functional), and the second, across all categories. First, is the order of prescription, with county design guides offering the most comprehensive guidance on residential design concerns, followed by the district/unitary guides (except for spatial concerns). The residential guides were generally followed by local plan/UDP policy (some way behind), reflecting the more general remit of residential design policy. Next (but often close), came site-specific design briefs, reflecting only those concerns relevant to particular sites, and therefore being less detailed overall. In all but the spatial and functional categories design standards (county and district/unitary) bring up the rear.[7]

The second broad pattern is the tendency for coverage across the different types of district/unitary guidance to catch and surpass the county design guides in terms of prescription. Thus, although county residential design guides are the single most comprehensive form of residential guidance in each design category (except social), taken together, design policies in local plans/UDPs and district/unitary design guidance,

---

[7] Design appraisals are difficult to include in this analysis because of the small numbers found.

*Table 7.6  Most frequently covered design issues*

| Area of design intervention | Plan policies | | Design guides | | Design standards | | Design appraisal | | Site briefs | | Overall coverage | |
|---|---|---|---|---|---|---|---|---|---|---|---|---|
| | C | D/U | C | D/U | C | D/U | C | D/U | C | D/U | C | D/U |
| *Spatial issues* | | | | | | | | | | | | |
| infrastructure | 50% | 24% | 50% | 16% | 71% | 7% | – | – | – | 43% | 67% | 38% |
| open space | 39% | 72% | 44% | 58% | – | 44% | – | 56% | – | 75% | 36% | 83% |
| public transport | 33% | 17% | 44% | 8% | 43% | 7% | – | 11% | – | 12% | 49% | 23% |
| road hierarchy | 6% | 9% | 81% | 34% | 100 | 7% | – | 33% | – | 30% | 76% | 32% |
| structure planting | 17% | 18% | 75% | 34% | 29% | 22% | – | 33% | – | 34% | 52% | 38% |
| *Morphological issues* | | | | | | | | | | | | |
| building line | – | 19% | 25% | 42% | 7% | 26% | – | 44% | – | 18% | 15% | 36% |
| development scale – infill | 22% | 37% | 13% | 37% | 7% | 15% | – | 33% | – | 5% | 21% | 48% |
| layout | 56% | 75% | 81% | 74% | 57% | 33% | – | 67% | – | 67% | 79% | 88% |
| permeability | 6% | 9% | 63% | 19% | 36% | – | – | – | – | 14% | 46% | 19% |
| route connectivity | 6% | 11% | 56% | 22% | 21% | 4% | – | 11% | – | 16% | 36% | 22% |
| *Contextual issues* | | | | | | | | | | | | |
| backland development | 6% | 27% | – | 22% | – | 19% | – | 44% | – | 2% | 3% | 34% |
| boundaries | – | 23% | 25% | 48% | 7% | 22% | – | 44% | – | 36% | 15% | 46% |
| building groups | 6% | 10% | 50% | 28% | 7% | – | – | 22% | – | 16% | 30% | 24% |
| character | 67% | 69% | 69% | 54% | 7% | 30% | – | 78% | – | 32% | 67% | 79% |
| context (respect for) | 78% | 78% | 63% | 65% | – | 19% | – | 33% | – | 42% | 64% | 84% |
| environmental quality | 50% | 31% | 56% | 28% | 14% | 11% | – | 22% | – | 9% | 55% | 36% |
| height | – | 38% | 25% | 47% | – | 7% | – | 44% | – | 42% | 12% | 55% |
| landscape (existing) | 61% | 66% | 81% | 65% | 27% | 37% | – | 33% | – | 66% | 73% | 80% |
| neighbourhood impact | 44% | 40% | 31% | 26% | – | 19% | – | 11% | – | 14% | 36% | 46% |
| relation to other buildings | 28% | 55% | 38% | 55% | – | 19% | – | 11% | – | 35% | 33% | 70% |
| siting | 50% | 27% | 19% | 28% | – | 4% | – | 33% | – | 10% | 33% | 38% |
| street scene/streetscape | – | 30% | 38% | 41% | – | 11% | – | 44% | – | 22% | 18% | 42% |
| topography | – | 28% | 69% | 49% | – | 22% | – | 33% | – | 29% | 33% | 48% |
| views/vistas | 17% | 31% | 69% | 38% | – | 7% | – | 56% | – | 25% | 42% | 45% |
| *Visual issues* | | | | | | | | | | | | |
| appearance | 11% | 40% | 31% | 39% | 7% | 7% | – | 14% | – | 17% | 24% | 47% |
| colour | – | 15% | 38% | 37% | – | 4% | – | 33% | – | 28% | 18% | 33% |
| details | – | 29% | 50% | 47% | – | 11% | – | 56% | – | 29% | 24% | 47% |
| fenestration | – | 14% | 31% | 46% | – | 15% | – | 33% | – | 20% | 15% | 36% |
| floorscape | – | 1% | 69% | 14% | – | 7% | – | – | – | 4% | 52% | 8% |
| form | 17% | 37% | 38% | 41% | 7% | 7% | – | 44% | – | 35% | 27% | 52% |
| landscaping | 50% | 73% | 81% | 71% | 71% | 37% | – | 67% | – | 83% | 79% | 87% |
| landscaping – hard | 6% | 29% | 75% | 49% | 43% | 22% | – | 56% | – | 33% | 55% | 49% |
| landscaping – soft | 6% | 33% | 75% | 49% | 50% | 30% | – | 67% | – | 39% | 55% | 54% |
| massing | 6% | 31% | 13% | 28% | – | 7% | – | 44% | – | 15% | 9% | 39% |
| materials | 44% | 74% | 56% | 67% | 7% | 11% | – | 56% | – | 65% | 49% | 84% |
| richness/visual interest | – | 20% | 44% | 33% | 36% | 11% | – | 33% | – | 16% | 33% | 33% |
| roofscape/roof forms | – | 16% | 31% | 42% | 7% | 15% | – | 44% | – | 39% | 18% | 42% |
| scale | 67% | 71% | 25% | 53% | 7% | 15% | – | 44% | – | 33% | 46% | 77% |
| screening | – | 16% | 38% | 34% | 7% | 33% | – | – | – | 20% | 21% | 34% |
| style – local (vernacular) | – | 22% | 17% | 34 | 38% | – | – | 22% | – | 20% | 24% | 35% |
| townscape | 17% | 30% | 31% | 21% | – | 4% | – | 22% | – | 12% | 24% | 35% |
| *Perceptual issues* | | | | | | | | | | | | |
| enclosure | – | 12% | 44% | 35% | – | 7% | – | 22% | – | 22% | 21% | 32% |
| identity | 6% | 13% | 63% | 31% | 7% | 7% | – | 22% | – | 17% | 33% | 23% |
| perception/sense of place | 6% | 12% | 44% | 17% | 21% | – | – | 11% | – | 14% | 33% | 20% |

*Social issues*

| | | | | | | | | | | | |
|---|---|---|---|---|---|---|---|---|---|---|---|
| community | 33% | 13% | 38% | 23% | – | – | – | – | – | 18% | 36% | 24% |
| crime prevention | 17% | 45% | 38% | 47% | 14% | 19% | – | 22% | – | 19% | 30% | 57% |
| disabled access | 11% | 49% | 25% | 40% | 7% | 48% | – | 11% | – | 20% | 18% | 55% |
| facilities and amenities | 22% | 42% | 19% | 30% | – | 19% | – | 33% | – | 32% | 18% | 56% |
| play space | 11% | 32% | 31% | 47% | – | 37% | – | 11% | – | 46% | 21% | 54% |

*Functional issues*

| | | | | | | | | | | | |
|---|---|---|---|---|---|---|---|---|---|---|---|
| access | 22% | 57% | 81% | 55% | 64% | 37% | – | 11% | – | 78% | 73% | 76% |
| access – cycles | 11% | 22% | 63% | 30% | 43% | 22% | – | – | – | 35% | 49% | 40% |
| access – pedestrian | 11% | 32% | 81% | 55% | 64% | 26% | – | – | – | 64% | 64% | 60% |
| access – vehicular | 17% | 36% | 81% | 55% | 71% | 33% | – | 11% | – | 76% | 70% | 63% |
| daylight | 6% | 35% | 44% | 43% | – | 63% | – | – | – | 6% | 24% | 47% |
| emergency access | – | 6% | 44% | 10% | 36% | 22% | – | – | – | 12% | 33% | 15% |
| footpath design | – | 24% | 75% | 45% | 71% | 30% | – | 22% | – | 48% | 61% | 51% |
| garden size | – | 42% | 25% | 69% | – | 74% | – | 44% | – | 25% | 12% | 64% |
| house size mix | 11% | 24% | 19% | 15% | – | – | – | 22% | – | 18% | 15% | 31% |
| house type mix | 28% | 33% | 50% | 32% | 7% | 4% | – | 44% | – | 47% | 36% | 51% |
| lighting (external) | 6% | 21% | 44% | 34% | 57% | 4% | – | – | – | 16% | 46% | 33% |
| overlooking | – | 38% | 38% | 52% | 7% | 56% | – | – | – | 25% | 21% | 56% |
| parking design | – | 10% | 63% | 27% | 21% | 19% | – | 33% | – | 10% | 39% | 22% |
| parking provision | 28% | 62% | 63% | 65% | 71% | 70% | – | 33% | – | 60% | 64% | 79% |
| privacy | – | 60% | 56% | 70% | 7% | 63% | – | 44% | – | 34% | 27% | 74% |
| residential amenity | 33% | 67% | 31% | 43% | 7% | 44% | – | 56% | – | 32% | 36% | 74% |
| road design | – | 31% | 88% | 48% | 100 | 22% | – | 22% | – | 59% | 79% | 59% |
| road safety | 17% | 33% | 88% | 42% | 100 | 11% | – | – | – | 20% | 76% | 38% |
| servicing | 44% | 34% | 81% | 29% | 86% | 30% | – | 22% | – | 46% | 82% | 51% |
| shared road surfaces | – | 3% | 75% | 20% | 57% | 15% | – | 11% | – | 15% | 58% | 18% |
| space around dwellings | – | 42% | 50% | 76% | – | 74% | – | 56% | – | 26% | 24% | 66% |
| sunlight | 1% | 29% | 38% | 40% | – | 56% | – | – | – | 10% | 18% | 45% |
| traffic calming | – | 14 | 44% | 20% | 29% | 15% | – | 11% | – | 12% | 33% | 24% |

*Sustainable issues*

| | | | | | | | | | | | |
|---|---|---|---|---|---|---|---|---|---|---|---|
| density | 56% | 63% | 56% | 50% | – | 33% | – | 44% | – | 62% | 49% | 77% |
| orientation/aspect | 11% | 26% | 38% | – | – | 22% | – | 11% | – | 26% | 24% | 44% |
| trees | 17% | 39% | 63% | 51% | 29% | 37% | – | 67% | – | 40% | 49% | 58% |
| wildlife habitats | 22% | 22% | 25% | 20% | 7% | 4% | – | – | – | 14% | 27% | 32% |

*Design and planning process issues*

| | | | | | | | | | | | |
|---|---|---|---|---|---|---|---|---|---|---|---|
| briefs (authority will prepare) | – | 34% | 25% | 14% | 7% | – | – | – | – | 6% | 15% | 36% |
| comply with DB32 | – | 5% | 56% | 25% | 36% | 7% | – | 11% | – | 6% | 42% | 15% |
| housing design (seek quality) | 89% | 71% | 63% | 55% | – | 15% | – | 11% | – | 48% | 67% | 78% |
| innovation (encourage) | 6% | 18% | 25% | 30% | 14% | 19% | – | 11% | – | 15% | 21% | 31% |
| site survey/analysis | – | 9% | 56% | 33% | 7% | 11% | – | 44% | – | 16% | 30% | 26% |

*Note:*
C = County authorities, D/U = District and Unitary authorities.
Design considerations are included in the table only if covered in over 30% of county design guidance or district/ unitary design guidance overall. The 'guidance type' percentages are given as a percentage of authorities with guidance of that particular type that contain particular design issues. The 'overall coverage' percentages are calculated as a percentage of the total number of authorities analysed that covered particular design issues across the guidance types.

standards, appraisal and briefs, exhibit more comprehensive coverage of residential design concerns than structure plan policy, country design guides and standards put together. Of course many district authorities also benefit from both the county guidance and from their own residential design guidance at the lower tier.

To the overarching patterns a number of key findings could be observed:

- reflecting government guidance in PPG12 – that all key design considerations should be in the plan (DoE, 1992c, para. 7.11) – the number of residential design concerns dealt with in design policy was often as many as in the design guides, but coverage in the latter was in greater depth, and, in the case of design briefs, more site-specific;
- because of the recent efforts directed towards the production of district-wide local plans and UDPs, the resulting policy showed evidence of incorporating a wider design agenda including social and sustainable considerations, as well as the dominant visual and functional concerns;
- coverage in residential design policy, however, tended to be motherhood at best, requiring design guides to elucidate the concepts introduced in plan policies;
- design guides also tended to deal most comprehensively with design and planning process considerations;
- where found, design appraisals were dominated by contextual and visual considerations, often based on defined character areas derived from established residential vernacular, but rarely on established urban form;
- design standards were comprehensively used to prescribe functional considerations, and, at the county level, to prescribe spatial concerns as well (particularly road hierarchy). Such considerations used easily measurable criteria for control;
- design standards were frequently incorporated into design policy, guides and briefs, as well as in standards published separately;
- site-specific briefs were commonly used to reflect spatial and functional considerations, and often little else. Social considerations were particularly (and surprisingly) poorly represented in briefs;
- coverage at the county level is still dominated by the statutory highways function, a function tempered, but not decisively, at the district level by a greater concern for local context: visual, social, amenity and environmental.

Examination of the issues covered most frequently across residential design guidance (see Table 7.6) reveals a continuing lack of confidence to extend design considerations from standards-based functional/spatial and motherhood-based contextual/visual considerations, to encompass the wider design agenda: morphological, perceptual, social, sustainable, design process; or even deeper (and less measurable) visual concerns – townscape, 3D articulation, visual richness, and so forth.

The emphasis on design criteria seen as more measurable – and therefore less 'subjective' – stands out, as does the emphasis on criteria clearly specified in government guidance at the time of survey (with the exception of materials). The generality of at least some of these terms – layout, character, scale, access, density, etc. – has always enabled great scope for interpretation (see p. 67) and provided a springboard for the development of a more comprehensive design agenda by more prescriptive authorities. Contrary to intention, therefore, it may also have helped to sustain the persistent charge of subjectivity on residential design control practice.

appraisal, on the other hand, tended to be glossy productions, aimed at a wider audience, so requiring the involvement of greater resources in their presentation. The intention with these latter forms of guidance was to sell the key message that quality residential design can be secured, and that, in achieving it, response to context is a key concern.

The poor quality of presentation found in the development plans reflects their nature as policy documents rather than design guidance. Nevertheless, in a highly visual subject such as design, it wastes a potential opportunity (and medium) through which to drive home the key design policy messages. It also makes the plans less accessible to a wider audience, thus, potentially undermining consultation efforts. The poor showing of design policy may, however, have been unduly influenced by the high percentage of consultation and deposit versions of plans examined, for which – because of their transient nature – authorities may not have been willing to invest in high quality presentation.

### Other sources of residential design guidance

In addition to local authority produced residential design policy and guidance, authorities draw from a range of other sources of design guidance. The frequency of such cross-references gives some indication of what informs local authority design policy and guidance. The six most popular sources were three government PPGs: PPG1 (1992), PPG3 and PPG12. In addition, three key standards-based documents were prioritised: DB32; guidance on 'Site Layout Planning for Daylight and Sunlight' from the Building Research Establishment (BRE, 1991); and the National Playing Fields Association (1992) 'Six Acre Standard, Minimum Standards for Outdoor Playing Space'.

This short list of the six most frequent sources referenced in residential design policy and guidance reveals two patterns: a focus on sources that offer easily extractable standards rather than theoretical design principles, and a predictable reliance on sources either produced or explicitly endorsed by central government (see Table 2.2); this despite the plethora of design sources readily available elsewhere (Punter *et al.*, 1994a). Besides standards on daylighting, road layout and open space, readily available standards-based approaches on designing out crime, internal space provision and disabled access were also referenced. In a very small number of cases county design guidance from outside an authority's area was openly referenced, including the 'Essex Design Guide' in Southampton (Hampshire), Thamesdown (Wiltshire), and Wokingham (Berkshire), and the 'Cheshire Design Guide', also in Wokingham.

### Consultation and/or appraisal on residential design

Only 9% of authorities exhibited any focused consultation on residential design and 20% any appraisal of existing residential design or residential areas. Although these figures do not include statutory consultation on plan policy generally (which might elicit comments on residential design) or the implicit appraisal necessary to produce even the most basic design briefs or design guidance, it is nevertheless surprising that the figures for explicit consultation and appraisal were so low. The figures may (and most likely do) hide much consultation and appraisal, which was simply not recorded in the resulting guidance. Thus, the desired product rather than the process leading to that product tends to be stressed. In light of advice in PPG1 that such consultation and appraisal can add extra weight to policy or guidance (DoE, 1997b, paras. A1 and A3), the failure to reference explicitly such efforts represents very poor practice. The failure to include the results of such efforts in, for example, design briefs also indicates a waste of a potentially important design resource.

The percentages in Table 7.8 relate only to the 9% of authorities that exhibited any form of consultation on residential design. Hence, explicit evidence of consultation in the preparation of any of the four forms of guidance was not widespread. Most frequently, design briefs were used as the basis for consultation on proposed residential developments, even though the results of those exercises were not always made clear in the briefs. Consultation on residential design policy was the next most frequent form of residential design consultation, usually as a discrete part of wider design based consultation. However, as consultation for general design policy preparation is rare (Punter and Carmona, 1997a, Ch. 6), that focusing specifically on residential design was inevitably even rarer. This situation persists despite the often substantial impact of private sector residential development on established residential areas in many authorities. Evidence for explicit consultation on the preparation of residential design guides and design appraisal was also extremely rare, a somewhat surprising finding given the legitimacy that such consultation can lend to guidance, as well as the need to engender support for such initiatives among local populations.

It may be that consultation is undertaken but not explicitly recorded in final guidance mechanisms. If this is the case, then the guidance contained in revised PPG1 that consultation statements should be included with guidance (if they are to benefit from the extra weight such efforts imbue), may finally lead to the more explicit recording of consultation on design when it occurs. Where found, residential design-specific consultation took two forms: first, market research as used in Rydale in the preparation of their design guides, or Halton through the use of a Gallup Poll to identify concerns for incorporation in policy; second, focused consultation with particular local groups and societies including with community groups in Ealing, village resident groups in East Staffordshire or with the disabled in Hammersmith and Fulham.

Appraisal on residential design was more common, but still rare, with approximately 7% of authorities publishing discrete design appraisals (see Table 7.2) and 13% offering some form of explicit appraisal on residential design/areas in other policy/guidance mechanisms – briefs, design guides and local plans/UDPs being the most common – in that order (see Table 7.9). Most design briefs contained at least some implicit appraisal of the site, but few contained explicit appraisal of the type useful to potential designers. Design guides also benefited from some implicit appraisal of character; even if based solely on planning officers' 'patch knowledge', rather than on systematic appraisal. Again, however, explicit appraisal was rarer with guides moving straight into prescription and bypassing (or at least failing to record) any analysis. Confirming earlier research (Punter and Carmona, 1997a, Ch. 6), explicit appraisal in local plans/UDPs was rare, particularly when appended design guidance and briefs are stripped out, with residential-specific appraisal even rarer.

*Table 7.8 Evidence of consultation on residential design*

| Use of consultation | Frequency |
| --- | --- |
| In the preparation of design briefs | 39% |
| In the preparation of design policy | 32% |
| In the preparation of design guides | 14% |
| In the preparation of appraisal | 8% |
| In the preparation of design standards | – |

*Note:*
Percentages relate to the frequency of the different types of consultation exhibited by the proportion (9%) of authorities with some explicit consultation on residential design policy/guidance.

*Table 7.9  Evidence of appraisal on residential design*

| Types of appraisal | Frequency |
|---|---|
| Established residential areas/character zones (in policy or guidance) | 31% |
| In the preparation of design briefs | 19% |
| In the preparation of design guides | 15% |
| Town/village local plan insets | 14% |
| Landscape character | 4% |
| In the preparation of design policy | 4% |
| Settlement appraisals | 4% |
| Wildlife habitat survey | 4% |

*Note*:
Percentages relate to the frequency of the different types of appraisal exhibited by the proportion (20%) of authorities with some explicit appraisal of residential design/residential areas.

Where found, appraisals took two forms: first, site-specific analysis of the type most often found in design briefs, good examples of which include briefs prepared by Peterborough or Sheffield. Such site-specific analysis was also occasionally found in other forms of guidance, most notably in the framework for an expanded settlement at Monkerton in Exeter or for an expanded and a new settlement in the East Purbeck Local Plan. Second, area appraisal, most often found as established residential area character analysis such as Guildford's 'Residential Areas Appendix' to their Local Plan, Wycombe's 'Residential Character Zone Study', Richmond Upon Thames' 'Environmental Character' analysis (see Fig. 7.3) or Kingston's 'Residential Environment and Amenity Study' (the latter two examples from London representing particularly comprehensive examples of the genre). Less common, and with a tendency towards description rather than analysis, are the town/village insets attached to local plans. The purpose of these was usually to provide a contextual framework for the integration of new housing allocations, such as in the East Lindsey or Forest of Dean local plans, where additional volumes of each plan contain numerous settlement insets – in the former for 94 insets and in the latter for 108 insets. Rarer still were the whole settlement appraisals found in a very small number of local plans including Purbeck's visual appraisals for its key settlements, or more comprehensive village appraisals, such as those prepared by North Kesteven.

### Indicative design proposals in residential policy or guidance

Evidence of any indicative design proposals were found in only 11% of the authorities examined, a low figure given the prevalence of design briefs in approaching 50% of authorities. The figure underlines the unwillingness of authorities to prescribe spatial solutions for sites even at the most basic level. Thus, besides site plans, sometimes basic appraisals, and indications of possible access positions, many design briefs fail to give any indication of desired design solutions.

Even where found, indicative solutions in design briefs tended to be in the form of very basic solutions to layout. Usually, such spatial solutions were restricted to access issues only in the form of proposed road and footpath layouts (based on county road hierarchies and adopted road standards). In a minority of cases, indicative open space and structure landscaping layouts were also included. Only rarely do briefs go beyond such broad based capital web concerns to encompass more detailed urban design considerations, examples being the coverage of townscape requirements and desired courtyard development forms

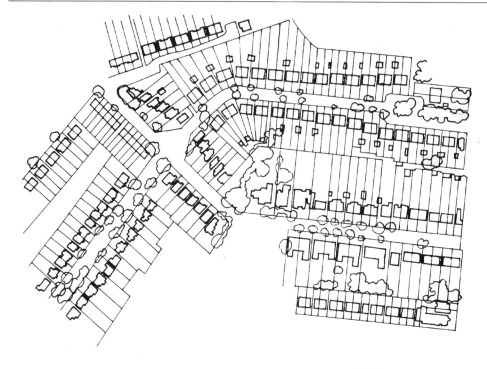

PLAN 1:2500

SECTION 1:2500

Space between buildings: ± 25-30m    Front gardens: 5-10m    Back gardens: up to 35m, most around 20m

- Streets of mixed age, design and style. 2,3,4 storey houses, terraced and semi-detached and some detached.
- Represent speculative estate building around old centres dating from 2nd half of 19th century to inter-war.
- Short streets of similar style.
- Enclosed views.
- Variety.
- Good vegetation/street trees.

PROBLEMS

- Redevelopment of some sites detracts from environment, if new building insensitive to surroundings.
- Demand for extensions - these can reduce quality of environment.
- Lack of garages leads to heavy on-street parking or forecourt parking.

EXAMPLES

- East and North Sheen: Sheen Common Drive, inter-war.
- East Twickenham: Park Road, Heathcote Road: Victorian and Edwardian.
- Barnes: Nassau Road: Victorian and Edwardian.
- Teddington: Park Road, Clarence Road: Victorian.

| AREA ANALYSIS | CATEGORIES OF RESIDENTIAL ENVIRONMENT<br>Small streets, uniform and or mixed designs, 2 storey, detached, semi-detached, terrace | Figure 9(3a) |

*Fig. 7.3  Area character analysis in Richmond (London Borough of Richmond Upon Thames, 1981).*

- a much lower emphasis on residential design at the county level (in every region), reflecting highways responsibilities rather than a wider design remit, but also a supplementary role to that at the lower tier;
- approximately 10% of authorities (of both types) exhibiting a very high emphasis on residential design;
- a low emphasis on sustainable design with approximately 80% of authorities (of both types) exhibiting either a low or very low emphasis on sustainable design, but with a small and increasing minority (4%) developing sustainable design policy/guidance mechanisms;
- that the majority (60%) of district/unitary authorities exhibited a high – although not total – consistency with government advice;
- that authorities have desired a greater control of residential design than government guidance – until 1997 – has sanctioned, with nearly a quarter of authorities clearly exceeding government advice;
- a north/south split in both county and district/unitary design emphasis, with authorities in the South giving a (marginally) higher emphasis to residential design than their Northern and Midlands counterparts;
- that more comprehensive residential design control practice at the county level would seem to influence beneficially practice at the district level, helping to ensure a more co-ordinated and rigorous response to residential design across authority types.

## Conclusions

If the objectives of the chapter are revisited, then the survey and content analysis suggests some overall conclusions. With 95% of authorities (county and district/unitary) boasting at least some form of residential design guidance (no matter how basic), the desire to influence the design of residential development remains strong among local authorities. Practice in the control of residential design, however, varies greatly between authorities, from reliance on individual policy or guidance mechanisms based on motherhood aspirations, implemented through rigid and unsophisticated standards, to the sophisticated use of the full range of design control mechanisms in hierarchy as a means to control all aspects of residential design.

Following the introduction of Section 54A to the 1990 Act, design policies in local plans/UDPs have clearly taken over from design guides as the primary mechanisms for setting out local authority aspirations on residential design, with the most sophisticated approaches allowing such policy to infuse through the plan and relate directly to other residential development policy. Other forms of guidance – particularly design guides and standards at the county level and design briefs at the district/unitary level – nevertheless, remain popular, so that well over 50% of authorities now benefit from the use of three or more forms of design guidance (strategic to site-specific) in combination, in an attempt to exert a more decisive influence on residential design.

In this process guidance produced at the county level continues to have a significant value, reducing the need for districts to produce their own design guides and standards, and – if comprehensive – encouraging an increased emphasis on design in district guidance as well. Unfortunately, although the traditional design guide is both alive and well, and benefiting from more innovative and specialist approaches being developed to meet the new challenges of sustainable urban design, under a third of residential design guides (outside the plan) can be considered full blown residential design guides, the reminder taking more partial or standards-based approaches to residential design. Nevertheless, the value of the traditional residential design guide seems unrivalled as an easily accessible mechanism for driving home the key message to a wide audience, that quality, contextually appropriate, residential design is required.

The full hierarchy of residential design guidance – county and district/unitary – continues to be produced, pushing towards 100% country-wide coverage of at least some form of preconceived residential design policy or guidance. The process also continues the updating of the significant percentage of design guides and standards that might be considered out-of-date, particularly at the county level. Together, the evidence illustrates a strong belief in the value of preconceived prescription as the basis for controlling residential design but tremendous variety in the chosen approaches used to prescribe that design.

Although country-wide coverage of residential design guidance was almost complete, and faith in the value of residential design guidance remained strong, the coverage of design considerations remained unsophisticated and locked into the standards-based, car dominated, functional tradition; tempered by motherhood contextual and visual aspirations and some concern for spatial design at the county level. Therefore, although signs of a developing design agenda were found, with some 10% of authorities exhibiting comprehensive coverage of much of the wider design agenda, the majority of authorities offered little morphological, perceptual, social, sustainable or process-oriented residential design advice and unsophisticated guidance across the board.

The low emphasis on theoretical principles to ensure that a comprehensive design agenda is addressed was compounded by the low priority given to both appraisal and consultation in the preparation of residential design guidance. Thus, few explicit design appraisals are published and explicit evidence for consultation or appraisal as the basis for other forms of guidance is rare, and where found remains unsophisticated, particularly in design briefs. Together with the seeming inability of authorities to suggest even broad indicative design solutions in design briefs, the low levels of confidence (and most probably competence) within local authorities to deal with residential design is clearly apparent.

Individually, different guidance mechanisms varied in the level of prescriptive advice offered, with the county guides out in front – offering the most comprehensive guidance on residential design – followed by the district/unitary guides, by local plan/UDP policy, by design briefs (with their more limited focus on matters affecting individual sites), and by design standards bringing up the rear. Much county guidance still remained locked into the standards-based highways function however, and when examined in hierarchical combination, coverage of residential design considerations at the district/unitary level clearly outstrip their county counterparts. At the district level motherhood design policies benefited from the more detailed development of concepts in the district design guides, in design briefs and standards and, where available, in design appraisals. Unfortunately, design guides at this level still articulate the standards-based space around dwellings approaches so heavily criticised in the past.

Unfortunately, only a small minority of authorities (approximately 10%) exhibit truly sophisticated design advice, and a smaller number (4%) any real attempt to promote sustainable solutions to residential development. The majority (particularly in the North and Midlands) remain tied to easily measurable design criteria, to rule-of-thumb guidance and sources of guidance, to car dominated policy and guidance (and therefore environments) and to criteria clearly specified in government design advice. Nevertheless, practice remains diverse, with many authorities taking advantage of the generality of government design advice to move at least some way beyond the strict limits of that agenda.

## INSET G: MANCHESTER CITY COUNCIL – HULME, THE 'DESIGN CODE' APPROACH[1]

As the regional capital, Manchester remains a dominant force in the economy of the North West, but like many other post-industrial cities has suffered a decline in fortunes brought about by a shift in its traditional industrial base. Until the early 1990s, the priority given to regeneration at all costs resulted in the marginalisation of design issues. This approach has been made explicit in various drafts of the unitary development plan which largely ignore design concerns beyond matters of conservation. The only policy aimed specifically to control the design of residential development in the 1992 deposit version of the plan, for example, offered little guidance to developers and just one criterion – avoidance of incidental open space – against which to review residential design (Manchester City Council, 1992a).

Nevertheless, in partnership with the private sector, the city has been instrumental in the success of an innovative 'design code', drawing from best practice in the US and Europe and developed to guide the regeneration of the notorious 1960s deck access flats in Hulme (one mile from Manchester city centre). The regeneration partners (Manchester City Council and local regeneration company – Hulme Regeneration Ltd) were determined not to make the same mistakes as earlier regeneration efforts, deciding instead to involve the communities in a round of participative meetings to gauge resident opinion (Hulme Regeneration Ltd, 1992, p. 1). The results showed a determination to acknowledge the largely gone (but not forgotten) history and social identity of the area prior to the 1960s redevelopment (Middleton, 1995, p. 7).

With these principles underpinning the design code (Hulme Regeneration Ltd/ Manchester City Council, 1994), the document aimed to:

- redevelop Hulme in an incremental, organic fashion, as a distinct residential quarter, physically and socially integrated once more into Manchester;
- encourage development which is both human in scale and urban in nature;
- encourage a diverse range of economic and social activities and uses within the area;
- nurture a quality public realm; and
- create a clear urban framework that produces streets, squares and buildings of variety and quality at a density that can sustain the local economy, be robust enough to last, but still be able to accommodate change over time.

The objective was once again to create Hulme as a network of self-policing streets, incorporating clearly defined public and private realms and giving the sense of a neighbourhood through which people can travel. The authors believed that most successful urban areas have a character, established through their own underlying code, which defines both the area in its parts and the relationship of those parts to the whole. Such codes, they argued, develop naturally over time, rather than as the result of high-speed clearance and comprehensive redevelopment. To create artificially a code in Hulme, a 'Development Strategy' prioritised a set of design guidelines to sit alongside a development masterplan (see Fig. G.1).

The first draft of the 'Urban Code for Hulme' was adopted by Manchester City Council in 1992 before the launch of the partnership. A second and slimmed down version was

---

[1] The Manchester case study is distinctly different from the other case studies because the context is urban rather than suburban or rural, because the tenure mix of the Hulme redevelopment includes substantial public housing, as well as private, and because the local authority acted as part of a public/private partnership company set up specifically to implement City Challenge. In addition, the emphasis on mixed use (although mixed use dominated by residential development) further distinguishes the case study.

*(1) Streets*
Buildings of all types should front onto streets, squares or parks.
Streets should be designed to encourage walking and cater for the needs of people with mobility problems.
There should be eyes on the street.
Doors onto streets should be at no more than 15 m intervals.
Ground floors of residential properties can be elevated 450 mm above pavement level.

*(2) Integration*
Housing must not be conceived and designed as estates.
All uses must be accommodated within an integrated pattern of streets.
Streets should contain a varierty of uses.
Space should be left to accommodate uses not currently viable.

*(3) Density*
Housing should be built to an average density of 90 units per hectare.
Developments should be concentrated along main routes and around focal points.

*(4) Permeability*
All streets should terminate in other streets.
Streets should encourage through movement.
There should be a variety of routes that people can choose when travelling through the area.
The grain of streets should become finer around nodes of activity.

*(5) Routes and transport*
Public transport should be planned as an integral part of the street layout.
Street design should reduce vehicle speed rather than ease traffic flow.
On-street parking is encouraged.
The impact of the car should be minimized.
The abuse of on-street parking must be avoided.
In-curtilage parking should be avoided in front of houses.
Traditional crossroads are encouraged.
Safe routes for cyclists will be provided.

*(6) Landmarks, vistas and focal points*
Development should be planned to optimize existing vistas and create new ones.
Corner buildings should consolidate the urban composition.
Street junctions should be designed as spaces rather than formless traffic interchanges.
Civic and community buildings will be located around public spaces.
Existing landmarks must be incorporated into Hulme's urban structures.
There will be no restriction on the height of buildings with footprints of less than 100 m.
Public art and street furniture should give character and life to urban spaces.

*(7) Definition of space*
A clearly defined building line should create a disciplined and largely unbroken urban edge.
Buildings which are set back a significant distance from a street should have sufficient presence to contribute to the street.
There should be clear definition between public and private space.
Streets, squares and parks should be defined by appropriately scaled buildings and good quality trees.
Street elevations should be scaled to the proportions of the street.

*(8) Identity*
Existing buildings should be enhanced and emphasized to avoid seeming all of the same age.
Large buildings should not overshadow or distort the scale of different streets.
Building design should respond to location.
The use of different materials and finishes is encouraged.
Diversity of design solutions is encouraged.

*(9) Sustainability*
Non-housing development should be designed with sufficient flexibility to enable change of use without major refurbishment works.
New buildings should be designed for ease of maintenance and with a view to refurbishment in 50–60 years' time.
New developments should cater for the retention of as much of the existing tree stock as is possible and streets and squares should incorporate street trees wherever appropriate.
Care should be taken to consider the maintenance burden of public open space.
High-quality landscaping is encouraged and urban nature conservation measures should be considered where possible.
All developments should have sufficient refuse storage space for segregated waste collection.
All new housing should attain 'good' on the BREEAM scale.
New homes should achieve the highest possible National Home Energy Rating: no less than 8.

*(10) Hierarchy*
Existing primary network.
High streets, secondary streets, residential streets.
Private areas are encouraged to create security within the blocks.

*Fig. G.1 Summary of Hulme development guidelines (Symes and Pauwels, 1999).*

University of Nottingham in 1996 and 1997. At these conferences, presentations were given by the key officers responsible for the particular innovative approach in nine of the ten case study authorities, each following a loose predetermined structure. Conference transcripts and subsequent informal interviews with the key officers helped to explore practice further.

2. *Direct practitioner input* – structured practitioner papers were subsequently commissioned from some of the innovative practice authorities as a further feed into the innovative case study work. These papers were disseminated in April 1997 as a special topic issue of 'Urban Design Quarterly' (Carmona, 1997b). During 1998 the case studies were written up in detail, and in 1999 were commented on and updated by each of the contributing officers.

3. *Wider practitioner discussion* – discussion of the innovative practice at the two arranged conferences and seven further (academic/CPD) conferences at which one or more of the innovative practice case studies were presented between 1997 and 1999. These events offered opportunity to gauge wider practitioner (and academic) reaction and feedback in both a formal and informal manner from audiences ranging across user groups. Conferences in the North and Midlands were deliberately targeted in order to give the research a better balance, reflecting practitioner views from around the country.

To draw conclusions from the collective experience and, where appropriate, to facilitate comparison, each case study was written following a predetermined structure:

- the unique and innovative characteristics of the approach;
- the approach taken to addressing context;
- how the practice relates to and is informed by other forms of guidance – the design guidance hierarchy;
- how the practice relates to and is informed by government guidance;
- reflections on implementation and effectiveness;
- resource implications of the approach;
- any external feedback received;
- an overview of the case study.

Space does not permit the full exposition of each case study, although the summaries as Insets at the end of each chapter are presented in comparative form as Table 8.2. A brief introduction to the individual studies follows however, before a comparative analysis of the case studies is made, overarching lessons from the innovative practice are drawn, and reflections presented from the wider practitioner study.

## The innovative case study authorities

### The county guides

The continuing existence of residential design guidance at the county tier represents something of an historical accident in England, a hangover from the pre-1974 planning system when county authorities also had responsibility for detailed development control. Nevertheless, counties have remained as strategic planning and highways authorities, and with so much of the residential environment determined by the delivery of an acceptable road layout, many highways authorities have considered it necessary to issue road hierarchy standards for residential road and footpath design. Such standards and the more elaborate design guides they gave rise to have often been the only guidance on residential design

*Table 8.2  Case study comparative evaluation*

|  | Essex | Suffolk | Cotswold | N. Norfolk |
|---|---|---|---|---|
| **Innovative characteristics** | updated county guide comprehensively adopts new urban design theory – responsive criteria, sustainability, mixed use – and abandons road hierarchies for 20 mph zones | new county guide adopts simple design conceptualisation advocated by HBF/ RIBA prioritising urban design over architectural design; joint county/districts initiative | use of a Cotswold Design Code to articulate local distinctiveness, very concisely, seven commandments; incorporated into policy to give extra weight | detailed design guide adopted as part of the local plan, as a means to interpret local distinctiveness and aid negotiation; used day-to-day in DC and widely accepted externally |
| **Addressing context** | lays down very detailed principles and processes in the guide to ensure contextually appropriate urban/architectural design, starting with site appraisal | attempts to encourage site-specific rather than county-specific approaches to context; but less prescriptive, i.e. flexible approach to style adopted | emphasis largely visual rather than social or functional, with heavy emphasis on materials and colours; main emphasis to control architecture rather than urban design | strong desire to respond to local inheritance by promoting the local vernacular; without discounting contemporary design; very architectural guide |
| **Guidance hierarchy** | efforts made to bring new county guide into line with local plans, but design standards more difficult to co-ordinate; in time plans likely to adopt much of the guide | county guide has been adopted by all district authorities and used by the highways authority for DC; guide to be referred to in all the local plans to boost its status | local plan organised into nine volumes (one general and eight sub-areas); attempt to incorporate policy/guidance/ standards as a one-stop-shop in the plan, but may have to move to SDG | design guide based on extensive development control experience and incorporated into the local plan to give extra weight; briefs used occasionally alongside guide |
| **Government guidance** | guide review coincided with reevaluation of gov't guidance so authorities are confident of the guide's compliance; guide received well by DoE | on publication the flexible approach was deliberately tailored to reflect gov't guidance; the approach drew heavily on gov't guidance to legitimise the guide | intention to persuade the DoE that the Cotswolds required special treatment – unsuccessful; used SoS speech and RIBA/RTPI joint statement to legitimise approach | recognised that the philosophy of promoting local vernacular was in sharp contrast to gov't guidance at time of writing; believed analysis added weight |
| **Implementation effectiveness** | revised guide based on an evaluation of what worked and what did not since 1973; new guide will benefit from positive gov't guidance and united approach among districts | co-ordinated approach to resolution of all design aspects to encourage effective implementation; use in DC and recent appeals success testifies to its utility | the authority's willingness to invest in design matters is shown in a willingness to fight appeals on even detailed design; aim to use code in all contexts of district | investment in design skills and time for pre-application negotiation increases effectiveness; inclusion in plan greatly increases effectiveness as do better house sales |
| **Resources implications** | continuing division of responsibility for design between county and districts makes agreement difficult, e.g. on standards, as little consistency in design resources, i.e. skills | new guide seen as opportunity to finally deliver co-ordination between the highway and planning authorities in the county; guide based on the work of multi-disciplinary team | long time to get plan adopted (seven years so far) because so detailed but concern for design as part of plan necessitates no extra work, i.e. part of statutory plan preparation process | process of design control gradually developed over 23-year period; use of negotiation as key tool requires resources, aided by good appeals record and economic case |
| **External feedback** | technical consultation favoured over full public participation in the preparation of the guide; negative response from RIBA, HBF, but better from locally-based housebuilders | some concern from developers over emphasis on urban design (they favour a market approach); very positive feedback from both national and local amenity societies | support of local architects gained by use in writing code; support from amenity and residents groups but concern for lack of flexibility by HBF; Inspector demoted code to SDG | strong local support for guide from local design and property interests as well as from the public; support also from local housebuilders; DoE support for inclusion in policy |
| **Overview** | although the core approach remains the same the guide incorporates the full range of theoretical advances since 1973 and learns from DC practice; failure to evaluate resident opinion may yet be a problem | the guide raises the consciousness of all those involved in residential design by pursuing a corporate approach; in achieving this a clear logical framework is adopted for design alongside a highly accessible format | the code promotes a very architectural approach to design based on a thorough understanding of the local vernacular which is nevertheless flexible encouraging innovation; the saga of policy v. SDG is still to be resolved | negotiation, prescription and investment in design skills sum up an effective approach based on day-to-day communication; the architectural approach is to be updated with urban design theory |

| Dacorum | Harrow | Manchester | Wycombe | W. Dorset | Sedgemoor |
|---|---|---|---|---|---|
| residential character/ design area approach taken, with systematic appraisal of residential areas used as a means to develop policy options for individual contexts | consultant analysis of borough's residential character to be used as a basis for revising local plan policies and as a means to strengthen design appeals performance | design code used to structure urban regeneration of large brownfield site; code underpinned by urban design theoretical structure aimed to reimpose traditional streets | development briefing process designed to break circle of confrontation in development process and establish design requirements before land purchase; policy defines process | design guides firmly rejected in favour of negotiation and site-specific footprints (masterplans) accompanied by site-specific design codes aimed at designing sympathetic layouts | negotiation and collaboration used as the basis to devise a design framework for residential expansion; public/private, multi-disciplinary team guided the work |
| approach based on exhaustive analysis of context at a very local level; detailed methodology devised to ensure consistency in analysis; resulting policy relates to small design areas | detailed appraisal and consultation undertaken to understand suburban character; borough divided into four environmental characterisations; landscape = the key | little context to respond to at the micro-scale, but attempt to replicate natural incremental growth patterns through the Code; flexible principles only promoted | methodology for brief preparation clearly defined including detailed appraisal of context as a means to ensure responsive design in both physical and community terms | footprint and design code intended to be three-dimensional site-specific design guide to ensure close contextual fit and avoid 'suburban' solutions; community facilities included | quality thresholds used to define response to context, with optimum threshold drawing from contextual analysis of surrounding areas to inform design |
| criteria-based policies provide first line of defence with environmental guidelines/standards as a separate volume of the plan; intend to adopt design area policy in next plan | analysis published as Report of Survey but not as SDG; used as a feed into DC and as a feed in to revised broad-brush design policies in UDP; supplement more detailed policy | design code used as basis for negotiation in Hulme, but resulting proposals go to Manchester DC; its success inspired design code for Manchester to supplement UDP | design briefing aims to interpret extensive local plan design policy for individual sites and given legitimacy through policy; methodology included as an appendix to the plan | general mistrust of design guides extends also to design policy, so little guidance beyond negotiated footprints used; very detailed footprints/design codes fill the gap | negotiation process used as a means to define a design brief for area, within which applications will be made; intention to produce better design policy and SDG in future |
| weak gov't guidance was the main spur to act and produce RACS; gained legitimacy from PPG3, PPG12 concern for established residential character | PPG12 concern for established residential character provided spur in otherwise hostile environment; but appraisal considered the key to legitimise control | writers did not feel directly confined by gov't guidance because outside strict remit of conventional planning; instead Quality in Town and Country drew from Hulme approach | briefing policy survived local plan inquiry intact on basis that site-specific guidance is thought helpful in PPG3; so making approach explicit in the plan is useful | weak gov't guidance gave spur for development of approach; in new context approach advocated as means to bridge private and public interests by negotiation | negative gov't advice has left district without any SDG or local plan policy, particularly PPG3; Town and Country inspired the re-evaluation |
| useful as DC resource and as justification in appeals but requires post-consultation adoption; aim to adopt as SDG to increase weight and later as policy | with the appraisal informing policy more effective control of design has been possible although design at a macro rather than micro-scale, i.e. open space not layout | effectiveness facilitated by public ownership of land and little context at a micro-scale, but also by flexibility and negotiation on site-by-site basis; new local climate for design | experience has shown that having the policy and process in the plan increases the status of briefs; design quality has improved in the district and developer certainty | great investment in skills by authority from preparing masterplans to advising on details and watching over implementation; used as positive tools for effective negotiation | the process has resulted in quality development on paper, although implementation will be the judge; success has depended on collaborative, team approach |
| the survey required considerable resources for the systematic survey of three towns; but no planned investment in skilled design staff to implement the results | a one-off investment in the survey has not been repeated despite its utility; lack of design skills within authority prevent improvements in the quality of individual residential dev'pts | £37.5 million of regeneration funds have underpinned the drive for good design; however design as a means for regeneration of the wider city is now accepted | developer-led design briefing has meant more rather than less staff time, but failure to invest in design skills has reduced effectiveness; briefs encourage more public objections | footprints and their implementation require extensive investment in staff skills and resources; but their economic benefits inspire better practice from all housebuilders | £40,000 required for the approach, with private and DoE contributions to employ multi-disciplinary team; greater cost than normative approach but clear benefits |
| criticism from outside the borough focuses on resource implications of survey and locally on the unwieldy nature of RACS; strong resident support for the approach | strong resident support for restraint policies and for maintaining a green environment; HBF concerned policy will reduce densities; standards removed from plan for inquiry | cross-professional input to code design sought, drawing from US practice; strong support gauged from local residents and from designers and housebuilders – increased certainty | approach developed in partnership with housebuilders; some local developers objected about delay and lack of flexibility but no DoE objection and plan inspector supported approach | strong support for the approach and its outcomes from local residents and housebuilders, reducing NIMBY reaction and increasing commercial returns | involvement from the start with landowners and housebuilders has maintained commercial realism; public consultation has resulted in strong public and amenity support as well |
| RACS represents a comprehensive approach to evaluate and safeguard the character of the borough's residential areas; the approach is time and labour intensive and largely visual in its scope, but shows promise | illustrates graphically the value of appraisal as a basis of design policy and the key importance of open space, landscape, and landscaping, but equally graphically the failure to invest in design skills | underpinned by public participation and a sophisticated urban design structure the flexible code is used as a basis for negotiation and promotion and to offer certainty; aims to replicate 'natural' development process | the approach offers the potential to secure better design, but paid for out of land values not developer profit margins; hence a potential for positive planning and conflict avoidance, but lack of LA design skills | turns the planning process on its head by LA forwarding pre-emptive design proposals; rejects district-wide approach to design in favour of site-specific intervention, but high resource costs | by harnessing collaboration and pre-empting the development process a consensus on quality was secured; in a context of tight margins the new framework offers potential to deliver that quality |

*Key*:

DC – Development Control, Gov't – Government, LA – Local Authority, RACS – Residential Areas Character Study, SDG – Supplementary Design Guidance, SoS – Secretary of State, UDP – Unitary Development Plan.

available in many areas. Their status has varied, but has never moved beyond the status of a 'material consideration'; in other words guidance rather than policy.

The research examined two county guides, the first – the 'Essex Design Guide' – (see Inset A) with a considerable (25-year) pedigree, re-written in the 1990s from the 1973 original (Essex Planning Officers' Association, 1997). The Essex Design guide was the first of its kind, and remains by far the most comprehensive, constituting, in effect, a detailed step-by-step guide to residential design in the county. 'At first welcomed, and then attacked by the architectural profession and the housebuilding industry, the Guide and its like have been the subject of intense *[negative]* lobbying of the government by these two interest groups' (Stones, 1992, p. 17). It continues to be controversial to the present day (Tollit and Tollit, 1998). Without the benefit of twenty-five years of design guide experience, the starting point for the second case study – the 'Suffolk Design Guide' (Suffolk Planning Officers' Group, 1993) was to seek some common understanding of what needed to be done between the planning authorities and the housebuilders (see Inset B). The hierarchy of design importance (layout before architecture) advocated by the HBF and RIBA (1990) seemed to offer a potential way forward (see p. 133). So, although detailed in its full extent, at the core of the Suffolk guide a simple logic was adopted.

### District-wide guidance

With all districts compelled to produce district-wide local plans at the district-wide scale, the local plan has now become the primary source of design policy and guidance (see p. 31). Therefore, although some district/unitary authorities prepare and actively utilise other forms of supplementary design guidance (local design guides, area appraisal and design briefs), almost all produce at least some form of policy statement on design in their local plans (see Table 7.2). Other forms of design guidance are rarer, with many district authorities seemingly preferring to leave general residential design guidance to the county-wide scale. Nevertheless, the district-wide residential design guide also remains, it seems, an important feature of such control, with practice ranging from standards-based space around dwellings criteria, to the full residential design and layout agenda in the 'Essex' mould. Although all the district/unitary authorities examined made (to a greater or lesser extent) explicit use of the local plan/UDP to control residential design, the case studies specifically examined one district making innovative use of the local plan to articulate and adapt their local design code – subsequently removed from the plan – (Cotswold – Inset C) and one, making use of a well-established local design guide – subsequently adopted as part of the plan (North Norfolk – Inset D).

Following the lead given by HRH the Prince of Wales (1989), Cotswold District resolved to structure their guidance on the 'Cotswold style' in the form of ten commandments – or a 'Cotswold Design Code'. The challenge for the policy writers was to relate the theoretical design principles to the local distinctiveness of the Cotswolds and to wording appropriate for the local plan and day-to-day development control. So, in 1993, the authority decided to write the code into policy, giving statutory force to what was previously just guidance, only to remove it from the 1999 adopted version of the plan following government Regional Office objections. In 2000, the code was finally published as a free-standing local design guide (Cotswold District Council, 2000). Similarly, to avoid making arbitrary judgements on the basis of personal taste, North Norfolk has favoured an approach that prioritises the appropriateness of buildings to their local context. Thus, the North Norfolk Design Guide is designed to be interpretative, indicating why the local vernacular takes the form it does, and how it has developed over the years. By this means, the guide forms the keystone of a system

the use of the site-specific approaches and explicitly outlined in the county guides. Other 'design process' concerns were not, however, widely prescribed.

Although the majority of the innovative approaches offered extensive guidance on their local vernacular traditions, contemporary solutions to residential design were also actively supported. A number of the authorities supported either/or approaches to architectural style, either local vernacular or contemporary design, but not housebuilder 'standard issue'. In the county guides and site-specific approaches, residential layout was identified as the key criterion for control, if roads were to be prevented from dominating developments and thus contextual fit achieved. Fundamental to achieving this seemed to be a recognition of the value placed by residents on the 'green' qualities of their environment, on the open spaces, trees and landscaping, and on the need to respect local materials. Hence, landscape (hard and especially soft) and materials were also regarded as key criteria to be controlled if an appropriate contextual response was to be secured.

### Design guidance hierarchy

The range of approaches advocated by the innovative case study authorities clearly had in common a belief in policy and/or guidance as the basis of securing a preconceived, and more objective means to control residential design. Only the form and scale of operation of that guidance changed – county-wide to site-specific. Thus, although the analysis tended to focus on a key 'innovative' mechanism for control, most of the authorities examined utilised more than one simple approach to control, instead, offering a hierarchy of control and guidance mechanisms.

The local plan/UDP was considered the first line of defence in nearly all of the authorities examined, although a minority had a healthy scepticism of its application to local contexts. Nevertheless, it was noticeable that authorities wished to include, wherever possible, often detailed design guidance and standards for controlling residential design in the plan as a means to gain for it the weight conferred by Section 54A (see pp. 31–2). As a minimum, authorities ensured appropriate reference was made to supplementary guidance/appraisal in the plan, and conversely, that the guidance/appraisal made reference to the plan. In this, the relation between county guides and plan policy was considered crucial, with district authorities either incorporating the essential components of county guides direct into their own plans and/or adopting the county guides as their own supplementary design guidance with appropriate reference in their plans. Considered fundamental to underpin these efforts (and the initiatives of other innovative case study authorities), were good and co-operative relations between both levels of statutory authority – county and district.

Beyond the issue of status, the feeling was that supplementary forms of guidance had their primary and very important role in interpreting and elaborating the local plan/UDP for particular contexts, sites and forms of development, i.e. residential. Thus, a hierarchy of guidance types was thought both appropriate and necessary, although the emphasis placed on each would differ between authorities, with some regarding site-specific forms of guidance as the most contextually-specific, and therefore relevant, with others preferring to look to the wider picture.

In preparing the guidance, the role of development control as the mechanism for implementing the guidance was prioritised, with most authorities seeing guidance, whether in the local plan or in supplementary documents, as having its *raison d'être* in providing a basis for negotiation, rather than as a statement of required residential form. Equally, the role of development control experience in informing policy/guidance writing was prioritised by many practitioners.

### Interpreting government guidance

For the majority of the authorities, the weakness of government advice throughout the 1980s and the first half of the 1990s had been the spur to action to develop their particular innovative practice. For most, the aim had been to create more effective control over residential design, working outwardly within the limits prescribed by established government guidance but implicitly pushing it to its limits and even beyond.

Thus, a minority were fastidious about staying within the letter of a strict interpretation of government design advice, but moved clearly beyond its spirit by offering advice on all aspects of design, detailed to general, and merely changing the expression (although not necessarily the implementation) of that advice in their guidance, being more flexible where required. Others used government guidance to legitimise their approach but chose to quote selectively from paragraphs that supported their efforts while ignoring those that did not. All used the woolly nature of many of the design concepts legitimised in government advice as a means to stretch legitimate control. Appraisal was also seen widely as a means to circumvent a strict interpretation of government advice by proving a local need for detailed intervention in residential design such as the control of materials, even if (nationally) advice suggested otherwise.

The different interpretations of government advice seemed, in part, to have been exacerbated by the variety of interpretations given to that advice by the DoE itself, through its Regional Offices and local plan inquiry Inspectors. Thus, while some authorities have been able to incorporate extensive and detailed design guidance and standards in the plan, others have been expressly dissuaded from including similar (or even less detailed) guidance. The inconsistency has encouraged persistent attempts by authorities to include more detailed advice in plans, and blurred the distinction between plan policy and supplementary design guidance. In some of the authorities, such attempts had clearly delayed the adoption of their district-wide local plans.

For all the authorities the changes to government advice inspired by the 'Quality in Town and Country Initiative' (DoE, 1994c) have been welcomed as a means to legitimise the practice developed locally. For a minority it acted as a belated spur to develop their own innovative approach to controlling residential design.

### Implementation and effectiveness

Authorities wished to give their design initiatives as much weight as possible to enhance their effectiveness as control devices, as well as their complementary role as guidance. A range of experience marked authorities' response to implementation and effectiveness, although all recognised that the new, positive, government advice offered the greatest boost to the effective implementation of their design aspirations. Directly related to this was widespread agreement that the relationship between the plan and supplementary forms of guidance remained crucial. Thus, some authorities advocated the inclusion of supplementary guidance in the plan to increase its status, or, failing that, clearly referencing the guidance in plan policy as a material consideration – alongside its formal adoption as supplementary planning guidance. Similarly, referencing the intention to prepare design briefs and advising of their subsequent material status in the plan was also considered to increase their status. Equally, the status, legitimacy and effective implementation of design policy was considered to increase clearly if underpinned by systematic design appraisal, including consultation on design. Beyond its utility as a means to underpin policy, design appraisal was also generally considered a valuable resource for development control and for justifying local authority design reviews of proposed residential developments.

For all the case study authorities, previous experience of controlling residential design informed their approaches, with some drawing on many years of collective experience of what had worked and what had not. Fundamentally, all the authorities prioritised the value of preconceived prescription on design in policy and guidance (of whatever form) as the basis for effective decision making and negotiation, and particularly, as a means to offer housebuilders certainty in making economic judgements based on the knowledge of an authority's design aspirations.

At the same time, authorities also recognised that improving residential design quality was not without its cost for the public sector, not least in the need for direct local authority investment in officers with design skills and in allowing officers time to negotiate on design. For a minority, investment in such resources had enabled a more flexible approach to design, so eliciting the co-operation of developers and designers in establishing a better climate for good design within their district. The desire to encourage collaborative, multi-disciplinary team approaches as a means to improve design was a strong theme of a number of the innovative case studies, both from public to private sector and within the public sector, from authority to authority and department to department – particularly highways and planning authorities – and in the case of 20 mph certification between local authorities and central government.

The value of involving professionals from across the built environment disciplines in developing design control mechanisms in the first place was also recognised. Crucial to negotiated approaches was considered the need for negotiation to be based on positive policy or guidance and for authorities to be prepared to use the stick where necessary through a willingness to fight appeals on design. All authorities agreed that winning appeals was the best test of effectiveness in controlling design.

### Resource implications

The main barriers to the continued effective implementation of the innovative strategies put in place by the case study authorities were clear and related to the availability of resources, or to the lack of them. Thus the tendency to see design initiatives as one-off investments, not requiring the ongoing commitment of resources offered some cause for concern; a tendency mirroring practice in central government such as the short lived 'Time for Design' (DoE, 1990) or 'Quality in Town and Country' initiatives. More importantly, the continued failure of even the innovative case study authorities to invest in design skills made effective implementation over the long term difficult. The clear correlation between effective implementation and investment in appropriate design skills was obvious to officers, but the case for more resources from cash-strapped councils for an essentially discretionary function (control of design) was a difficult one to make.

Nevertheless, the key resource made available by the innovative case study authorities has been staff time, and all have secured (or expect to secure) considerable benefit in reduced environmental cost from the investment. Not all boasted permanent dedicated design staff in their authority, however, and a minority recognised that this continues to be the single biggest factor undermining the effectiveness of their attempts to improve residential design. In these authorities, the time, ability and confidence to negotiate on design is seriously compromised and hence their commitment undermined to achieving quality outcomes, to fighting appeals on design, or to further developing their particular design initiative. However, all of the innovative case studies recognised the value of enlisting dedicated advice on design and the negative impact of failing to do so.

Variation in practice was stark, even in these authorities concerned to improve residential design quality, from no dedicated design skills, to teams resourced to comment on every planning application. In part, the variation in practice between authorities had spurred the production of the county guides as a means to co-ordinate residential design control practice across district authorities through guidance at the strategic level. The most resource intensive approaches to raising residential design quality involved:

- extensive design appraisals;
- site-specific approaches to design;
- adopting detailed design advice in the local plan.

Of these, the first tended to require one-off large investments and the second smaller but ongoing resources. Both have been considered extremely desirable and effective means of improving the design of residential development. The third has been expensive because of the extra time and resources required to take detailed policy through the statutory adoption process. For these authorities, however, the bonus has come in the resources being viewed internally by councillors as part of the statutory plan-making process and not therefore as extra discretionary resources directed towards improving design. Other means of reducing the short-term resource burden of design have been the linkage of design to a wider regeneration strategy or by the gradual investment, over many years, in design guidance and review.

### External feedback

Feedback received by the authorities on the development and implementation of the innovative case study experiences largely reflects the well-established positions of the key stakeholders in the development process (see pp. 87–9). Thus, in broad terms, feedback from the HBF and local RIBA chapters has been mainly negative, with particular concerns expressed about the possible delays, potential to stifle initiative and dangers of over-prescription (in architectural and urban design). Conversely, feedback from local residents and amenity societies has been universally positive in nature, with particular support for restraint policies aimed at preserving the character of established residential areas.

At a very local level, however, when particular housebuilders and designers were targeted, reactions to the various initiatives seemed more positive. Local housebuilders, in particular, perceived that local design initiatives gave them a potential competitive advantage (or at least levelled the playing field) over the standardised products of their national and regional counterparts. For the same reason, individual local architects also tend to be more positive, particularly when directly involved in the preparation of design guidance through consultation or participation exercises. Feedback from central government, through the Regional Offices and development plan inspectors, has, at best, been extremely variable, however, with different authorities receiving conflicting advice on both the level of prescription appropriate in plans, and on the relationship between plans and other forms of design advice.

Most authorities were aware that to truly influence residential design the approaches advocated had to offer marketing dividends to the housebuilder as well as environmental dividends to the authority. Evidence from a number of the case studies that the two were compatible and achievable therefore represented a significant finding. Perhaps as a consequence, attempts to bring development groups along with the new agendas were often more tangible than those aimed at winning over public support. In part, such efforts were built on the knowledge that any resulting policy or guidance had to be economically advantageous (or at least economically benign) to the housebuilders if they were to succeed in the long term. In this context, the case study authorities confirmed the need to base policy and guidance preparation on an awareness of established design/development control practice. Thus, policy and guidance should reflect development control experience in policy as well as the realities of controlling residential design within the context of local housing markets. Nevertheless, based on the experience of the innovative case studies, authorities more widely might confidently pursue more locally distinctive residential developments in the knowledge that better design can command a premium for housebuilder and house buyer, in both price and time taken to sell. In some places, including Essex (Anon., 1975), this much has long been understood.

## Evaluation: the innovative case study authorities

The comparative evaluation of ten innovative case study authorities reveals a number of distinctive themes, some of which may indicate possible directions for future mainstream residential design control practice in the UK.

Regarding the outcomes of residential design control, in the form of priorities identified by the innovative case study authorities as contributing to the creation of quality residential environments, the following trends were revealed (some of which confirm research findings elsewhere – Cowan, 1997; DETR, 1998a; Thorne, 1998):

- an ongoing emphasis on local distinctiveness and an overarching desire to preserve distinctiveness where it exists and create it anew where it does not;
- related to this, an emphasis on preserving the character of established residential neighbourhoods;
- attempts to move beyond the theoretical limitations of the townscape movement (visual/contextual) to encompass the other urban design dimensions – spatial, morphological, social, perceptual, sustainable and process concerns;
- the value of mixed-use development as opposed to single-use residential development as a theme beginning to filter into guidance;
- still a strong desire not to abandon control of the visual dimension of urban design and control of architectural design in particular;
- recognition of the value placed by residents on the 'green' qualities of their residential environments – open space, trees, landscaping;
- attempts to move away from strictly hierarchical road layouts in favour of traditional street patterns, particularly the connected street grid;
- on a related theme, attempts to reduce the dominance of roads and the car, and to stress the vital importance of layout as a control mechanism.

Regarding the development of effective means to deliver these quality outcomes through residential design control, the following were revealed (some of which again confirm research findings elsewhere – BDOR, 1992; RICS, 1996; Punter and Carmona, 1997a; POS *et al.*, 1998):

- the value of preconceived policy and guidance as a means of controlling residential design;
- a recognition of the weight attached to local plan policy, and therefore a desire to incorporate as much relevant control criteria as possible in the plan;

- the value of supplementary forms of guidance in interpreting and elaborating the local plan, with appropriate reference to that relationship in each;
- the value of appraisal as a basis for developing and legitimising policy and guidance on residential design;
- related to this, the need to confirm new policy directions through public consultation, although not necessarily to set those directions in the first place;
- the need to learn from development control experience in writing residential design policy and guidance;
- the need to be aware of the economic implications of design interventions in the knowledge that locally distinctive residential developments potentially command a premium for housebuilder and buyer;
- that corporate approaches between departments and authorities (particularly between highways and planning) and multi-disciplinary approaches were particularly effective as means to set policy directions and build consensus on outcomes;
- the need (at the time) for 20 mph certification responsibilities to be streamlined;
- that all policy/guidance mechanisms have particular value as a means to structure negotiation on design;
- that site-specific approaches are particularly effective but also resource intensive to deliver;
- that such approaches offer the potential to pre-empt the development process by ensuring that better design quality is financed out of increased land values and not from housebuilder profit margins;
- that both 'comprehensive' and 'concise' models of guidance offer potential for effective control of housing design.

Regarding the main barriers to the continued effective implementation of the innovative strategies put in place by the case study authorities, the pattern was clear:

- the tendency to see design initiatives as one-off investments that do not require ongoing resources for their continued effective implementation;
- related to this, a clear correlation between effective implementation and investment in appropriate design skills. Despite the great potential demonstrated by many of the case study approaches, the continued low level of design skills in some of the case study authorities, made effective implementation difficult.

**Wider practitioner discussion**

The discussion of the individual case studies at a number of professional conferences offered an opportunity to gauge wider practitioner feedback on the range of innovative practice. Audiences included academics and professionals from across the range of user groups – planners (public and private), highways engineers, designers (architects, urban designers, landscape architects), and representatives from housebuilders/development companies, and amenity groups. Of these, however, by far the largest group (approx. 75%) were local authority planning officers (development controllers and policy writers, conservation/design officers).

Concerns, therefore, largely reflect the day-to-day experience of officers in the front-line controlling residential design and their frustrations about what many perceive to be a very difficult task in authorities devoid of specialist design skills and with little design policy or guidance tailored to address residential design. All the concerns listed (see Figs 8.1–8.7) were widely held by delegates across the various conferences but are deliberately generalised and do not address individual case studies directly.[2]

The groups of comments are structured under headings, adapted from those used to structure the analysis of individual case studies. Each is briefly discussed:

1. Design characteristics
2. Addressing context
3. Design guidance hierarchy
4. Government guidance
5. Implementation and effectiveness
6. Resource implications
7. Stakeholder input.

## Design characteristics

Discussion of desirable design characteristics (like much of the feedback) bordered on the negative, with comments focusing on the negative design consequences of current house building practice, but also implying an inherent resistance, on all sides, to innovation (see Fig. 8.1). In this respect, many of the innovative design characteristics advocated by the case study authorities, such as the value of the street grid or 20 mph zones, were completely new to wider practice. Thus, although accepted as offering important theoretical lessons, and even being desirable in practice, innovative approaches tended to be dismissed as impractical in the local planning context of most mainstream authorities. Instead, wider practice still relied heavily on control through functional and amenity standards, sometimes through visual concerns, but rarely, if ever, by examining the social context created by suburban residential development.

Other considerations such as mixing uses or designing for sustainability were also considered well beyond the core remit of general residential design control practice. This was still seen in terms of a battle between developers and authorities, with developers offering their most profitable market solutions to sites and aiming to maximise individual unit amenity – regardless of inherent design quality – while authorities attempt to 'improve' design with the blunt instruments of design standards, road adoption standards foremost amongst these. On one matter agreement was unanimous, that the design quality of private sector residential development was poor and needed to be improved. Too often, it seems, developments remained road and parking dominated, with poorly thought out open space provision and minimum levels of landscaping.

## Addressing context

With regard to context, the reactions were again largely negative in character, with comments suggesting that although context should provide the primary basis for residential design (urban and architectural), the reality remained that housebuilders tended to build the same product everywhere, irrespective of context (see Fig. 8.2). The impression was that

---

[2] The wider practitioner discussion was not intended to be an exhaustive discussion of practitioner experience, nor does it represent comprehensive coverage of the subject matter. It merely reflects the most frequent concerns raised at the conferences at which the innovative case study work was presented to a collective audience of some 500+. Some of the comments directly addressed the practice presented, whilst others represented reflections on the wider practice of the particular authorities and practitioners attending the conferences. Where comments contradicted each other both points of view have been given.

*Key comments*:
1. difficult to define 'quality development' or what makes 'a good place to live'
2. dealing with the car is the fundamental issue
3. a design concept is required before anyone draws roads
4. torturous routes around estates are common
5. cul-de-sacs have their place and customers value them
6. 20 mph zones are valuable, and make other design innovations possible
7. layouts are dominated by the requirements of car parking
8. car parking places rather than open spaces are provided by developers
9. standard house types undermine innovation in urban and architectural design
10. developers fight hard to avoid constructing terraced housing
11. authorities always have to fight to get landscaping in a development
12. open spaces are usually afterthoughts, tagged on to fill undevelopable space
13. open spaces are not strategically thought out to make them accessible
14. frequently residents want open spaces removed after completion
15. houses don't always overlook open space or streetspace
16. variety is undermined by housebuilders reluctance to build other uses
17. little commitment to mixed-use development from local authorities
18. sustainable considerations not considered by local authorities
19. sustainable considerations are difficult for authorities to integrate in suburban locations
20. no set of simple answers to securing sustainable development
21. integrated transport policy required to undermine car dominance
22. tendency to look at functional, amenity and visual concerns, social dimension ignored
23. social considerations need to be considered
24. too often the public's answer to security problems is – 'we want walls around the development'
25. the housebuilder's task is to maximise individual unity amenity, hence standardisation in layout and product is inevitable
26. terraced housing is becoming more popular (particularly town houses) for small and large units
27. industrial manufacturing processes might begin to inform housebuilding more and more in the future

*Fig. 8.1 Views on design characteristics.*

*Key comments*:
1. architectural and urban design should reinforce the characteristics of the area
2. 'suburban' housing is built anywhere – whether in rural, urban or suburban contexts
3. housebuilders build in isolation of context, often deliberately to differentiate and shelter a development from surrounding deprived areas
4. site planning tends to be introspective and unresponsive to context, often in response to resident objections and to reduce impact on surrounding established residential areas
5. little effort is made to utilise established site features
6. officers find it difficult to demand proof that designers have actually visited sites
7. the context of the authority determines response, with a greater emphasis on controlling suburban design in rural authorities (as opposed to urban or suburban)
8. the location of the authority determines response, greater emphasis on controlling suburban design in the South, less emphasis in the North
9. well formulated appraisal of context is the key to better residential design
10. there is nothing wrong with standardised house types, it just depends how good they are
11. the distinction between town and country is an artificial one as often the design problems are the same and the physical boundaries are not distinct

*Fig. 8.2 Views on addressing context.*

designers working for housebuilders rarely visited sites and that design appraisal (which was considered vital to ensure an appropriate response to context) was rarely undertaken. Hence, context, external to the site and even the internal characteristics of the site itself, tend to be ignored.

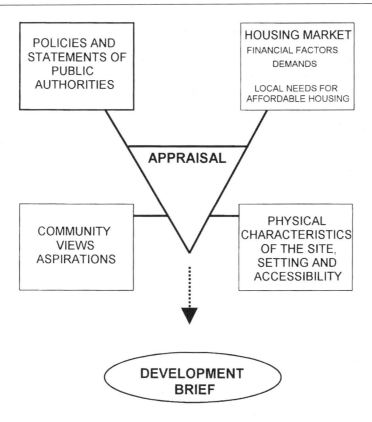

*Fig. H.1 Development briefing.*

Following adoption of the process, a number of briefs have emerged through the system. Developers have generally been co-operative and experience has shown that having the policy and guidance in the local plan enhances the status of the development briefs and the consistency of brief preparation. The approach established that as standard practice the council would expect development briefs to be prepared and approved for housing sites of over one hectare in size, but that these briefs could be initiated either by the local planning authority or by the landowner or developer. To provide a consistent framework for brief preparation the procedures and checklists were clearly set out in a 'Practice Manual' (Wycombe District Council, n.d.).

To date, application of the approach has been for small- to medium-sized sites in the five to twenty-five acre range. Many have been urban redevelopment 'windfall' sites that spring up unexpectedly and hence until the approach was adopted did not benefit from a systematic assessment of issues at an early stage. Thus, officers argue, the process has offered:

- increased certainty for the development industry about the local authority stance on design;
- a forum for the local community to become involved earlier in the design process;
- an opportunity for the market/financial implications of ideas to be assessed in conjunction with the landowner/developer; and
- a framework for promoting better quality developments.

The briefs have also proved useful in filling the gap between broad local plan policy and site-specific development control. Previously in the same role outline planning applications proved to be inflexible and comparatively poor instruments for consideration of design

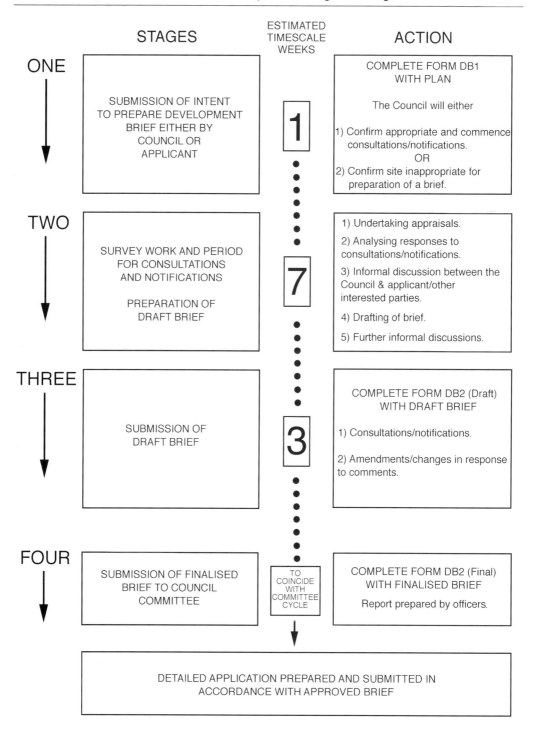

*Fig. H.2 Stages in the development briefing process.*

matters. Hence, the authority is now convinced of the utility of an intermediate approach for larger and more complex sites.

However, the approach has not been without its problems. The lack of design skills until the appointment of an urban designer in 1996 meant that the 'design' content of early briefs was rarely developed to its full potential and developer initiated briefs have not been the time savers it was thought that they would be (the same quality control is still required from officers). Therefore, in the context of ubiquitous staff shortages and other work pressures, sustaining the briefing initiative has proved difficult.

Furthermore, it quickly became apparent that the very procedural approach laid out in the Practice Manual was somewhat cumbersome and that following government guidance on the preparation of development briefs (DETR, 1998d), a more flexible approach to briefing was required. Nevertheless, a commitment across the department to the approach, and to its long-term benefits and time savings has kept the process alive, with simplified guidance outlined in an appendix to the 1998 deposit draft of the local plan (Wycombe District Council, 1998). The Practice Manual is no longer used, but developers, agents or landowners can still prepare briefs, with the district council responsible for consultation.

The new approach is aided by the enhanced availability of urban design skills in the authority, by clear planning gain 'shopping lists' outlined in the plan for each of the major allocated sites and by extended design policies and supplementary guidance on residential design (the latter also in the plan). Internal review processes have also been enhanced, with cross-departmental project teams (including highways representation from the county level) established to promote key development opportunities in the borough. Briefs are now seen as a starting point for dialogue with developers rather than as ends in themselves (Jackson, 1997).

As advocated in Wycombe, the development briefing process is beginning to deliver a local acceptance that through early focused intervention 'win–win' solutions are possible and that 'housing plus', in the form of better design, can be delivered without the unnecessary confrontation caused by the usual determination of private developers to maintain profit margins in the face of public sector requirements. The development briefing approach has proved useful at Wycombe despite revision to the process, and alongside a re-investment in design skills is beginning to pay dividends in influencing a better quality of residential design (see Fig. H.3).

*Fig. H.3 Dolphin Court, Kingsmead Road, High Wycombe.*

# Part Three:
# The challenge for control

# Chapter 9

# An agenda for delivering housing quality

In this, the penultimate chapter of the book, the discussion and findings from the earlier chapters are brought together as a means to address the key research aim by making recommendations on improving the practice and effectiveness of residential design control. One of the key recommendations to emanate from the research has been the need to re-write government planning guidance on residential design. Based on the research, and pre-empting the revised guidance contained in the 2000 version of PPG3 (discussed in Chapter 10), a suggested re-working of the design paragraphs of that note was published in Town & Country Planning (Carmona, 1998) and is included as Appendix 1. The re-working directly addressed the final research objective: to propose a new government framework for controlling the design of residential development.

The chapter concludes by postulating an agenda to further the research effort, as a means to extend the research findings into a definitive study of residential design control effectiveness. The chapter begins with the presentation of the key research recommendations.

## Recommendations for improving effectiveness

In Chapter 1 the research aim and seven objectives were outlined as a means to structure the work. The aim was: to evaluate current practice and innovation in local authority control of private sector residential design through the planning system, as a means to make recommendations on improving the effectiveness of residential design control.

Research objectives 1 to 6 have been addressed consecutively in Chapters 6, 7 and 8 by means of the empirical research outlined in Part 2 of the book, informed in turn by the theoretical review in Part 1. The discussion addressing the research objectives (in the conclusions to the Part 2 chapters), together with the research 'evaluations' throughout the book (at the end of each sub-section), constitute the key research findings. They also directly address the first part of the research aim – evaluating current practice and innovation in residential design control. Recommendations on improving the effectiveness of residential design control – the second half of the aim – flow directly from these findings.

The research has proved increasingly topical as the work commenced. Through its focus on the potential local authorities possess through their planning powers to influence the design of private sector residential development, it directly addresses a key opportunity to ameliorate the environmental impact of continued massive housing projections (see p. 4). The key research recommendations are structured under five headings:

1. Overarching recommendations
2. Criteria for residential design control
3. The hierarchy of residential design guidance
4. Residential design process and review
5. Central government's role and guidance.

### *Overarching recommendations*

#### *Quality not compromise*

Residential design and its control through planning action has frequently been characterised as a 'compromise' process; as a compromise between the often conflicting requirements of the different interests involved in delivering new residential environments (landowners, housebuilders, planning and highway authorities), and as a compromise indirectly espoused in government guidance as recently as 1992 (DoE and DoT, 1992, p. V). The result has been residential development in the UK which is widely and consistently berated on design grounds (most recently in 'Kerb Appeal' – see pp. 121–2) and which, in the light of housing projections, is becoming increasingly unsustainable (Manley and Guise, 1995; Rudlin and Falk, 1995). However, widespread cross-development industry agreement now seems to exist (POS *et al.*, 1998, p. 4) that action is required to improve the design of speculative residential development and that intervention through the planning system offers at least one appropriate response.

To move beyond 'compromise' solutions towards 'design quality' as a non-negotiable pre-requisite for residential development, central government has argued for a two-pronged approach. First, that the housebuilding industry's widely recognised (and in a purely free market situation, understandable) product-oriented disregard for context needs to be overcome. Second, that so does the contextually unresponsive and over-rigid control mechanisms used by too many planning authorities (Raynsford in POS *et al.*, 1998). In part, it seems this process might already be underway, after the adoption by central government of a revised design agenda in PPG1. PPG1 prioritises urban design, local distinctiveness, decision making on the basis of policy, prescription on the basis of appraisal, and public sector intervention wherever required in the cause of better design. Cross-disciplinary consensus around these principles came through strongly from the analysis of key stakeholder responses to PPG1 (see Chapter 6).

In implementing the new agenda, the key stakeholder organisations were clear that the local authority role in controlling design is a legitimate one. However, they argued that the wide variety in practice between local authorities needs to be addressed as a means to avoid further discord and offer greater certainty to housebuilders and local populations (a valuable commodity to developers – HBF, 1998, p. 11). In this context, the content analysis of residential design policy and guidance revealed that many of the 90% of authorities failing to exhibit a 'very high' emphasis on residential design have a long way to go to come up to the best practice of the 10% who do. In particular, authorities need to value good design in those areas with which the majority of their populations most readily associate – their home environments – and not just in their town and city centres, rural areas, and areas of established historic value.

#### *Understand the process to influence the product*

To achieve this, however, planning authorities need to possess an in-depth understanding of the processes that give rise to speculatively built residential environments, as well as taking a view about the desired end products. Thus, the prime movers shaping the design of new housing are first, the housebuilders, and second, the house buyers who purchase their products. In turn, these products are shaped by land, construction and housing markets, and by complex planning and development processes. In particular, authorities need to understand that the perceptions of housebuilders are largely determined by the profit motive and by manufacturing and market constraints in an industry characterised by significant commercial pressures and uncertainties and not always by high profit margins.

To housebuilders the product is therefore the individual house, and standardisation and conservative approaches to design the logical response to uncertainty (to which the planning system can unwittingly contribute). Similarly, to house buyers, price, location and value, rather than design are often the primary concerns driving decision making, while unsustainable modes of living remain overwhelmingly the choice of most buyers of new housing; who, once in occupation, are generally satisfied with the product they purchase. Thus, to improve the design of volume built residential development for the wider public interest, local authorities are often faced with considerable in-built resistance, and with complex development processes that defy simple intervention with 'blunt' (and too often entirely negative) policy instruments.

The need, then, is for processes that deliver desired design outcomes by combining early 'positive' intervention with realistic market assumptions. The objective should be to bridge complex and often contradictory stakeholder aspirations, not by forcing unwilling parties to accept the authority's line (although sometimes this may be necessary and policy tools should be robust enough to cope), but instead by creating a framework that actually rewards better design – more profitable development, better marketability, faster planning permission, better re-sale values, and so forth. By such means, a shared commitment to better design might be nurtured. However, this will only be achieved locally in the light of local circumstances and objectives, and in such a context the contribution of national guidance can only ever be limited.

### Criteria for residential design control

#### Urban design not standard(s) design

The research confirmed key findings elsewhere (DETR, 1998a; POS *et al.*, 1998), that there is need to move beyond standards-based approaches to residential design on both sides of the development process – planning and highways standards from local authorities and standard products from the housebuilders. Furthermore, that the main thrust of design control practice still awaits a shift from the limiting concern with aesthetics and over-simplistic emphasis on 'residential amenity'. Unfortunately, during the case studies and wider practitioner debates, the number one complaint from planning officers about housebuilders concerned their determination to impose standard house types in all locations, and about their highways colleagues, that inflexibility in the interpretation of road standards still marked the usual response. For their part, a review of the most frequently covered design considerations in residential design policy and guidance (see Chapter 7) helps to illustrate the limited standards, amenity and 'motherhood'-based contextual perspective still taken by most planning authorities.

To move toward more sophisticated approaches to residential design, first, the perception that local authorities are mere guardians of basic amenity and road safety will need to be overcome, to be replaced by a broader conceptualisation of design as the basis of any adopted design strategy. To develop such a conceptualisation based on cross-professional/stakeholder consensus, the review of innovative practice authorities confirmed the fast developing received wisdom that urban design, rather than architectural design, should become the primary focus of attempts to control residential design (strategic to site-specific). In this context, guidance issued by Essex, Suffolk, Manchester, West Dorset and Wycombe, all emphasised the significance of urban design over the architectural character of development. Based on the full agenda revealed after analysis of urban design theory and over 300 authorities' design policy and guidance, Fig. 9.1 illustrates how such a broad urban design conceptualisation might be addressed.

*Local distinctiveness in architecture and landscape*
Although a wide ranging conceptualisation of urban design may provide the basis of residential design control strategies, the new government emphasis on local distinctiveness (DoE, 1997b, para. 18) would nevertheless seem to require a response to architectural and landscape design as well. As regards the former, policy and guidance can emphasise that respecting or creating local distinctiveness is not a simple stylistic concern. Nevertheless, in choosing to emphasise the key characteristics of the local vernacular, many authorities (including West Dorset and Dacorum) are, they argue, addressing a clearly expressed

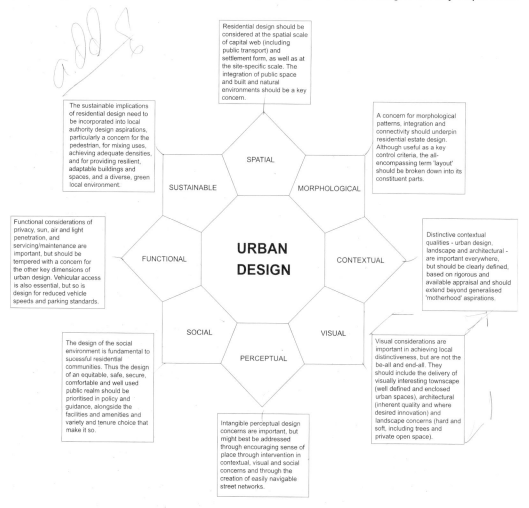

*Fig. 9.1  Addressing the broad urban design agenda.*

preference of their local populations. In such a context, some of the innovative practice authorities, particularly Cotswold and North Norfolk, successfully promote 'either/or' approaches to architectural style, either local vernacular or contextually inspired contemporary design, but not anonymous standard house-type solutions. Such approaches, the authorities contend, clearly satisfy the public demand that the architecture of new residential development should reflect the well-established character of the locality, but also respect the legitimate need to allow scope for innovation in design. The latter has been consistently supported in government guidance but is rarely promoted by developers.

Regarding landscape in residential design, the green qualities of residential environments – open space, trees and landscaping – are also fundamental to their character and to house buyers' perceptions of the same. Correspondingly, landscape concerns featured strongly in local authority area appraisals that reflected residents' perceptions of their environments, most notably Harrow's categorisation of the borough by four (predominantly landscape-oriented) environmental categorisations. Supporting advice elsewhere (Baines, 1990), such concerns should be given due consideration at the start of the design/development process and as an integral part of the design concept, not as a means to hide bland architecture or as uses for left-over (undevelopable) space (a common criticism made by development controllers of submitted layouts). Policy and guidance should therefore aim to ensure both an appropriate response of residential design to landscape character (including in suburban contexts) but also the rigorous implementation of landscaping proposals once agreed (DPOS, 1993).

### 'Pedestrian-friendly' not car-dominated environments

As part of the pursuit of quality residential layouts, authorities (planning and highways) need to reject explicitly car-dominated visions of future residential form and the stranglehold of road hierarchy and parking standards. This clear message from the wider practitioner discussion (see Chapter 8) is also now reflected in the most sophisticated design guides – including those in Essex and Hulme. These suggest that highways considerations in residential areas should move beyond matters of safety and vehicle flow efficiency to encompass a concern for environmental quality, pedestrian permeability and three-dimensional space design. In achieving this, hierarchical approaches to residential road design are being increasingly seen as over-simplistic and encouraging of car dominance, whilst traditional, connected, street patterns are once again being promoted. Nevertheless, participants in the wider practitioner discussions were clear that no universal solutions exist, and that cul-de-sacs are always likely to have a place.

In this pursuit, road design and layout represents an integral part of residential design and never an independent concern (too often the picture revealed by the content analysis). Thus, joint Planning Officer's Society, HBF and DETR research firmly recommended that the limited perspective of the highways authority should no longer be allowed to dominate the design of residential environments (POS *et al.*, 1998, p. 8). To achieve this, highways authorities will need to move their concerns for residential design beyond their statutory responsibilities for safe and cost-effective road adoption to support the creation of streets and places for people rather than cars. In the meantime, planning authorities can creatively interpret highways guidance, and actively seek innovation (and where necessary exemptions from highway authority standards) in pursuit of coherent 'pedestrian-friendly' residential urban design. Imagination and flexibility in the interpretation of advice would seem to be the key message in the new government guidance on residential road design (DETR, 1998a, p. 5 – see pp. 305–6).

*Innovation not formulaic approaches*

Easily measurable, and therefore arguably more objective criteria (RIBA, 1995), were popular in policy and guidance, including density, access, privacy, height and daylight. But, reflecting the broader conceptualisation of urban design revealed in urban design theory (Fig. 9.1) and now adopted in government guidance (DoE, 1997b, para. 14), such criteria can be supplemented beneficially by a confidence to use more intangible, less formulaic, design considerations as well, concerns such as visual interest, enclosure, community, route connectivity and sense of place, for example.

As a starting point, authorities could reflect in their policy and guidance the new design agenda outlined in PPG1. The 'general' design criteria contained in that note could then be used as a springboard to interpret, extend and legitimise policy and guidance in the light of local circumstances (but not as the definitive statement on design). Selective quoting from government advice, use of appraisal and consultation to justify departures, taking advantage of the woolly nature of many of the concepts used in government advice, altering the expression of policy and guidance, and referring to external sources of advice (particularly government endorsed advice), were all used by surveyed authorities as means to extend the range of local authority policy and guidance beyond a strict interpretation of government design advice, while remaining within its spirit.

Widespread support now exists for authorities to promote mixed-use development through policy (see Chapter 6). The innovative practice authorities, including, most notably, Essex, Manchester and Sedgemoor, were increasingly coming to realise that the mixing of uses offers one further means to move beyond formulaic approaches to residential design towards more sustainable and socially vibrant development. Therefore, following the lead given in government guidance (DoE, 1997b, paras. 10–12), authorities might promote explicitly specific mixed-use areas and the incorporation of a range of uses in otherwise residential areas. At the time of survey only small proportions of authorities considered the value of mixing uses in policy and/or guidance. Nevertheless, the renaming of the Essex guide – 'A Design Guide for Residential and Mixed Use Areas' – sets a valuable example.

### The hierarchy of residential design guidance

*Combining policy approaches*

The detailed content analysis of residential design policy and guidance revealed that when used in combination, either within individual authorities, or across the upper and lower planning tiers (county to district), the combined scope of policy and guidance mechanisms can be far more comprehensive than if used in isolation. Discussion with the innovative practice authorities subsequently confirmed hierarchical approaches (combining policy and guidance from across the different levels in the design guidance hierarchy – see Chapter 5) to be the most effective means to deliver policy aspirations. A key recommendation, therefore, is that a variety of approaches should be used, in combination, to make design objectives explicit and to ensure district-wide design policies are adequately related to design guidance on an area-wide and/or site-specific basis.

To take full advantage of the status imbued by Section 54A of the 1990 Town and Country Planning Act (see p. 31) all fundamental design concerns, including 'process' concerns, should be in the plan. Such concerns should subsequently be elucidated in supplementary design guidance to avoid overloading the plan with detailed advice and hence slowing down the adoption process. This was a problem highlighted by some of the more ambitious authorities studied, in particular by Cotswold, although North Norfolk reported few problems in incorporating their detailed design guidance into the plan. Nevertheless, adopting detailed

## Places, Streets and Movement

Back in the era of a mass public sector housebuilding programme the 'Design Bulletin' series was conceived and developed throughout the 1960s and 1970s into a comprehensive catalogue of 'information and advice on current housing problems' (DoE, 1972). The series covered – in tremendous detail – subjects as diverse as house construction technologies, space in the home, housing for special needs, and the design and layout of the external environment: roads, parking, landscaping, density issues and so forth. Unsurprisingly, the series withered when the Conservative administrations of the 1980s instigated a very different response to both housing (the public sector building programme was slashed), and to planning and design (both of which were marginalised). 'Design Bulletin 32: Residential Roads and Footpaths, Layout Considerations' was among the last of the original Bulletins (DoE and DoT, 1977).

Perhaps because of the particularly significant role roads play in determining the environmental quality of residential areas, but more likely because of the resource and safety implications the design of roads has on the public sector, while the other Design Bulletins have long since faded into oblivion, DB32 has survived, being republished in 1992 – see pp. 42–4.

In 1994, the decision was taken to review DB32 as part of the 'Quality in Town and Country Initiative'. The decision recognised a similar ground-swell of opinion in the 1990s to that which had instigated the original Design Bulletin 32 in the 1970s – that in design terms most speculative residential development leaves much to be desired. Four years later, the fruits of that work were finally published in *Places, Streets and Movement* (DETR, 1998a), described in the sub-title as a 'Companion Guide' to DB32; the Bulletin itself receiving an endorsement in the new guide and so securing a new lease of life.

Illustrations in the new guide reveal a sense of its primary inspirations: the 'Urban Villages' movement in the UK and neo-traditional (new urbanist) design generally. Indeed, the design philosophy promoted is essentially one of working with context, promoting 'pedestrian-friendly' environments, returning to traditional perimeter block systems, and, where possible, mixing uses. Furthermore, most of the examples in the guide illustrate housing of relatively high density (although this is not an explicit recommendation).

Launching the guide, the Minister argued: 'We need to ensure that to build is to enhance and that local authorities, planners, highways engineers and developers consider the needs of all users, not just car users, in the design of new development' (Raynsford, 1998). Perhaps taking a leaf out of the 'Birmingham Urban Design Studies' approach (see pp. 160–2), the philosophy is boiled down into a series of questions. In summary they are:

- Have the main characteristics of the locality been understood fully and taken into account?
- Has a framework for development been drawn up and agreed?
- Does the framework design aim to create a distinctive place through the density and layout of buildings and spaces?
- Has every effort been made to introduce or retain mixed use?
- Do streets and spaces contribute to making a high-quality public realm?
- Does the framework provide for all forms of travel including walking, cycling and public transport?
- Has full account been taken of the need to create places which will be safe and well cared for?

Thus, although the scope of DB32 was explicitly limited to the design and integration of residential roads and footpaths, the new guide introduces the concepts of 'place' and 'streets' (as opposed to roads) into its title, although fails to advise on any of the three-dimensional aspects of space design, on density issues, or on the contribution of buildings and landscape to defining the public realm. The result is a guide that is neither a fully comprehensive guide to road and footpath design – for that it needs to be read with DB32 as well – nor a comprehensive guide to the urban design of residential areas. Nevertheless, the principles contained in the new guide broadly reflect those promoted in Chapter 9, while the guide itself is glossy, readable and accessible. Undoubtedly it will have an important role to play in curbing some of the worst commercial excesses of speculative residential development and standards-based design control. The latter, in part, has been perpetuated by DB32 as the new guide itself implies through its stated aim '. . . to ensure that DB32 is used more imaginatively than has previously been the case' (p. 5). The guidance may even spur a new round of contextually-driven design guides at local authority level.

In fact the new guide already shares a variety of the updated principles contained in the new 'Essex Design Guide', suggesting a continuing symbiotic relationship between the two (see Inset A). These include:

- advice that spaces come first, with buildings arranged to fit the context, and that roads should be plumbed in later (see Fig. 10.1);
- support for the designation of 20 mph zones;
- rejection of hierarchical road solutions in favour of basing the design of residential areas on a network of spaces, rather than on a hierarchy of roads;
- relation to a sustainable movement framework and integration of a mix of uses; and
- promotion of connected, rather than cul-de-sac, road layouts.

Significantly, when published, a range of headlines across the national press portended the 'end of the road' for the suburban cul-de-sac: 'Dead end mooted for the baffling cul-de-sac' (*The Guardian*, 4 April 1998), or 'Planners drive cul-de-sac into suburban impasse' (*The Times*, 3 April, 1998). In reality, the guidance is nowhere near as equivocal as the headlines would have us believe.

## Towards an Urban Renaissance

The second report, *Towards an Urban Renaissance* delivered by the Secretary of State's Urban Task Force (1999b) has a much broader remit: to recommend practical solutions to bring people back to urban areas through 'joined-up' urban governance aimed at delivering design excellence, social well-being, economic strength and environmental responsibility. For residential design, the report is significant as the work originated from the need to deliver the government's projected housing requirements in a sustainable manner (see p. 4) – the dominant planning issue of the 1990s.

The elevation of design to among the key means of delivering the required 'Urban Renaissance' has a particular significance alluded to by the Secretary of State, John Prescott (1999), when launching the document. He argued 'we need more vision to create places and communities that will be cherished'. This case for more positive, proactive thinking is made throughout the report and relates to the lack of creative thinking across all urban scales, city-wide to local; to the paucity of expertise in both public and private sectors to turn visions into realities; and therefore to the lack of 'joined-up' thinking among the key stakeholders in urban regeneration.

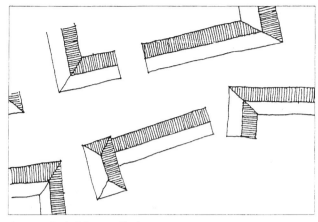

*Arrange the buildings to fit the local context*

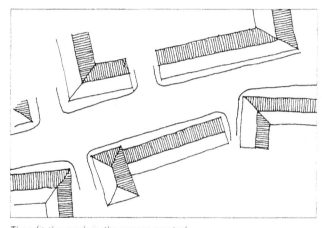

*Then fit the roads in the spaces created.*

*Fig. 10.1  Plumbing the roads in after the spaces (DETR, 1998a).*

If the main thrust of the report represents an attempt to join up the diversity of contributions to deliver an urban renaissance, then for urban design, its major contribution lies in mixing design into this melting pot. Among a whole series of detailed design-based strategies – not least the expected call to amend density standards upwards to support more sustainable environments – the report delivers a number of ideas of direct significance to residential design. These largely focus on the process of delivering better design, and include:

- a national urban design framework;
- integrated design-led demonstration projects and competitions;
- the value of Home Zones;
- integrated spatial masterplans; and
- regional skills base resource centres.

The national urban design framework is, on the face of it, the most ambitious of these, although also one of the least developed recommendations. At the heart of the framework is the idea of bringing together in one place responsibility for a concern which crosses administrative boundaries (three government departments – DETR, DCMS, DfEE – and the new Commission for Architecture and the Built Environment). This, for a subject that too often falls between the gaps (see pp. 54–5), has great merit in itself; although the failure to expand significantly on the nature and scope of such a framework leaves this powerful idea somewhat hanging in the air. A network of architecture centres to encourage discussion and engage local communities and a series of design bulletins to promote best practice, begin to put some meat on the bones of the idea (the latter already tried in the 1960s and 1970s – see p. 305 – not always to good effect).

To further promote best practice, the Task Force suggest that a series of national demonstration projects be launched in the Millennium Villages[1] mode. The aim is to demonstrate the value of innovation and to push forward the frontiers in delivering more sustainable urban regeneration projects. The observation is made that of the projects visited by the Urban Task Force, the most successful were the result of competitions. The result is a recommendation that all significant regeneration projects should be the subject of a design competition. Significantly, despite the public sector investment, the first two Millennium Villages at Greenwich (see Fig. 9.4) and Allerton Bywater have faced major problems in turning the competition winning visions into financially deliverable development proposals (Fairs, 2000c; DETR, 2000c).

Less ambitious locally, but far more ambitious if adopted nationally, is the explicit support given to the value of 'Home Zones', an idea promoted by the Children's Play Council (1999) and the subject of six trial schemes funded by the DETR. Based on the Dutch 'Woonerf' concept, Home Zones aim to restore streets to pedestrians and make them more sociable places to live (see Fig. 10.2). In large part, this involves removing vehicle priority and parking and replacing it with enhanced landscaping, street furniture and public space. The major aim is to change public perceptions of established urban areas and to guide incremental urban change in a positive manner. Nevertheless, the principles apply equally to the design of new residential developments.

The advocacy of integrated spatial masterplans is directed towards a different goal – to promote successful and sustainable urban developments in areas requiring comprehensive development (or redevelopment). The Urban Task Force argued that the spatial masterplan differs from two-dimensional zoning plans by establishing a three-dimensional framework

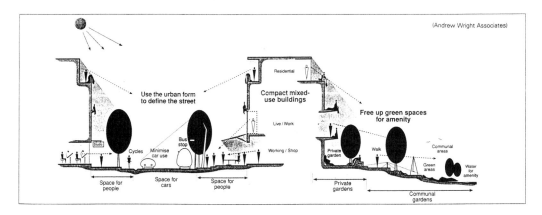

*Fig. 10.2 Streets as places (Urban Task Force, 1999b).*

[1] The Millennium Village projects have been established with significant public sector regeneration investment to deliver sustainable communities through public/private partnership.

for buildings, spaces and the defined design principles. Consequently, the full range of design professionals are involved in preparing a spatial masterplan, encouraging consensus and placing at the heart of the decision-making process the quality of the end product (see Fig. 10.3).

The aim is to create a visionary, flexible, participative and fully integrated mechanism (integrated with the land use planning system); a mechanism able to define at an early stage issues of urban form and public space, movement, community requirements, environmental design and building design (access, massing, orientation, etc., but not elevational treatment). The recommendation that any public funding and planning permission for area regeneration schemes should be tied to production of such a masterplan and to other accompanying forms of supplementary design guidance (briefs or codes) is therefore positive. It recognises clearly the need to tie economic regeneration objectives firmly to urban quality concerns. Such masterplans form the final level in the hierarchy of design guidance outlined in Table 5.4.

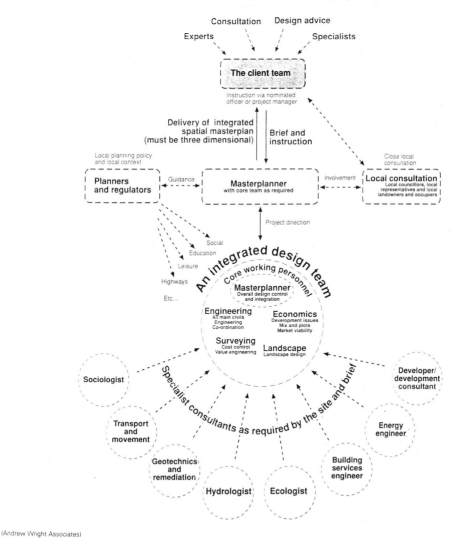

(Andrew Wright Associates)

*Fig. 10.3 An integrated spatial masterplan requires an integrated design team (Urban Task Froce, 1999b).*

Unfortunately, the paucity of skills across a wide range of fronts in the urban development and regeneration field, but particularly in urban design and the ability to deliver complex projects, represents a major focus of the report. The Task Force argued 'there is the need for a clearer understanding of the role of design within development' and that this awareness needs to spread to a wider audience, including: 'funding institution managers, elected members, housing association officers, managers of utilities, and urban regeneration partnership managers – as well as the more traditional list of architects, planners, highway engineers, landscape architects and conservation officers' (p. 158). The solution (adding to those presented in Chapter 6) is the development of a network of regional centres for urban development, tied to enhanced skills development in urban-related issues from the national curriculum to established professional training to CPD.

Nevertheless, potential for conflict with the design aspirations of the Urban Task Force may unintentionally exist in the support given in the report for streamlined planning consents, this despite the clear recommendation that greater speed should not come at the expense of design quality. To achieve such a balance, the report supports local authorities doing more of the groundwork up front, utilising design guides, briefs and masterplans. Partially supporting a key recommendation of the research (see p. 293), it argues that 'the emphasis of the planning system should be on rewarding authorities which perform well, in terms of quality of development, level of public acceptance and speed of decision-making, with more freedom and powers' (p. 198).

The danger is that as the last of these three objectives – speed – is the easiest to measure (as the Audit Commission annually confirm in their league tables), it too easily becomes the primary measure of planning system effectiveness. In the case of design, such a view is highly dangerous, because achieving better design will inevitably take time. Nevertheless, if the Urban Task Force recommendations are successful in moving the time required for good design forward in the process and on to the shoulders of the public sector in the form of a more proactive and positive planning process then, reflecting the experience of some of the innovative practice case studies (see Insets D, G and I), the danger may be avoided.

## PPG3: Housing

The third piece of guidance is also perhaps the most significant from the perspective of residential design and the planning process. A key recommendation of the research has been that the guidance on residential design operating throughout the research period – PPG3 (DoE, 1992b) – required a radical overhaul to bring it into line with evolving government policy on design and the planning system (see p. 296). As this book was completed, a revised version of the guidance was published (DETR, 2000a), hailed (optimistically) by the Secretary of State as the 'most radical change in town planning since the 1947 Town and Country Planning Act' (John Prescott in Lewis, 2000).

As significant for what it omits as for what it includes, in design terms, the latest draft of PPG3 (eight years after the last) represents a substantial move forward. The move is reflected up-front in the statement of 'government objectives', where local authorities are advised to 'promote good design in new housing developments in order to create attractive, high-quality living environments in which people will choose to live' (para. 2).

Looking back at the 1992 version of PPG3, the impression given is one of lip-service to design, while the free hand extended to housebuilders throughout the 1980s received a further lease of life. Repeating almost word for word advice given in the now infamous Circular 22/80, the tone and emphasis of the 1992 note amounted, in effect, to the continued support of market-driven approaches to residential design. Conversely, the latest version of

PPG3 makes no mention of marketing needs as a driver of design solutions and places no obvious limits on the design aspirations of authorities (except to avoid low density, mono-use development). Instead, the note outlines a somewhat disjointed, but nevertheless wide-ranging design agenda, with more comprehensive advice than its predecessor ranging across a far broader range of issues.

The design advice covers five main areas (see Table 10.1), and underpinning the new design emphasis is the first of these: an overarching objective to encourage environmentally and socially sustainable communities by breaking away decisively from single use, socially-zoned residential ghettos. Mixed developments are seen as the answer: mixed uses, mixed tenures, mixed housing types and sizes, and socially mixed communities. Indeed, the notion of community receives an endorsement in the guidance, an objective to be pursued through design and layout and the allocation of space around development, but also through better accessibility by public transport and an explicit link between housing design and delivery of the urban renaissance agenda.

The second area, the new emphasis on urban design, marks a decisive shift away from the former guidance and an acceptance that urban design exists in predominantly residential areas as well as in more urban contexts. Although far from comprehensive, the advice encompasses visual (townscape), social usage, morphological (urban form), and functional conceptualisations of urban design, and briefly addresses many of the perceived problems with contemporary residential development discussed in Chapter 4. Significantly, however, useful statements in the consultation draft of the new note (DETR, 1999), that developments should connect into their wider locality and that housing layouts should be established before road designs (see Fig. 10.1) were removed from the text.

The third area, landscape design, recognises the perceptually significant role of landscaping and open space in living environments and encourages the 'greening' of developments to promote quality, enhance drainage and increase bio-diversity. The landscape setting of new development receives a mention as a legitimate issue for local authority concern, as does the need to provide and retain public open space within easy reach of new housing. Noticeably, little mention is made of private open space and specifically of the important contribution of private or commercial gardens and hard landscaping (including boundary treatments).

Architectural design, the fourth area of concern, marks a further departure from the hands-off approaches of the past. Thus, local building traditions and materials are recognised specifically as legitimate contextual considerations (previously considered matters of detail) and more energy efficient housing designs (and layouts) are promoted. New building technologies are also promoted as means to deliver still acceptable building forms more efficiently.

The final area relates to housing design and the planning process, advice which largely repeats that given in PPG1 that applicants should demonstrate how they have taken the need for good design and layout into account and that authorities should review applications in the light of clear plan policies and adopted supplementary design guidance, including design briefs. Consequently, authorities are encouraged to review their existing design standards in favour of more flexible policy mechanisms that aim to reduce land-take. In preparing their guidance, authorities are also encouraged to 'develop a shared vision with their local communities of the types of residential environments they wish to see in their area' (para. 55) – a departure that recognises the importance of the human as well as physical context for new residential development.

Although not as comprehensive as the suggested re-working of the design paragraphs of PPG3 emanating from the research (see Appendix 1), slowly and surely the PPGs are filling

*Table 10.1  Design aspects of the PPG3s compared*

| PPG3 – 1992 | PPG3 – 1999 |
|---|---|
| **Sustainable communities** | |

| PPG3 – 1992 | PPG3 – 1999 |
|---|---|
| good design – encourages community acceptance | accessibility – by public transport |
| mix of houses – regulate only with good reason | communities – create socially mixed, inclusive and |
| – regulate if large allocation | balanced |
| – consider marketing consideration | – promote through design, layout and |
| new settlements – high design/layout standards | space allocation |
| – landscaping and sense of place | mix uses – for more sustainable development patterns |
| – create community | mix of houses – size and type |
| – walking/cycling/public transport | mono-tenure – avoid |
| | new settlements – high design/layout standards |
| | urban renaissance – promote through housing design |
| | to improve quality of life |

**Urban design**

| PPG3 – 1992 | PPG3 – 1999 |
|---|---|
| access and parking – relevant considerations | density – avoid less than 30 dph (promote 30–50 dph) |
| density – relevant consideration (if flexible) | – avoid restrictive policies |
| – avoid town cramming | – based on capacity studies |
| design – aim for high quality | – imaginative increases without compromising |
| – good schemes respect context and purpose | quality |
| – reject poor design (out of scale/character) | – increase around transport nodes |
| development setting – consider | layout – consider context, streets and spaces |
| existing development patterns – relation to | – contribute to energy efficiency |
| functional aspects – for marketing judgement | – facilitate pedestrian and cyclist movement to |
| – garage provision | reduce car dependence |
| – internal space standards | – for people not traffic movement or parking |
| – size of gardens | – safe, healthy, crime free |
| infrastructure – relation to | local character – respect and enhance |
| layout – relevant consideration | parking – frame policies with design in mind (not more |
| – imaginative layouts required in rural areas | than 1.5 spaces per unit) |
| local environment – character and quality | – less off-street parking |
| village character – respect including scale/density | – more flexible parking standards (not |
| | minimums) |
| | places and spaces – with attractive, distinctive identity |
| | quality living environments – where people will choose |
| | to live |
| | road design – design to reduce traffic speeds and |
| | increase pedestrian safety |
| | – reduce road width |
| | townscape context – consider |
| | village character – respect including layout |

**Landscape design**

| PPG3 – 1992 | PPG3 – 1999 |
|---|---|
| landscaping – aim for high quality | ecology – consider context |
| – relevant consideration | greening – to promote quality, enhance drainage, |
| – allow space in rural areas | increase bio-diversity |
| open space – adequate provision required | landscape context – consider |
| – parks, allotments, gardens, informal | landscaping – new and existing |
| – safe play space | – trees |
| | open space – retain existing open space |
| | – provide sufficient open space |
| | – within easy reach |

**Architectural design**

| | |
|---|---|
| building style/character – of low cost rural housing | building style/character – of low cost rural housing |
| detailed design – rarely relevant | building traditions – consider context |
| disabled access – for building regulations | energy efficiency – promote |
| materials – in sensitive areas | materials – consider context |
| neighbouring buildings – consider context | neighbouring buildings – consider context |
| scale, height, massing – relevant considerations | new building technologies – acceptable and efficient |

**Planning process**

| | |
|---|---|
| have regard to – 'Design Bulletin 32' | applicants – to demonstrate delivery of good design |
| – 'PPG1' | design briefs – for new residential and mixed use design |
| planning briefs – can advise on site characteristics | design guidance – for new residential design |
| rigid formulae – avoid, i.e. house location/relation | have regard to – sources of good practice guidance |
| planning policies – flexible, avoid over prescription | – PPG1, PPG17 |
| | planning policies/standards – review to reduce land use and increase flexibility |
| | planning policies – for new residential design |
| | poor design – reject |
| | shared vision – develop with local communities |
| | village design statements – useful |

the gap left by the 'hands-off' approaches to design advocated in the 1980s (the 1992 and 2000 versions of the note are compared in Table 10.1). If related to the six principles underpinning the suggested advice in the Appendix, then the new advice accepts:

- explicitly, that new residential development, like other development, should and can achieve the highest standards of design whether in urban, suburban or rural locations;
- implicitly, that the problem of poor quality residential design has been as much a consequence of inappropriate central and local government action as of the actions of the housebuilders;
- explicitly, that the role of local government in intervening to improve the design of residential development is an important and legitimate one;
- explicitly, that the current housing allocations will need to be implemented on the ground in environmentally and socially sustainable, locally acceptable and contextually compatible ways;
- explicitly, that to achieve this, authorities will need first to invest in the necessary policy tools with which to do the job and implicitly in skilled manpower as well.

Significantly, however, no mention is made of the value of 'consensus' over more 'adversarial' approaches to negotiating residential design solutions as the best means to deliver high-quality design by bringing commercial as well as community stakeholders along with any preconceived design policy objectives.

## Beyond 2000 – moving on

The research on which this book is based has been undertaken on the shifting sands of government design policy objectives throughout the 1990s. Originally conceived shortly after the publication of the 1992 version of PPG3, the work concludes as that guidance is superseded with a note that turns almost full circle in its treatment of design. In this respect the work reports on a period in transition and outlines an agenda to respond to a changed policy context at the start of the new century.

From the government perspective, this agenda is laid out most comprehensively in 'By Design', the long awaited good practice guide on urban design in the planning system (DETR and CABE, 2000). The document makes the case for better design and the role of the planning system in helping to realise it. It outlines a series of urban design objectives, explores a policy 'toolkit' to help articulate these, and discusses a range of complementary processes as a means to deliver the toolkit and urban design objectives. At the launch of the guide, Stuart Lipton the Chairman of CABE, argued:

> The guide has been drawn around a limited number of simple but compelling principles. First, good design is important everywhere. Second, while the planning system has a key role to play in delivering better design, the creation of successful places depends on the skills of designers and the vision and commitment of those who employ them. Finally, no two places are identical and there is no such thing as a blueprint for good design. Good design always arises from a thorough and caring understanding of place and context (DETR and CABE, 2000).

To that extent the guide offers a restatement and considerable deepening of the advice contained in PPG1 (1997), this time with a perceived audience of local councillors as well as planning officers (a summary leaflet produced specifically for the former). Nevertheless, in its detail, the force of its key messages, and through its comprehensive coverage of urban design and design policy tools, the guide breaks new ground at least for the English planning system. Significantly, however, a gap was still perceived in the area of residential design, particularly following the publication of PPG3. Therefore, to relate and extend the general advice in 'By Design' specifically to housing, a 'Good Practice Guide on Improving Housing Design' was also commissioned by the DETR for publication in 2001.

## By design, urban design in the planning system

'By Design' continues the process of putting in place the right tools for a more effective role for the planning system in helping to improve standards of urban design. The guide itself is sizeable – at least when compared to the individual pieces of advice scattered across the PPGs. Extending to 99 pages, it contains often detailed advice on the preparation of new policy tools. Yet the underlying messages are simple: that some thought needs to go into defining in any particular context what is meant by good urban design; that this needs to be reflected in policy tools (whichever form these take); and that some investment is required to ensure the careful delivery and use of these tools thereafter. 'By Design' is split into four sections, followed by a series of appendices including a glossary and checklist of information required with planning applications.

### The need for better design
In the first section the case is made that the planning system has an important role to play in delivering better standards of design, that the guide builds on established planning policy guidance in PPG1, and that efforts should concentrate on the making of 'better places' through urban design. Ultimately, however, it is argued 'achieving good design depends on the skills of the designer and the commitment to good design of all those concerned with new development' (DETR and CABE, 2000, p. 10).

### Thinking about urban design
The second section reads a little like an urban design textbook and establishes a set of objectives for urban design which, it is suggested, are characteristics common to most successful places. Seven mutually reinforcing objectives are outlined:

- *Character* – to promote character in townscape and landscape by responding to and reinforcing locally distinctive patterns of development and culture.
- *Continuity and enclosure* – to promote the continuity of street frontages and the enclosure of space by development which clearly defines private and public areas.
- *Quality of the public realm* – to promote public spaces and routes that are attractive, safe, uncluttered and work effectively for all in society, including disabled and elderly people.
- *Ease of movement* – to promote accessibility and local permeability by making places that connect with each other and are easy to move through, putting people before traffic and integrating land uses and transport.
- *Legibility* – to promote legibility through development that provides recognisable routes, intersections and landmarks to help people find their way around.
- *Adaptability* – to promote adaptability through development that can respond to changing social, technological and economic conditions.
- *Diversity* – to promote diversity and choice through a mix of compatible developments and uses that work together to create viable place that respond to local needs.

An eighth objective – 'efficiency' – relating to sustainable development principles and urban design was dropped from the earlier drafts of the document on the contestable grounds that such concerns more appropriately infuse the remaining objectives. The objectives of urban design are subsequently related to aspects of development form through eight characteristics of physical form (expanding on those outlined in PPG1 (DoE, 1997b, para. A1) – layout (urban structure), layout (urban grain), landscape, density and mix, scale (height), scale (massing), appearance (details), and appearance (materials)). Urban design objectives and aspects of form are then combined in a series of 'prompts to thinking', followed by more detailed 'pointers to good design', the intention being to support good practice rather than create hard and fast rules.

*Urban design and the planning toolkit*
The third section begins by arguing that a guide to better practice can only hope to 'offer prompts for better designs, but successful development depends on tailoring these to local circumstances' (DETR and CABE, 2000, p. 36) through understanding the local context via appraisal, and implementing principles through locally derived policy and guidance. The section outlines the array of techniques available to appraise the qualities of locality, including to the non-designer a (no doubt) baffling range of approaches, each in little detail and with no clear attempt to define a recommended method or set of methodologies. This is the most unsatisfactory part of the guide, but perhaps merely heralds the arrival of UDAL's 'Placecheck' initiative which aims to fill the gap (Cowan, 2000 – see p. 147). Detailed advice is subsequently offered on how to address urban design in development plans, urban design frameworks, development briefs and design guides. The section concludes with an examination of design and development control, advising on the consistent application of design principles throughout the negotiation and control processes. A rather unresolved discussion of reviewing design outcomes is tacked on to the end.

*Raising standards in urban design*
The 'toolkit' forms the heart of the guidance and recommends a more proactive and positive approach to design than thus far has been seen in government guidance. The message continues through to the last and much shorter section on the planning process. In this, the case is made that 'the effectiveness of the planning tools in raising the standards of urban

design will depend on how they are used and the management style and ability of the people who use them' (DETR and CABE, 2000, p. 72). The section includes discussion on proactive management, collaboration, developing the right skills, design initiatives and on means to monitor the delivery of design services and objectives.

It is argued 'Everyone who makes policy, shapes opinion, sets budgets, selects designers, writes briefs or assesses proposals can play a part in raising standards' (DETR and CABE, 2000, p. 72). If only a fraction of these people read and digest the key messages in 'By Design', the chances of delivering better urban design will undoubtedly be enhanced. Along with revised PPG3, 'By Design' comes closest to reflecting the key messages outlined in this book.

Nevertheless, throughout the period covered by the research (as previously), many of the debates discussed in Chapter 3 have remained stubbornly the same. Thus in reaction to the publication of 'By Design' the letters pages of the architectural press reflected 'business as usual':

> Our planning system is crucial in deciding what makes up our environment. Who studies and practises for decades, sincerely searching for, and understanding, 'good design'? Architects. Who makes the final judgement in planning committees? Dustmen, taxi-drivers, shopkeepers, retired WI-types etc. – any pot-luck combination of people unqualified in the sphere of architecture. . . . In my opinion, if you are not innovative, but are conservative, conventional and pander to the average common denominator, i.e. don't do anything really bad or really good, then you will get a quicker positive result. . . . A better way than trying to explain design rules would be to have a more informed panel of judges (Ford, 2000).

This comment, inspired by a committee rejection of a 'traditional, but different, house design' and the others it in turn inspired, merely reflect some of the eternal problems presented by any system charged with the regulation of private interests in the name of a common community 'good'. As government initiatives come and go, such debates are unlikely to subside. Nevertheless, for a variety of reasons, the context within which such decisions on residential design are made is likely to change quickly, offering a further rationale for a democratic engagement in design.

In Chapter 1, one of the major drivers leading to this change was outlined, namely the massive housing projections needing to be accommodated in England over the next twenty years. Underpinning these projections, but also moving well beyond them are a whole series of sometimes contradictory trends, influences and developing policy objectives that together will make the context for housing design and development up to 2021 (the period covered by the most recent housing projections), very different from that faced before. These include the following.

1. *The sustainable agenda*: The increasing importance attached to the sustainability agenda, both nationally and locally, with the changes that the drive to more sustainable patterns of living imply on current consumer-driven patterns of development. In time, this broad policy objective is likely to deliver the most profound changes to planning and development processes since the Garden Cities movement around the turn of the previous century.
2. *Higher density living*: A necessity to help deliver more sustainable patterns of development, but also physically to fit the required new housing into the limited land available in the light of broader countryside conservation objectives. The move will leave more extensive 'suburban' patterns of development as exceptions rather than norms and

may require a move away from standard house type solutions to more bespoke solutions to housing design. Extensive research commissioned by the government Office for London and the London Planning Advisory Committee on 'Sustainable Residential Quality' (1998; 2000), has confirmed the viability of design-led approaches to increasing density.

3. *Mixing uses*: Again, to deliver more sustainable forms of development, housebuilders who have seen themselves traditionally as housing specialists are likely in the future to become more generalists, perhaps even deriving significant parts of their profit from development other than housing. Such approaches would mark a move from viewing these parts of developments as loss leaders to be resisted if at all possible.

4. *Increased personal mobility*: Because as patterns of work change, so do patterns of living, with far more extensive migration and less attached to individual homes, neighbourhoods or even towns. In turn, these trends away from 'settling down' and permanence may impact on what is expected from housing and even on patterns of home-ownership.

5. *Home-ownership*: This remains as popular as ever, but a climate of housing shortages and spiralling prices (at least in some parts of the country) may lead in time to reduced levels of home-ownership among certain sections of society, and therefore to different patterns of tenure and perceptions about what good housing should offer.

6. *Social housing*: This is increasingly becoming the purview of private developers, as the contribution of the state to providing social and affordable housing shows little sign of revival, and as market housing is increasingly out of the reach of significant sections of society.

7. *The impact of the car*: Because as levels of car ownership continue to rise and environmental quality (and accessibility) locally continues to decline, alternative car-free or car-reduced housing may in turn become more viable. Impending gridlock might even force greater investment in public transport, so helping to free new housing developments from dominating parking requirements.

8. *Cultural change*: As the UK becomes more of a European state, sizeable sections of the population increasingly hail from cultures with less tradition of home-ownership, a greater acceptance of urban living and from housing stock of greater inherent quality. Such experiences, and the experiences of UK citizens as they travel abroad and compare lifestyles overseas with their own, may in time lead to a demand for different types of living environment and for greater housing quality.

9. *Changing demographic patterns*: Because social patterns and household sizes are changing fast as people are living longer, having children later and getting divorced more often, the result may inspire alternatives to the traditional family home.

10. *Working from home*: As technology changes and the Internet increasingly links homes to work, working from home is likely to become more the norm in a service-oriented economy. Such trends may not undermine demand for work environments, but may require more adaptable housing environments and environments which offer more of the facilities and social experiences foregone. The changes inspired by these new technologies may be far more profound than we yet realise (Mitchell, 1996).

11. *Breakdown of traditional communities*: Increasingly global patterns of living and communication mean that friends and relations are just as likely to live around the world as around the corner, so potentially undermining the need for, and use of, public space and facilities as venues for social interaction.

12. *Postmodern attitudes*: Despite globalisation trends, postmodern attitudes increasingly seem to find expression in neo-traditional design models (urban villages in the UK, the

new urbanism in the US). Such trends may increasingly reconstruct the trappings of community, even if criticised for not always supporting its substance.

13. *Construction technologies*: Contemporary forms are used to great effect in Europe, Japan and the US to bring down the cost of housing. Modularisation and prefabrication, for example, are likely to play an increasing role in the UK (see pp. 111–14). Indeed, some of Britain's biggest housebuilders – Wimpey, Westbury and Beazer Homes – are currently exploring factory-built technologies as means to increase quality and reduce construction times and costs (Fairs, 2000b).

14. *Public sector involvement:* This is increasingly taking a more 'hands-on' role in guiding the design of development at the national level, not least to deliver sustainable objectives. This is likely increasingly to inform local practice, as planning authorities revive their interest and abilities to engage constructively in design concerns.

15. *The third way*: As a political philosophy, the third way is in the ascendancy, and likely to dominate the political scene for at least the first decade of the new century. Inherent in these philosophies is a much greater emphasis on a partnership between the public and private sectors to deliver development, and perhaps therefore on less autonomy for private housing providers.

16. *Public involvement*: As individuals become better informed about environmental concerns, and as pressures (not least intensification) on local environments increase, greater public involvement may increasingly become the norm as communities attempt to play a more central role in the design of their neighbourhoods.

The Urban Task Force (1999b, p. 27) combined a number of these into what they saw as three key drivers for change which in turn confirm the need for more fundamental approaches to the design and integration of residential development. They identified:

- The technical revolution: centred on information technology and the establishment of new networks connecting people from the local to the global level;
- The ecological threat: greater understanding of the global implications of mankind's consumption of natural resources and the importance of sustainable development; and,
- The social transformation: changing life patterns reflecting increasing life expectancy and the development of new lifestyle choices.

These factors are likely increasingly to come to bear on decisions made by planning authorities in considering residential design, as well as by housing providers, particularly developers. Already a switch from extensive to more compact forms of residential development is obvious, with the latest PPG3 attempting to drive-up new-build residential densities from the English average of 25 dwellings per hectare (dph) – half of all dwellings built in the period of research were built at densities of below 20 dph – to advocated densities of no less than 30 dph and if possible up to 50 dph. Increasingly this new housing is also having to be delivered on brownfield rather than greenfield sites, with all the contextual and development process constraints that this implies (even in the most pressured and constrained context – the English South East – the target for brownfield reuse remains 60% – Prescott, 2000).

With these influences driving forward change, it is possible that we could be entering one of the most significant periods of innovation and change in housing design since the 'heroic', if in hindsight fatally flawed, residential developments of the post-war modernist designers. It is hoped the changes will conspire to deliver better design and that the mistakes of the mid-twentieth century will be avoided by grounding the process in the sometimes painfully learnt lessons about what constitutes good urban design. To achieve this, the role of the planning system will be fundamental as the only truly legitimate means to establish a public design agenda and reconcile the conflicting interests: new technologies with context; context with housing requirements; housing requirements with sustainability; sustainability with market forces; market forces with public interests; public interests with private expectations; and so forth. In these evolving relationships better urban design should represent a constant whatever the context – urban, suburban, rural; North, Midlands, South; high or low established quality; high, medium or low density. This will only be possible, however, if the whole planning process is re-cast as a 'positive' force for change, through which local vision can combine with environmentally responsible national objectives and informed and balanced local objectives, to encourage and deliver a truly sustainable residential renaissance.

## Addendum

As the book went to press the Urban White Paper – *Our Towns and Cities: The Future, Delivering an Urban Renaissance* (DETR, 2000e) was published promising a new vision for urban living, building on the recommendations of the Urban Task Force. In detail, the White Paper accepts the arguments for more 'Millennium Village' demonstration projects, the value of masterplans and of regional resource centres – 'Centres of Excellence' to tackle the skills deficit. The National Urban Design Framework envisaged by the Urban Task Force is not, however, delivered, although significantly, in its place a plan to further revise PPG1 to put 'Urban Renaissance' at the heart of the planning system is proposed. Clearly, the shifting sands of government policy on planning, design and residential provision continue to shift. It is hoped that the principles outlined in this book will in some way help to inform the process.

## INSET J: SEDGEMOOR DISTRICT COUNCIL – NEGOTIATING QUALITY[1]

As one of only three larger urban centres in Somerset, Bridgwater has been the recipient of a large proportion of the county's housing allocations in the 1980s, most of which developed in a fragmented manner resulting in poor quality urban sprawl with little sense of place, community or inherent quality. In recent years, the expansion of the town has become physically constrained as the town's edges have spread further into the surrounding countryside. Nevertheless, in the face of mounting pressure for new residential development, two significant parcels of greenfield land were allocated for 1,400 new homes in the local plan (Sedgemoor District Council, 1991). The scenario faced by officers – with fragmented ownerships and heavy infrastructure costs – promised to deliver yet more suburban sprawl, with little chance of delivering the required infrastructure improvements or sustainable environment the authority wished to see. Fortunately, a successful bid to the 'Quality in Town and Country, Urban Design Campaign' (DoE, 1995a) fund gave the council the spur it needed to re-think their approach to residential design.

Officers argued that a positive approach to residential development was required, an approach which avoided the confrontational and reactive review of residential design. They were concerned that the sequential process of private developer proposal, followed by local authority intervention, based, in the case of Sedgemoor, on little preconceived design policy or guidance, would inevitably end in an appeals lottery in which the authority took its chances along with the developer.

The solution was to involve housebuilders at the start of the process (pre-application) in a collaboration with the council in order to build a culture of co-operation in which all parties could achieve shared objectives – high quality, contextually appropriate, profitable residential development (see Fig. 9.2). To pursue the aim, a steering group was convened representing the broad range of stakeholders in the area: the county, district and town councils; representatives of the landowners and developers; together with an academic input to act as an independent arbitrator when required. A project specification was drawn-up to identify the roles, interests and needs of the different stakeholders, together with the benefits each expected from the process. This key innovation to which all parties signed-up, clarified issues, ways of working and decision-making as well as common aims, objectives and outputs. An appendix to the specification laid out these concerns and meant that there was less room for disagreement during the later stages (see Fig. J.1 – Sedgemoor District Council, 1996). The aim was to create a team capable of solving problems in a collaborative way, to avoid defensive posturing and to utilise the resources and skills of both public and private sectors effectively. So, from the start, one of the public/private taboos was broken with members of the team sharing knowledge and information, as well as operational costs.

In the context of different interpretations of what was meant by quality, the team had to consider how agreement could be reached on what they were trying to achieve. To reach an understanding, the team went back to first principles and identified the concept of 'Quality Thresholds' as a means to measure the satisfaction of differing aspirations by alternative courses of action. Quality, it was decided, would be achieved when the resultant proposal exceeded expectations of the greatest number of stakeholders. Three quality thresholds were postulated:

[1] The Sedgemoor case study originates from work undertaken for the 'Quality in Town and Country Urban Design Exhibition' (DoE, 1996h). Because the Bridgwater work was the only scheme of the twenty-one exhibition case studies to focus on predominantly residential development, the authority was invited to contribute with an article to the research (Carmona, 1997b). This final case study is largely based on that work and on subsequent discussions held with the authority. It is the only case study not to have been presented at one of the two research conferences.

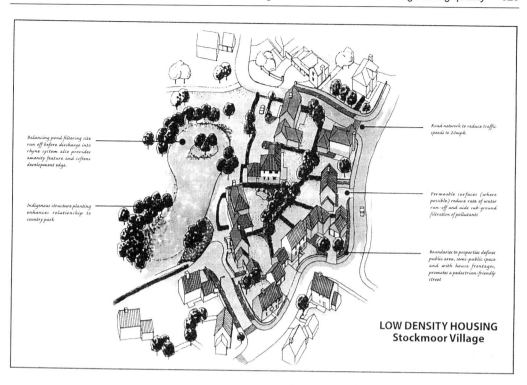

Balancing pond filtering site run off before discharge into rhyne system also provides amenity feature and softens development edge.

Indigenous structure planting enhances relationship to country park

Road network to reduce traffic speeds to 20mph

Permeable surfaces (where possible) reduce rate of water run-off and aids sub-ground filtration of pollutants

Boundaries to properties defines public area, semi-public space and with house frontages, promotes a pedestrian-friendly street

**LOW DENSITY HOUSING**
**Stockmoor Village**

# Appendix

# Proposed re-working of PPG3

Based on the research findings, a suggested re-working of the design paragraphs of PPG3: Housing (see Fig. 2.8 for the 1992 version of the text) was published in Town & Country Planning (Carmona, 1998) and is included below. It represented an attempt at extending the framework outlined in 1997 in PPG 1 to the residential context. Although some text was taken directly from the then current paragraphs of PPG3 (DoE, 1992b, paras. 4–7), other text was strategically edited and so new and old text is deliberately not distinguished. The revised paragraphs for PPG3 were intended as a supplement – specifically relating to residential development – of the revised 'general' guidance on design contained in PPG1. The revised text reflects many of the recommendations in Chapter 9 and in so doing extends the advice on design in PPG3 (1992) from four to fifteen paragraphs. The reworked guidance effectively addressed the final research objective.

The advice is based on six overarching principles:

- That new residential development, like other development, should and could achieve the highest standards of design whether in urban, suburban or rural locations.
- That the problem of poor quality residential design in the past has been as much a consequence of inappropriate central and local government (planning and highways) action as of the actions of the volume housebuilders themselves.
- That the role of local government in intervening to improve the design of residential development is an important and legitimate one, but one requiring clear and consistent political backing from central government above.
- That to secure the provision of the required housing without alienating the populations it is intended to serve, the current housing allocations will need to be implemented on the ground in environmentally and socially sustainable, locally acceptable and contextually compatible ways.
- That consensus, rather than adversarial means will need to be found before high quality residential design in urban, landscape and architectural terms can be delivered.
- That to achieve this, authorities will need to co-ordinate highways and planning action aimed at achieving quality; invest in the necessary tools with which to do the job – comprehensive design policies in development plans, design briefs that interpret design requirements on a site-specific basis, and local design guidance to expand on principles outlined in the development plan; as well as in the necessary skilled manpower to

interpret, implement and monitor any adopted principles on an application by application basis, through the planning process.

## PPG3: Housing – good design in new residential development

1.  Developers should aim for a high quality of urban, architectural and landscape design in all new housing developments and in all contexts. A well-designed scheme that respects the local environment can do much to make new housing more acceptable to the local community. A good scheme will produce buildings that are well designed for their purpose and for their surroundings. General advice on the control of design is given in paragraphs 13 to 20 and Annex A to PPG1. The principles outlined in PPG1 apply equally to new residential development as to other forms of development and to development in suburban locations as well as in urban or rural areas. In particular, local authorities and applicants should prioritise the value of good urban design and of securing locally distinctive development, based – through appraisal – on a thorough understanding of context.

2.  Local authority interest in the design of residential development is clearly legitimate, although the disparity in practice between authorities in both outlining their design aspirations and in intervening – where necessary – to improve residential design needs to be addressed. All authorities should value design in those areas with which their populations most directly associate – their home environment. Henceforward, the DETR will be making strong representations at development plan public inquiries if plans fail to address design issues adequately in relation to all land uses and contexts.

3.  Reflecting the new plan-led planning system, authorities should base their assessments of residential design proposals on preconceived adopted policies and guidance and not simply on discretionary and potentially arbitrary case-by-case design evaluations. Hierarchical approaches to residential design policy and guidance have proved most effective in delivering such an approach, with comprehensive policy in development plans establishing a 'positive' overarching framework covering all key design concerns at the district-wide level for detailed interpretation in local design guides and subsequently in site-specific design briefs. Within the development plan, consideration of residential design should make direct and desirable links to wider residential development policy.

4.  Authority-wide residential design guides are of particular value in explaining the full design agenda, in relating that agenda to the local context and therefore in offering increased certainty to both housebuilders and local populations. Specialist residential design guides are also encouraged to emphasise key themes such as the principles of sustainable housing design or of reducing crime through better design. The production of residential design guides at the county level (or across unitary authorities) has proved a consistently valuable and resource efficient means to co-ordinate practice across district authorities. Such guidance should aim to integrate residential road design requirements with broader urban design objectives and should have the backing of both planning (county and district) and highways authorities.

5.  Purely standards-based approaches to residential design will rarely be appropriate, either from local authorities in the form of rigid design standards, or from housebuilders in the form of standard house types and layouts. If residential design standards are used it may be more appropriate to publish such standards alongside broader design guidance in the development plan or in local design guides and/or design briefs, rather than in isolation. Design briefs are of particular value, both in helping developers by

Ball M. (1999) 'Chasing the Snail: Innovation and Housebuilding Firms' Strategies', *Housing Studies*, **14**, 1, 9–12.

Barlow J. (1999) 'From Craft Production to Mass Customisation, Innovation Requirements for the UK Housebuilding Industry', *Housing Studies*, **14**, 1, 23–42.

Baron T. (1983) 'The Challenge for the UK Housing Industry in the 1980s and the Planning System', *Construction Management and Economics*, **1**, 1, 17–29.

Barrett H. and Phillips J. (1993) *Suburban Style: The British Home 1840–1960*, London, Little Brown and Company.

Barton H., Davis G. and Guise R. (1995) *Sustainable Settlements: A Guide for Planners, Designers, and Developers*, Luton, Local Government Management Board.

Bateman A. (1995) 'Planning in the 1990's – A Developer's Perspective Report', 1, February, pp. 26–29.

Bath City Council (1993) *Cherishing Outdoor Places, A Landscape Strategy for Bath*, Bath, Bath C.C.

Batty S., Davoudi S. and Layard A. (Eds) (2001) *Planning for a Sustainable Future*, London, Spon Press.

Bazlinton C. and Bartlett K. (Eds) (1997) *Rethinking Housebuilding*, York, Joseph Rowntree Foundation.

BDOR (1992) *Development Briefing Project, Stage Two Report*, London, The Housing Research Foundation.

Beer A. (1982) 'The Development Control Process and the Quality of the External Environment in Residential Areas', *Landscape Research*, **7**, 3, 14–21.

Beer A. (1983) 'Development Control and Design Quality, Part 2: Attitudes to Design', *Town Planning Review*, **54**, 4, 383–404.

Beer A. (1990) *Environmental Planning for Site Development*, London, Chapman & Hall.

Beer A. and Booth P. (1981a) *Development Control and Design Quality, Five Reports*, Sheffield, Sheffield Centre for Environmental Research.

Beer A. and Booth P. (1981b) *Development Control and Design Quality, a Report on an Investigation into the Effectiveness of Architectural and Landscape Design Conditions – Report One*, Sheffield, Sheffield Centre for Environmental Research.

Bentley I. (1990) 'Urban Design, 3 Ecological Urban Design', *Architects' Journal*, **192**, 17, 69–71.

Bentley I., Alcock A., Murrain P., McGlynn S. and Smith G. (1985) *Responsive Environments: A Manual for Designers*, London, Architectural Press.

Best A. (1978) 'Essex Assessed', *The Architects Journal*, **167**, 20, 949–959.

Biddulph M. (1996) 'An Evaluation of a Private Sector Residential Layout Guide', *Urban Design International*, **1**, 2, 145–162.

Billingham J. (1996) 'Street Patterns Stitch Urban Fabric Together', *Planning*, 1162, 22–23.

Birkbeck D. (1997) 'Very Bury', *Building Homes*, 1, January, 8–11.

Birkbeck D. (1999) 'Top 50 Housebuilders', *Building Homes*, 65, May, 20–22.

Birmingham City Council (1987) *City Centre Strategy*, Birmingham, Birmingham City Council.

Birmingham City Council (1991) *Birmingham Unitary Development Plan, Revised Draft for Public Deposit*, Birmingham, Birmingham City Council.

Birmingham City Council (1993a) *Giving the Streets Back to the People Reviving Cities Urban Design in Action Exhibition*, London, Royal Institute of British Architects.

Birmingham City Council (1993b) *The Birmingham Plan*, Birmingham, Birmingham City Council.

Birmingham City Council (1997) *Digbeth Millennium Quarter Plan*, Birmingham, Birmingham City Council.

Birmingham City Council (2000) *Places for Living, Revised Residential Design Guide for Birmingham*, Birmingham, Birmingham City Council.

Birmingham City Council (n.d.) *New Residential Development Design Guidelines*, Birmingham, Birmingham City Council.

Bishop J. and Davison I. (1989) *Good Product; Could the Service be Better?*, London, The Housing Research Foundation.

Black J. (1997) 'Quality in Development, by Design or Process?', *TCPSS Proceedings*, 1997, London, RTPI, pp. 80–82.

Blakely E. and Snyder M. (1997) *Fortress America: Gated Communities in the United States*, Washington D.C., Brookings Institution Press.

Blaney T. (1993) *Experience Mounts on Development Plan Lead Planning*, 1031, 13 August, 26–7.

Blowers A. (Ed.) (1993) *Planning for a Sustainable Environment*, London, Earthscan Publications Ltd.

Booth P. (1982) 'Housing as a Product: Design Guidance and Residential Satisfaction in the Private Sector', *Built Environment*, **8**, 1, 20–24.

Booth P. (1996) *Controlling Development, Certainty and Discretion in Europe, the USA and Hong Kong*, London, UCL Press.

Brackenbury M. (1994) 'Design in the Development Process', *TCPSS Proceedings*, London, RTPI.

Bramley G., Bartlett W. and Lambert C. (1995) *Planning, the Market and Private Housebuilding*, London, UCL Press.

Breheny M. and Hall P. (1996) 'Four Million Households – Where Will They Go?', *Town and Country Planning*, **65**, 2, 39–41.

Broadbent G. (1990) *Emerging Concepts in Urban Space Design*, New York, Van Nostrand Reinhold.

Brooke Rt. Hon. H. (1958) 'Aesthetic Control; Minister's Statement to RIBA Symposium', *The Architects Journal*, **127**, 681.

Buchanan P. (1989) 'What City, A Plea for Place in the Public Realm', *Architectural Review*, **184**, 1101, 31–33.

Building Profile (1997) *Marketing Architectural Services in the UK*, Gloucester, Building Profile.

Building Research Establishment (1991) *Site Layout Planning for Daylight and Sunlight: A Good Practice Guide*, Garston, Watford, BRE.

Butina Watson G. (1997) 'The Future of Urban Design Education', *Urban Design Quarterly*, 64, October, 16–18.

Buxton P. (1997) 'Design and Build Groupies: Join the Quality Club', *Building Design*, 1324, 10 October, 3.

Cabinet Office (1997) *The Contribution of Good Architectural Design and the Use of Materials to Sustainable Living*, Working Paper Commissioned by Cabinet Office for the Government Panel on Sustainable Development, London, Cabinet Office.

Calthorpe P. (1993) *The Next American Metropolis, Ecology, Community and the American Dream*, New York, Princeton Architectural Press.

Carmona M. (1991) *The London Docklands, An Experiment in Incremental Urban Planning*, unpublished MA dissertation, Nottingham, University of Nottingham.

Carmona M. (1996a) 'Controlling Urban Design – Part 1: A Possible Renaissance', *Journal of Urban Design*, **1**, 1, 47–73.

Carmona M. (1996b) 'Controlling Urban Design – Part 2: Realizing the Potential', *Journal of Urban Design*, **1**, 2, 179–200.

Carmona M. (1996c) 'Squaring the Design Control Circle – Prescription Without Interference', *Town and Country Planning*, **65**, 9, 240–243.

Carmona M. (1997a) 'Design Issues Return to the Drawing Board', *Planning*, 1210, 21 March, 20–21.

Carmona M. (Ed) (1997b) 'Special Topic: Residential Design Guidance', *Urban Design Quarterly*, 62, 16–35.

Carmona M. (1998) 'Residential Design – Not an Optional Extra', *Town and Country Planning*, **67**, 6, 227–229.

Case Scheer B. and Preiser W. (1994) *Design Review, Challenging Urban Aesthetic Control*, London, Chapman & Hall.

Chadwin J. (1997) 'Brindleyplace Implementation', *Urban Design Quarterly*, 62, April, 12–15.

Chamberlain R. (1994) 'Residential Design Guides: Time for a New Wave?', *TCPSS Proceedings*, London, RTPI.

Chapman D. and Larkham P. (1992) *Discovering the Art of Relationship: Urban Design, Aesthetic Control and Design Guidance*, Birmingham, UCE.

Chapman D. and Larkham P. (1999) 'Urban Design, Urban Quality and the Quality of Life: Reviewing the Department of the Environment's Urban Design Campaign', *Journal of Urban Design*, **4**, 2, 211–232.

Cheltenham Borough Council (1992) *Cheltenham Borough Local Plan, Deposit Copy*, Cheltenham, Cheltenham B.C.

Cherry G. E. (1988) *Cities and Plans: The Shaping of Urban Britain in the Nineteenth and Twentieth Centuries*, London, Edward Arnold.

Cheshire County Council (1974) *Planning Standards, Residential Roads*, Cheshire, Cheshire County Council.

Cheshire County Council (1976) *Design Aid, Housing: Roads*, Cheshire, Cheshire County Council.

Children's Play Council (1999) *Home Zones, Reclaiming Residential Streets*, London, Children's Play Council.

Cockshaw A. (1997) 'Quality in the Urban Environment', *Built Environment*, **22**, 4, 278–282.

Construction Industry Board (1997) *Construction Industry Board Memorandum of Understanding (Accreditation/Validation)*, London, CIB.

Construction Industry Council (1997) *Partners in Building Prosperity: A Manifesto for the UK Construction Industry*, London, CIC.

Cooper K. (1993) Design Guidance in Local Plans, paper given to the 'Design Guidance Conference', London, RTPI.

Cooper, Marcus C. and Sarkissian W. (1986) *Housing as if People Mattered, Site Design Guidelines for Medium-Density Family Houses*, Berkeley, University of California Press.

Cotswold District Council (1992) *Cotswold District Local Plan, Consultation Draft*, Cirencester, Cotswold District Council.

Cotswold District Council (1993) *Cotswold District Local Plan, Deposit Draft*, Cirencester, Cotswold District Council.

Cotswold District Council (1996) *Cotswold District Local Plan Inquiry, Inspector's Report*, Cirencester, Cotswold District Council.

Cotswold District Council (1999) *Cotswold District Local Plan*, Cirencester, Cotswold District Council.

Cotswold District Council (2000) *Cotswold Design Code*, Cirencester, Cotswold District Council.

Couch C. (1986) *MSc Report: What's Happening to the Local Housebuilder*, London, Bartlett School of Architecture and Planning, University College, London.

Countryside Commission (1989) *Planning for a Greener Countryside*, Cheltenham, Countryside Commission.

Countryside Commission (1993) *Design in the Countryside*, Cheltenham, Countryside Commission.

Countryside Commission (1994) *Countryside Design Experiments, Report on a Programme to Pilot Countryside Design Summaries and Village Design Statements*, Cheltenham, Countryside Commission.

Coupland A. (1996) *Reclaiming the City, Mixed Use Development*, London, E & FN Spon.

Cowan R. (1995) *The Cities Design Forgot, A Manifesto*, London, Urban Initiatives.

Cowan R (1997) *The Connected City, A New Approach to Making Cities Work*, London, Urban Initiatives.

Cowan R. (2000) *Placecheck, A Users' Guide*, London, UDAL.

Cowburn W. (1967) 'Housing in a Consumer Society', *Architectural Review*, **142**, 849, 398–400.

CPRE (1995) *Local Attraction: The Design of New Housing in the Countryside*, London, CPRE.

Cronin A. (1993) 'The Elusive Quality of Certainty', *Planning Week*, **1**, 4, 16–17.

Cullen G. (1961) *Townscape*, London, Architectural Press.

Cullen G. (1967) *Notation*, London, Alcan.

Dacorum Borough Council (1995a) *Dacorum Borough Local Plan*, Hemel Hempstead, Dacorum Borough Council.

Dacorum Borough Council (1995b) *Residential Areas Character Study*, Hemel Hempstead, Dacorum Borough Council.

Dacorum Borough Council (1996) *Exhibition Text: Residential Areas Character Study*, Hemel Hempstead, Dacorum Borough Council.

Dacorum Borough Council (1998a) *Dacorum Borough Local Plan First Review to 2011*, Hemel Hempstead, Dacorum Borough Council.

Dacorum Borough Council (1998b) *Supplementary Planning Guidance on Development in Residential Areas Character Study*, Hemel Hempstead, Dacorum Borough Council.

Davison I. (1987a) 'Volume Housing, 1 Rules of the Game', *Architects' Journal*, 2 September, 63–67.

Davison I. (1987b) 'Volume Housing, 2 Urban Designs', *Architects' Journal*, 9 September, 59–65.

Davison I. (1989) 'Designs on Customers', *House Builder*, February, 38–44.

Davison I. (1991) 'Land Values, Part of the Design Equation', *House Builder*, March, 38–44.

DCMS (2000) *Better Public Buildings, A Proud Legacy for the Future*, London, DCMS.

Dean J. (1997) 'Joint Perspectives in Planning and Architectural Education', *Planning*, 1222, 13 June, 20.

DEGW (1988) *The Highbury Initiative: Proceedings of the Birmingham City Centre Challenge Symposium*, Birmingham, Birmingham City Council.

Delafons J. (1990) *Aesthetic Control: a Report on Methods Used in the USA to Control the Design of Buildings*, Berkeley, University of California, Institute of Urban and Regional Development, Monograph 41.

Delafons J. (1991) 'Design Control – The American Experience', *The Planner TCPSS Proceedings*, 13 December.

Delafons J. (1997) *Politics and Preservation: A Policy History of the Built Heritage 1882–1996*, London, E & FN Spon.

DEMOS (1999) *Living Together, Community Life on Mixed Tenure Estates*, London, DEMOS.

DETR (1997) *Land Use Change in England No. 12*, London, DETR.

DETR (1998a) *Places, Streets and Movement, A Companion Guide to Design Bulletin 32 Residential Roads and Footpaths*, London, DETR.

DETR (1998b) *Planning for the Communities of the Future*, London, DETR.

DETR (1998c) *Rethinking Construction, The Report of the Construction Task Force to the Deputy Prime Minster, John Prescott, on the Scope for Improving the Quality and Effectiveness of UK Construction*, London, DETR.

DETR (1998d) *Planning and Development Briefs: A Guide to Better Practice*, London, DETR.

DETR (1999) *Revision of Planning Policy Guidance Note 3: Housing, Public Consultation Draft*, London, DETR.

DETR (2000a) *Planning Policy Guidance (PPG3): Housing*, London, The Stationery Office.

DETR (2000b) *Planning Policy Guidance (PPG12): Development Plans*, London, The Stationery Office.

DETR (2000c) *Millennium Villages and Sustainable Communities*, London, DETR.

DETR (2000d) *Government Gives Pointer to Better Urban Design, News Release 355:15 May*, London DETR.

DETR (2000e) *Our Towns and Cities: The Future, Delivering an Urban Renaissance*, London, DETR.

DETR and CABE (2000) *By Design, Urban Design in the Planning System: Towards Better Practice*, London, DETR.

Dimbleby J. (1995) 'Design is Key to Problems of "Dreary Suburbia"', *Planning Week*, **3**, 18, 8.

District Planning Officers Society (1993) *Landscape – Raising the Profile*, London, DPOS.

DoE (1971) *Sunlight and Daylight: Planning Criteria and the Design of Buildngs*, London, HMSO.

DoE (1972) *Design Bulletin 25: The Estate Outside the Dwelling, Reactions of Residents to Aspects of Housing Layout*, London, HMSO, 128.

DoE (1975) *Review of the Development Control System, Final Report*, London, HMSO.

DoE (1976) *Research Report 6: The Value of Standards for the External Residential Environment*, London, DoE.

DoE (1977) *Circular 72/77: Residential Roads and Footpaths*, London, HMSO.

DoE (1978) *Circular 36/78: Trees and Forestry*, London, HMSO.

DoE (1980) *Circular 22/80: Development Control and Practice*, London, HMSO.

DoE (1983) *Draft Circular on Good Design and Development Control*, London, HMSO.

DoE (1985) *Circular 31/85: Aesthetic Control*, London, HMSO.

DoE (1988a) *Planning Policy Guidance (PPG1): General Policy and Principles*, London, HMSO.

DoE (1988b) *Planning Policy Guidance (PPG3): Land for Housing*, London, HMSO.

DoE (1988c) *Planning Policy Guidance (PPG12): Local Plans*, London, HMSO.

DoE (1990) *Time for Design, Monitoring the Initiative*, London, HMSO.

DoE (1991) *Planning Policy Guidance (PPG17): Sport and Recreation*, London, HMSO.

DoE (1992a) *Planning Policy Guidance (PPG1): General Policy and Principles*, London, HMSO.

DoE (1992b) *Planning Policy Guidance (PPG3): Housing*, London, HMSO.

DoE (1992c) *Planning Policy Guidance (PPG12): Development Plans and Regional Planning Guidance*, London, HMSO.

DoE (1992d) *Development Plans: A Good Practice Guide*, London, HMSO.

DoE (1992e) *Planning Policy Guidance (PPG4): Industrial and Commercial Development and Small Firms*, London, HMSO.

DoE (1993a) *Alternative Development Patterns: New Settlements*, London, HMSO.

DoE (1993b) *Circular 8/93: Awards of Costs Incurred in Planning and Other (Including Compulsory Purchase Order) Proceedings*, London, HMSO.

DoE (1994a) *Planning Policy Guidance (PPG13): Transport*, London, HMSO.

DoE (1994b) *Circular 5/94: Planning Out Crime*, London, HMSO.

DoE (1994c) *Quality in Town and Country, A Discussion Document*, London, DoE.

DoE (1995a) *Quality in Town and Country, Urban Design Campaign*, London, DoE.

DoE (1995b) *Circular 11/95: The Use of Conditions in Planning Permissions*, London, HMSO.

DoE (1996a) *Sustainable Settlements and Shelter, The United Kingdom National Report Habitat II*, London, HMSO.

DoE (1996b) *Analysis of Responses to the Discussion Document 'Quality in Town and Country'*, London, HMSO.

DoE (1996c) *Household Growth: Where Shall We Live?*, London, The Stationery Office.

DoE (1996d) *Planning Policy Guidance (PPG6): Town Centres and Retail Development*, London, HMSO.

DoE (1996e) *Consultation Paper: Planning Policy Guidance (PPG1): General Policy and Principles*, London, DoE.

DoE (1996f) *PPG1: Public Consultation Exercise: List of Responses* (unpublished internal distribution list), London, DoE.

DoE (1996g) *Regional Planning Guidance (RPG 3): Strategic Guidance for London Planning Authorities*, London, HMSO.

DoE (1996h) *Quality in Town and County: Urban Design Exhibition*, London, DoE.

DoE (1997a) *UK Round Table on Sustainable Development: Housing and Urban Capacity*, London, DoE.

DoE (1997b) *Planning Policy Guidance (PPG1): General Policy and Principles*, London, The Stationery Office.

DoE (1997c) *Planning Policy Guidance (PPG7): The Countryside – Environmental Quality and Economic and Social Development*, London, The Stationery Office.

DoE and DoT (1977) *Design Bulletin 32: Residential Roads and Footpaths: Layout Considerations*, London, HMSO.

DoE and DoT (1992) *Design Bulletin 32 Second Edition: Residential Roads and Footpaths: Layout Considerations (Second Edition)*, London, HMSO.

DoE and Housing Research Foundation (HRF) (1976) *Design Guidance Survey*, London, DoE.

DoE Eastern Regional Office (1994) *DoE Response to the Pre-Deposit Draft for Public Consultation of the North Norfolk Local Plan*, DoE.

Donovan J. and Larkham P. (1996) 'Rethinking Design Guidance', *Planning Practice and Research*, **11**, 3, 303–318.

Edwards A. (1981) *The Design of Suburbia, A Critical Study in Environmental History*, London, Pembridge Press.

English Heritage (1993) *Conservation Area Appraisals, Defining the Special Architectural or Historic Interest of Conservation Areas*, London, English Heritage.

English Heritage (1997) *Conservation Area Practice*, London, English Heritage.

English Partnerships (1996) *Time for Design: Good Practice Guide in Building, Landscape and Urban Design*, London, English Partnerships.

English Partnerships (1998) *Time for Design 2, Good Practice in Building, Landscape and Urban Design*, London, English Partnerships.

Epping Forest District Council (1994) *Epping Forest District: Local Plan, Deposit Draft*, Epping, Epping Forest District Council.

Essex County Council (1973) *A Design Guide for Residential Areas*, Chelmsford, Essex County Council.

Essex Planning Officers Association (1997) *A Design Guide for Residential and Mixed Use Areas*, Essex, EPOA.

Fairs M. (1998) 'End of Road for the Cul-de-sac', *Building Design*, 1373, 1.

Fairs M. (1999) 'House Factory Opens', *Building Design*, 1417, 1 October, 4.

Fairs M. (2000a) 'Wimpey Goes Modular', *Building Design*, 1429, 2 February, 2.

Fairs M. (2000b) 'Housing Giant Goes prefab', *Building Design*, 1438, 28 April, 5.

Fairs M. (2000c) 'Rescue Bid for 2000 Village', *Building Design*, 1431, 10 March, 1.

Fathing S. and Winter J. (1988) *Residential Density and Levels of Satisfaction with the External Residential Environment, A Research Report on New Private Sector Housing Schemes in West Totton Hampshire*, Bristol, Bristol Polytechnic.

Field J. (1996) 'Silent Supporters Stand Firm on Design Guidance', *Planning*, 22 November, 1196, 26.

Fisher J. (1998) 'Homes are a Family Affair', *Building Design*, 1362, 21 August, 21.

Ford V. (2000) 'Planning Chaos', *Building Design*, 1443, 2 June, 15.

Forrest R., Kennett T. and Leather P. (1997) *Home Owners on New Estates in the 1990s*, The Policy Press, Bristol.

Frey H. (1999) *Designing the City: Towards a More Sustainable Urban Form*, London, E & FN Spon.

Gardner J. (1998) 'New Housing "History in the Making", The Developer's Viewpoint' paper given to the Institute of Historic Building Conservation, Annual Conference, 5 June, Nottingham.

Garreau J. (1991) *Edge City, Life on the New Frontier*, New York, Doubleday.

Gehl J. (1987) *Life Between Buildings: Using Public Space*, New York, Van Nostrand Reinhold.

Gibberd F. (1953) *Town Design*, London, The Architectural Press.

Ginsburg L. (1973) 'The Reality: Outlaw into By-law', *The Architectural Review*, **154**, 919, 219–266.

Gleave S. (1990) 'Urban Design, 1. Introduction', *Architects' Journal*, **192**, 17, 63–4.

Gloucestershire County Council (1994) *Design Guide for Residential Roads in Gloucestershire*, Gloucester, Gloucestershire County Council.

Godwin G. (1976) *Private Housing and Public Need*, London, National House-Building Council.

Goodchild B. (1991) 'Postmodernism and Housing: A Guide to Design Theory', *Housing Studies*, **6**, 2, 131–144.

Goodchild B. (1997) *Housing and the Urban Environment, a Guide to Housing Design, Renewal and Urban Planning*, Oxford, Blackwell Science.

Gosling D. (1984) 'Definitions of Urban Design', *Architectural Design*, **54**, 1/2, 16–25.

Gosling D. and Maitland B. (1984) *Concepts of Urban Design*, London, Academy Editions.

Goss A. (1965) The Architect and Town Planning, report presented to the Council of the RIBA, London, RIBA.

Gould S. (1992) 'London's Unitary Development Plans: Design Policy Content', *Urban Design Quarterly*, Issue 44, 10–16.

Government Office for London and the London Planning Advisory Committee (1998) *Sustainable Residential Quality: New Approaches to Urban Living*, London, LPAC.

Government Office for London and the London Planning Advisory Committee (2000) *Sustainable Residential Quality: Exploring the Potential of Large Sites*, London, LPAC.

Grant I. (1998) 'Best Value, Implications for Planning', *Scottish Planner*, April, 6–7.

Greed C. and Roberts M. (Eds) (1998) *Introducing Urban Design, Interventions and Responses*, Harlow, Addison Wesley Longman.

Griffiths J. (1995) 'Griffiths Flies Kite for Role in Improving Urban Design', *Planning*, 1125, 30 June, 6–7.

Gummer J. (1994) DoE Press Release 713: More Quality in Town and Country, London, DoE, 12 December.

Gummer J. (1995) DoE Press Release 162: The Way to Achieve 'Quality' in Urban Design, London, DoE, 30 March.

Gupta T. (1989) 'Designs for Volume Production', *House Builder*, May, 28–30.

Hall A. (1990) *Generation of Objectives for Design Control*, Chelmsford, Anglia College Enterprises Ltd.

Hall A. (1996a) *Design Control, Towards A New Approach*, Oxford, Butterworth Heinemann.

Hall A. (1996b) Design Control for Local Areas: A Morphological Approach, paper presented to the ACSP/AESOP Joint International Conference, July 1996, Toronto.

Hamilton J. (1976) 'Alan Reason's Rationale for the Essex Design Guide', *House Builder*, **35**, September.

Hanson J. (1999) *Decoding Homes and Houses*, Cambridge, Cambridge University Press.

Hawkins R. (1993) 'The Planning Process: What Goes on Behind Closed Doors', *Architects' Journal*, **197**, 3, 16–18.

Hayward R. and McGlynn S. (1993) *Making Better Places, Urban Design Now*, Oxford, Butterworth Architecture.

HBF (1996) *Families Matter*, London, The Housebuilders Federation.

HBF (1998) *Urban Life, Breaking Down the Barriers to Brownfield Development*, London, HBF.

HBF and RIBA (1990) *Good Design in Housing*, London, HBF/RIBA.

Hedges B. and Clemens S. (1994) *Housing Attitudes Survey*, London, HMSO.

Hellman L. (1995) 'A Century of Development', *Building Design*, 1236, 29 September, 9.

Hillier B. (1996) *Space is the Machine: A Configurational Theory of Architecture*, Cambridge, Cambridge University Press.

Hillman J. for the RFAC (1990) *Planning for Beauty, The Case for Design Guidelines*, London, HMSO.

Hirst C. (1997) 'Campaigning on the Home Front', *Planning Week*, **4**, 19, 9.

HM Government (1990) *This Common Inheritance: Britain's Environmental Strategy*, London, HMSO.

HM Government (1994) *Sustainable Development: the UK Strategy*, London, HMSO.

HM Government (1995a) *Our Future Homes: Opportunity, Choice, Responsibility: Command 2901, Housing White Paper*, London, HMSO.

HM Government (1995b) *Rural England, A Nation Committed to a Living Countryside*, London, HMSO.

Holt G. (Ed) (1988 with updates) *Development Control Practice*, Gloucester, Ambit Publications.

Hooper A. (1994) 'House Adaptability for Sustainable Change', *Town and Country Planning*, **63**, 5, 142–4.

Hooper A. (1999) *Design for Living, Constructing the Residential Built Environment in the 21st Century*, London, Town & Country Planning Association.

Hooper A. and Nicol C. (1999) 'The Design and Planning of Residential Development: Standard House Types in the Speculative Housebuilding Industry', *Environment and Planning B: Planning and Design*, **26**, 6, 793–805.

Hough M. (1990) *Out of Place: Restoring Identity to the Regional Landscape*, London, Yale University Press.

House of Commons (1977) *Eighth Report from the Expenditure Committee: Session 1976–77; Planning Procedures*, Vols. I–III, London, HMSO.

House of Commons (1985a) *Lifting the Burden*, London, HMSO.

House of Commons, (1985b) *Royal Fine Art Commission; Twenty Second Report, October 1971– December 1984*, London, HMSO.

Housing Research Foundation (1983) *Local Standards for the Layout of Residential Roads: A Review*, London, Housing Research Foundation.

Howard E. (1898) *Tomorrow: A Peaceful Path to Real Reform*, London, Swan Sonnenschein.

Howard E. (1976) *Garden Cities of Tomorrow*, London, Faber & Faber.

HRH, The Prince of Wales (1989) *A Vision of Britain: A Personal View of Architecture*, London, Doubleday.

Hubbard P. (1994a) 'Recognising Design Quality in Development Control', *Town and Country Planning*, **6**, 11, 311–313.

Hubbard P. (1994b) 'Professional vs. Lay Tastes in Design Control – An Empirical Investigation', *Planning Practice and Research*, **9**, 4, 271–28.

Hulme Regeneration Ltd (1992) *The Shape of Hulme to Come, Consultation Report*, Manchester, HRL.

Hulme Regeneration Ltd and Manchester City Council (1994) *A Guide to Development: Hulme, Manchester*, Manchester, HRL/MCC.

Jackson L. (1997) *Discussion Paper, Review of Development Briefing*, High Wycombe, Wycombe District Council.

Jacobs J. (1961) *The Death and Life of Great American Cities*, New York, Random House.

James S. (1992) 'Pinning the Blame for Stifling Design', *Planning*, 22 October, 991, 15.

Jarvis R. (1980) 'Urban Environments as Visual Art or Social Settings?', *Town Planning Review*, **51**, 1, 51–66.

Jenks M., Burton E. and Williams K. (1996) *The Compact City, A Sustainable Urban Form?*, London, E & FN Spon.

Joint Centre for Urban Design, Oxford Brookes University (1994) *Quality in Town and Country: Analysis of Responses to the Discussion Document*, London, DoE.

Katz P. (1994) *The New Urbanism, Towards an Architecture of Community*, New York, McGraw-Hill.

Keeble L. (1971) *Town Planning at the Crossroads*, London, Estates Gazette.

Kingswood Borough Council (1996) *Design Guidance for Residential Development in Kingswood*, Bristol, Kingswood B.C.

Krier R (1979) *Urban Space*, London, Academy Editions.

Landis J. (1982) 'Why Homebuilders Don't Innovate', *Built Environment*, **8**, 1, 46–53.

Lang J. (1994) *Urban Design, The American Experience*, New York, Van Nostrand Reinhold.

Larkham P. (1996) *Conservation and the City.* London, Routledge.

LDR/HLN Consultancy (1988) *Pedestrian Movement and Open Space Framework*, Birmingham, City of Birmingham.

Le Corbusier (1967) *The Radiant City*, London, Faber.

Leopold E. and Bishop D. (1983) 'Design Philosophy and Practice in Speculative Hosebuilding: Part 1', *Construction Management and Economics*, **1**, 2, 119–144.

Lewis J. (1998) 'Get Ready for Some Extra Housework', *Building Design*, 1353, 29 May, 8.

Lewis J. (2000) 'Wimpey Goes Modular', *Building Design*, 1429, 25 February, 2.

Llewelyn-Davies (1999) *Gallions Reach Urban Village Thamesmead, Design Guidance*, London, L.B. Greenwich.

Loew S. (1997) 'Developers Call for More Precise Design Guidance', *Planning*, 22 March, 1211, 20.

London Borough of Bexley (1996) *London Borough of Bexley Unitary Development Plan*, London, L.B. Bexley.

London Borough of Greenwich (1989) *Thamesmead Residential Development Guidelines*, London, L.B. Greenwich.

London Borough of Greenwich (1994) *London Borough of Greenwich Unitary Development Plan*, London, L.B. Greenwich.

London Borough of Greenwich (1995) *Greenwich Waterfront Strategy*, London, L.B. Greenwich.

London Borough of Harrow (1986) *Harrow Borough Local Plan*, London, L.B. Harrow.

London Borough of Harrow (1988) *Housing Development Strategy – Issues Paper*, London, L.B. Harrow.

London Borough of Harrow (1992) *Harrow Unitary Development Plan, Deposit Version*, London, L.B. Harrow.

London Borough of Harrow (1994) *Harrow Unitary Development Plan*, London, L.B. Harrow.

London Borough of Merton (n.d) *Designing Out Crime*, London, L.B. Merton.

London Borough of Richmond Upon Thames (1981) *District Plan Topic Study Report – 7 Environmental Character*, London, L.B. Richmond Upon Thames.

London Planning Advisory Committee (LPAC) (1994) *The Quality of London's Residential Environment*, Romford, LPAC.

Loukaitou-Sideris A and T. Banerjee T, (1998) *Urban Design Downtown – Poetics and Politics of Form*, Berkeley, University of California Press.

Lyall S. (1985) 'From Rags to Riches', *A Building Supplement*, 22 March, 28–31.

Lynch K. (1960) *The Image of the City*, Cambridge Mass, MIT Press.

Lynch K. (1976) *Managing the Sense of a Region*, Cambridge Mass, MIT Press.

Lynch K. and Hack G. (1984) *Site Planning* (3rd edn), Cambridge Mass, MIT Press.

Madanipour A. (1996) *Design of Urban Space, An Inquiry into a Socio-spatial Process*, Chichester, John Wiley & Sons.

Madanipour A., Lally M. and Underwood G. (1993) *Design Briefs in Planning Practice*, Working Paper No. 26, Newcastle, University of Newcastle Upon Tyne.

Madden L. (1982) 'The Volume House-Builders', *Building*, 16 April, 26–33.

Mallett L. (1997a) 'Curbing the Committees', *Building Design*, 28 February, 1297, 7.

Mallett L. (1997b) 'Design and the Planning Process', *Town and Country Planning Summer School Proceeding, 1997*, London, RTPI, 78–79.

Manchester City Council (1992a) *Manchester City Unitary Development Plan, Draft Deposit*, Manchester, Manchester City Council.

Manchester City Council (1992b) *Urban Code for Hulme*, Manchester, Manchester City Council.

Manchester City Council (1994) *City Pride, a Focus for the Future*, Manchester, Manchester City Council.

Manchester City Council (1995) *City Development Guide*, Manchester, Manchester City Council.

Manchester City Council (1997) *A Guide to Development in Manchester*, Manchester, Manchester City Council.

Manley S. and Guise R. (1995) 'Achieving Quality in the Housing Environment', *Report*, 1, February, 33–35.

Manser M. (1980) 'An Excuse for Lousy Buildings', *RIBA Journal*, **87**, 2, 49.

Manser M. and Adam R (1992) *Application of Aesthetic Control and Conservation Area Legislation, in the Town and Country Planning System*, London (mimeo).

Matheou D. and Field M. (1993) 'How a Conciliatory Approach Can Win Over the Planners', *The Architects' Journal*, 17 February, 19–21.

Middleton L. (1995) 'Lessons from Hulme', *Report*, 10, November, 6–7.

Milne R. (1996) 'Lock Turns the Planning Key to Affordable Homes', *Planning*, 1160, 15 March, 8–9.

Ministry of Health (1933) *Circular 1305: Town and Country Planning Act*, London, HMSO.

Ministry of Housing and Local Government (MHLG) (1961) *Homes for Today and Tomorrow* (the Parker Morris Report), London, HMSO.

Ministry of Housing and Local Government (MHLG) (1966) *Circular 28/66: Elevational Control*, London, HMSO.

Ministry of Housing and Local Government (MHLG) (1968) *Circular 61/68: Town and Country Planning Act 1968: Part V: Historic Buildings and Conservation*, London, HMSO.

Ministry of Housing and Local Government (MHLG) (1969) *Development Control Policy Note 10: Design*, London, HMSO.

Ministry of Town and Country Planning (MTCP) (1951) *Command 8204, Town and Country Planning 1943–51*, London, HMSO.

Mitchell W. (1996) *City of Bits, Space, Place and the Infobahn*, Cambridge Mass., MIT Press.

Monk S. (1991a) *Discussion Paper 33: Planning, Land Supply and House prices, The National and Regional Picture*, Cambridge, Department of Land Economy, University of Cambridge.

Monk S. (1991b) *Discussion Paper 31: The Speculative Housebuilder, A Review of Empirical Research*, Cambridge, Department of Land Economy, University of Cambridge.

Monk S. and Whitehead C. (1999) 'Land Supply and Housing: A Case-Study', *Housing Studies*, **11**, 3, 407–423.

Moro P. (1958) 'Elevational Control', *Architects' Journal*, **127**, 203.

Morris J. (1996) 'Beware the Perils of the Brownfield Path', *Planning Week*, **4**, 48, 8.

Moughtin C (1992) *Urban Planning: Street and Square*, Oxford, Butterworths Architecture.

Mulholland Research Associates Limited (1995) *Towns or leafier Environments' A Survey of Family Home Buying Choices*, London.

Munro B. and Lane R. (1990) 'An Environmental Assessment of the Residential Areas of Harrow', *The Planner*, **76**, 1, 15–18.

Murray K. (1997) 'RTPI Participation in New Urban Design Initiative', *Planning*, 1235, 12 September, 20.

Murray K. and Willie D. (1991) 'Choosing the Right Approach', *Landscape Design*, May, 21–23.

Nairn I. (1955) *Outrage*, London, Architectural Press.

Nairn I. (1957) *Counter Attack Against Subtopia*, London, Architectural Press.

National Playing Fields Association (1992) *The Six Acre Standard, Minimum Standards for Outdoor Playing Space*, London, NPFA.

Newman O. (1972) *Defensible Space: Crime Prevention Through Urban Design*, New York, Macmillan.

Nicol C. and Hooper A. (1999) 'Contemporary Change and the Housebuilding Industry: Concentration and Standardisation in Production', *Housing Studies*, **14**, 1, 57–76.

Norberg-Schulz C. (1980) *Genius Loci*, London, Academy Editions.

Norfolk County Council (1998) *Norfolk Residential Design Guide*, Norwich, Norfolk County Council.

North Norfolk District Council (1993) *North Norfolk Design Guide*, Cromer, North Norfolk District Council.

North Norfolk District Council (1998) *North Norfolk Local Plan*, Cromer, North Norfolk District Council.

Nottingham City Council (1998) *Design Guide, Community Safety in Residential Areas*, Nottingham, Nottingham City Council.

Oliver P., Davis I. and Bentley I. (1981) *Drunroamin, The Suburban Semi and its Enemies*, London, Pimlico.

Osborne T. (1991) 'The Developer's Role in Design and the Environment', *The Planner TCPSS Proceedings*, 13 December, 26–30.

Owen S. (1995) 'Local Distinctiveness in Villages, Overcoming Some Impediments to Clear Thinking about Village Planning', *Town Planning Review*, **66**, 2, 143–161.

Owen S. (1999) 'Village Design Statements, Some Aspects of the Evolution of a Planning Tool in the UK', *Town Planning Review*, **70**, 1, 41–59.

Pacione M. (1989) 'The Site Selection Process of Speculative Residential Developers in an Urban Area', *Housing Studies*, **5**, 4, 219–228.

Peak District Advisory Panel (1934) *Housing in the Peak District*, Sheffield, CPRE & Peak District Committee.

Pearman H. (1998) 'Home is Sweeter When Detached', *The Sunday Times*, 20 September.

Planning Officers Society (1999) *Planning and Design, Achieving Good Practice Through the Planning Process*, Crawley, POS.

Planning Officers Society, Housebuilders Federation and DETR (1998) *Housing Layouts – Lifting the Quality*, London, HBF.

Popular Housing Forum (1998) *Kerb Appeal, The External Appearance and Site Layout of New Houses*, Winchester, The Popular Housing Forum.

Prescott J. (1999) Press Release 625: Government Welcomes Urban Task Force Final Report, London, DETR, 29th June.

Prescott J. (2000) Press Release 164: Prescott Announces More Responsive Approach to Meeting South East's Housing Needs, London, DETR, 7th March.

Punter J. (1985) *Office Development in the Borough of Reading 1954–1984, A Case History of the Role of Aesthetic Control Within the Planning Process, Working Papers Environmental Policy No. 6*, Reading, University of Reading.

Punter J. (1986) 'A History of Aesthetic Control: Part 1, 1909–1953', *Town Planning Review*, **57**, 4, 351–381.

Punter J. (1987) 'A History of Aesthetic Control: Part 2, 1953–1985', *Town Planning Review*, **58**, 1, 29–62.

Punter J. (1990) *Design Control in Bristol 1940–1990*, Bristol, Redcliffe Press Ltd.

Punter J. (Ed.) (1994) 'Design Control in Europe', *Built Environment*, **20**, 2, 85–87.

Punter J. (1996) 'Developments in Urban Design Review: The Lessons of West Coast Cities of the United States for British Practice', *Journal of Urban Design*, **1**, 1, 23–45.

Punter J. (1999) *Design Guidelines in American Cities, A Review of Design Policies and Guidance in Five West Coast Cities*, Liverpool, Liverpool University Press.

Punter J. and Bell A. (1997) *Design Appeals in English Planning: An Introduction and Aggregate Analysis*, Cardiff, Department of City and Regional Planning Cardiff University.

Punter J. and Carmona M. (1996a) 'Design Policies in English Local Plans: The Search for Substantive Principles and Appropriate Procedures', *Urban Design International*, **1**, 2, 125–143.

Punter J. and Carmona M (1996b) 'Urban Design Policies in English Local Plans: Content and Prescriptions', *Urban Design International*, **1**, 3, 201–234.

Punter J. and Carmona M. (1997a) *The Design Dimension of Planning: Theory, Content, and Best Practice for Design Policies*, London, E & FN Spon.

Punter J. and Carmona M. (1997b) 'Design Policies in Local Plans: Recommendations for Good Practice', *Town Planning Review*, **68**, 2, 165–193.

Punter J., Carmona M. and Platts A. (1994a) *Sources for Design Policy: A Bibliographic Guide*, Glasgow, University of Strathclyde.

Punter J., Carmona M. and Platts A. (1994b) 'The Design Content of Development Plans', *Planning Practice and Research*, **9**, 3, 199–220.

Punter J., Carmona M. and Platts A. (1996) *Design Policies in Local Plans; A Research Report*, London, DoE.

Rapoport A. (1982) *The Meaning of the Built Environment: A Nonverbal Communication Approach*, University of Arizona Press, Tucson.

Ravetz A. (1995) *The Place of Home, English Domestic Environments 1914–2000*, London, E&FN Spon.

Raynsford N. (1997a) *Launch of the Urban Design Alliance: Keynote Address*, London, DETR, 1 December.

Raynsford N. (1997b) *Royal Fine Art Commission Seminar: Good Design in Speculative Housing*, London, DETR, 3 December.

Raynsford N. (1998) Press Release 755, Pedestrians Needs Must Come First, London DETR, 16th September.

Raynsford N. (1999) quoted in 'Raynsford Slams Pastiche', *Building Design*, Issue 1388, 26 March, 1.

Raynsford N. (2000) Press Release 0057, Government Targets Better Quality Housing Design, London, DETR, 27th January.

RFAC (1980) *Building in Context*, London, RFAC.

RFAC (1990) *Planning for Beauty: The Case for Design Guidelines*, London, HMSO.

RFAC (1994) *What Makes a Good Building? An Inquiry by the Royal Fine Art Commission*, London, HMSO.

RIBA (1965) 'The Case for and Against Control', *RIBA Journal*, **72**, 323–324.

RIBA (1993) *Before and After Planning*, London, RIBA.

RIBA (1995) *Quality in Town and Country: A Response to the Secretary of State for the Environment*, London, RIBA.

RIBA (1996) *Guidance for Clients on Fees*, London, RIBA.

RICS (1996) *Quality of Urban Design, A Study of the Involvement of Private Property Decision-Makers in Urban Design*, London, RICS.

Roger Tym & Partners (1989) *The Incidence & Effects of Planning Delays*, London, Housebuilders Federation.

Rogers R. (1990) *Architecture A Modern View*, London, Thames and Hudson.

Rogers L. (1994) 'Gazumping the Housebuilders', *RIBA Journal*, **101**, 11, 6–11.

Rogers L. (1997a) *Cities for a Small Planet*, London, Faber and Faber.

Rogers L. (1997b) 'Homes Fit for Heritage', *Building Design*, 1321, 19 September, 7.

Roskrow B. (1997) 'The Great Subjective Subject', *HouseBuilder*, October, 30–32.

Roskrow B. (1998) 'Housing Snobs are Out of Touch', *HouseBuilder*, October, 3.

Rouse R. (1998) 'The Seven Clamps of Urban Design', *Planning*, 1293, 6 November, 18–19.

Rowland J. (1997) 'Time for Change', *Urban Design Quarterly*, 64, October, 21–26.

Rowley A. (1994) 'Definitions of Urban Design: The Nature and Concerns of Urban Design', *Planning Practice and Research*, **9**, 3, 179–197.

Rowley A. (1996) Private Property Decision-Making and the Quality of Urban Design, paper presented to the ACSP/AESOP Conference, July 1996, Toronto.

RTPI and RIBA (1980) *Joint Policy Statement on Design*, London, RTPI/RIBA.

Rudlin D. and Falk N. (1995) *21st Century Homes, Building to Last*, London, URBED.

Rudlin D. and Falk N. (1999) *Building the 21st Century Home, The Sustainable Urban Neighbourhood*, Oxford, Architectural Press.

Schurch T. (1999) 'Reconsidering Urban Design: Thoughts About its Definition and Status as a Field or Profession', *Journal of Urban Design*, **4**, 1, 5–28.

Scorpio (1997) 'Design Meets its Makers', *Building Design*, 1321, 19 September, 10.

Scottish Office (1994) *Planning Advice Note (PAN 44): Fitting New Housing Development into the Landscape*, Edinburgh, The Scottish Office.

Sedgemoor District Council (1991) *Bridgwater Area Local Plan*, Bridgwater, Sedgemoor District Council.

Sedgemoor District Council (1996) *Project Specification, Urban Design Campaign: Housing Development at South Bridgwater*, Bridgwater, Sedgemoor District Council.

Sedgemoor District Council (1998) *Development & Design Guide for Housing, South Bridgwater Somerset*, Bridgwater, Sedgemoor District Council.

SERSCPOC (South East Region Senior Crime Prevention Officers Conference) (n.d.) *Secured by Design*, Hassocks West Sussex, REA Publicity.

Sharp T. (1946) *The Anatomy of the Village*, Harmondsworth Middlesex, Penguin.

Short J., Fleming S. and Witt S. (1986) *Housebuilding, Planning and Community Action*, London, Routledge.

Sim D. (1993) *British Housing Design*, Harlow Essex, Longman and the Institute of Housing.

Sitte C. (from 1889 original) *City Planning According to Artistic Principles*, London, Phaidon Press.

Smales L. (1991) Unpublished PhD Thesis, *An Appraisal of the History, Impact and Effectiveness of the Essex Design Guide for Residential Areas*, Oxford, The Joint Centre for Urban Design, Oxford Polytechnic.

Smith D. (1974) *Amenity and Urban Planning*, London, Crosby Lockwood Staples.

Southworth M. (1989) 'Theory and Practice of Contemporary Urban Design, A Review of Urban Design Plans in the United States', *Town Planning Review*, **60**, 4, 369–402.

Southworth M. and Parthasarathy B. (1996) 'The Suburban Public Realm 1: Its Emergence, Growth and Transformation in the American Metropolis', *Journal of Urban Design*, **1**, 3.

Sparks L. (1993) 'Local Plans and Urban Design', *Urban Design Quarterly*, 46, April, 32–37.

Sparks L. (1994) 'The Role of Briefing in Urban Regeneration', *Urban Design Quarterly*, 51, July, 16–19.

Sparks L. (1997) 'Birmingham – Regional Capital', *Urban Design Quarterly*, 63, July, 24–27.

St Edmundsbury Borough Council (1992) *St Edmundsbury Borough Local Plan, Deposit Draft*, Bury St. Edmunds, St Edmundsbury Borough Council.

St Edmundsbury Borough Council (1993) *Supplementary Planning Guidance No. 4: Open Space Provision*, Bury St Edmunds, St Edmundsbury Borough Council.

St Edmundsbury Borough Council (1994) *Drovers West Moreton Hall, Bury St Edmunds Residential Development Brief*, Bury St Edmunds, St Edmundsbury Borough Council.

Steel M. (1995) 'Development Costs: The Economics of Design Controls', *Report*, September, 8, 20–22.

Steventon G. (1996) 'Defensible Space: A Critical Review of the Theory and Practice of a Crime Prevention Strategy', *Urban Design International*, **1**, 3, 235–245.

Stewart I. (1991) 'Birmingham Urban Design Studies', *The Planner*, **77**, 31, 5–6.

Stones A. (1992) 'Revising the Essex Design Guide', *Urban Design Quarterly*, 44, September, 17–19.

Storah A. (1997) 'Good Design is in the Beholder's Eye', *Planning*, 1217, 9 May, 16.

Strelitz Z, Henderson G. and Cowan R. (Eds) (1996) *Making Cities Better*, Leicester, Vision for Cities.

Stungo N. (1996) 'Conflict Resolution', *RIBA Journal*, **103**, 8, 6–11.

Suffolk Building Preservation Trust (1993) *Patterns for Suffolk Buildings, A Simple Design Guide*, Lavenham, The Suffolk Building Preservation Trust Ltd.

Suffolk Planning Officers' Group (1993) *Suffolk Design Guide for Residential Areas*, Ipswich, Suffolk County Council.

Suffolk Planning Officers' Group (n.d.) *Suffolk Design Guide for Residential Areas, Consultation Draft*, Ipswich, Suffolk County Council.

Symes M. and Pauwels S. (1999) 'The Diffusion of Innovations in Urban Design: The Case of Sustainability in the Hulme Development Guide', *Journal of Urban Design*, **4**, 1, 97–117.

Tetlow J. (1996) 'Everything Connects Across the Design Divide', *Planning*, 6 September, 1185, 20.

Thorne R (1998). 'Places People and Movement', *Mxd*, 4, 6–7.

Tibbalds F. (1988a) '"Mind the Gap" A Personal View of the Value of Urban Design in the Late Twentieth Century', *The Planner*, **74**, 3, 11–15.

Tibbalds F. (1988b) 'Urban Design: Tibbalds Offers the Prince His Ten Commandments', *The Planner* (mid-month supplement), **74**, 12, 1.

Tibbalds F. (1991) 'Planning – An Architect's View – Grasping the "Nettle" of Design', *The Planner TCPSS Proceedings*, 13 December, 71–74, London, RTPI.

Tibbalds F. (1992) *Making People-Friendly Towns, Improving the Public Environment in Towns and Cities*, Harlow, Longman.

Tibbalds, Colbourne, Karski, Williams (1990) *City Centre Design Strategy (BUDS)*, Birmingham, City of Birmingham.

Tibbalds, Colbourne, Karski, Williams (1993) *Urban Design Framework, Area 1: St. Paul's and Environs*, Birmingham, Birmingham City Council.

Tollit P. and Tollit M. (1998) 'The "New" Essex Design Guide?', *Urban Design Quarterly*, 67, July, 10–14.

Townsend T. (1995) *Representing the Past*, unpublished paper given to the 'Teaching and Research in Urban Design' conference, University of Manchester.

Tugnutt A. (1991) 'Design – The Wider Aspects of Townscapes', *The Planner TCPSS Proceedings*, 13 December.

Tugnutt A. and Robertson M. (1987) *Making Townscape, A Contextual Approach to Building in an Urban Setting*, London, Mitchell.

Unwin R. (1909) *Town Planning in Practice, An Introduction to the Art of Designing Cities and Suburbs*, London, Ernest Benn.

Urban Design Group (1994) *Urban Design Source Book*, Abingdon Oxon, UDG.

Urban Design Group (1996) *Urban Design Source Book 1996*, Blewbury, UDG.

Urban Task Force (1999a) *Regional Centres of Urban Development: A Feasibility Study*, London, Urban Task Force.

Urban Task Force (1999b) *Towards an Urban Renaissance*, London, E & FN Spon.

Urban Villages Group (1992) *Urban Villages, A Concept for Creating Mixed-use Urban Developments on a Sustainable Scale*, London, Urban Villages Group.

URBED, MORI and University of Bristol (1999) *But Would You Live There' Shaping Attitudes to Urban Living*, London, Urban Task Force.

Vernez Moudon A. (1992) 'A Catholic Approach to Organizing What Urban Designers Should Know', *Journal of Planning Literature*, **6**, 4, 331–349.

Villars P. (1993) 'Before and After Shot', *Planning*, 1002, 22 January, 6–7.

Walker P. and Davison T. (1997) 'A Divided City Seeks Top Quality Quarters', *Planning*, 1208, 7 March, 20–21.

Waller R. (1998) 'Modern? Innovative? Not in our Backyard', *Building Design*, 1365, 18 September, 6–7.

Welsh J. (1994) 'Tick for Tat', *RIBA Journal*, **101**, 11, 5.

West Dorset District Council (1991) *Herrison Development Brief and Design Code*, Dorchester, West Dorset District Council.

West Dorset District Council (1992) *West Dorset District Consultative Local Plan*, Dorchester, West Dorset District Council.

West Dorset District Council (1994) *West Dorset District Deposit Local Plan*, Dorchester, West Dorset District Council.

Western Australian Planning Commission (1997) *Liveable Neighbourhoods, Community Design Code*, Perth, Western Australian Planning Commission.

Whitehand J. (Ed) *The Urban Landscape: Historical Development and Management, Papers by M.R.G. Cozen*, New York, Academic Press.

Whyte W. (1980) *The Social Life of Small Urban Spaces*, Washington D.C., Conservation Foundation.

Whyte W. (1988) *City: Rediscovering the Centre*, New York, Doubleday.

Wigfall V. (1997) *Thamesmead, Back to the Future*, London, Greenwich Community College Press.

Winter J, Coombes T. and Farthing S. (1993) 'Satisfaction with Space Around the Home on Large Private Sector Estates', *Town Planning Review*, **64**, 1, 65–88.

Wooton Jeffreys Consultants (1989) *Harrow: An Environmental Assessment of Residential Areas*, Harrow, London Borough of Harrow.

Worskett R. (1969) *The Character of Towns, An Approach to Conservation*, London, The Architectural Press.

Wycombe District Council (1983) *Wycombe District Local Plan, to 2011*, High Wycombe, Wycombe District Council.

Wycombe District Council (1993) *Wycombe District Local Plan, Consolidated Version*, High Wycombe, Wycombe District Council.

Wycombe District Council (1994) *Wycombe District Local Plan Inquiry, Inspector's Report*, High Wycombe, Wycombe District Council.

Wycombe District Council (1998) *Wycombe District Local Plan to 2011*, High Wycombe, Wycombe District Council.

Wycombe District Council (n.d.) *Development Briefing for Housing, A Practice Manual*, High Wycombe, Wycombe District Council.

# Index